Psychology at the Movies

# Psychology at the Movies

### Skip Dine Young

*Professor of Psychology, Hanover College, Indiana, USA*

**WILEY-BLACKWELL**

A John Wiley & Sons, Ltd., Publication

This edition first published 2012
© 2012 Skip Dine Young

Wiley-Blackwell is an imprint of John Wiley & Sons, formed by the merger of Wiley's global Scientific, Technical and Medical business with Blackwell Publishing.

*Registered Office*
John Wiley & Sons Ltd, The Atrium, Southern Gate, Chichester, West Sussex, PO19 8SQ, UK

*Editorial Offices*
350 Main Street, Malden, MA 02148-5020, USA
9600 Garsington Road, Oxford, OX4 2DQ, UK
The Atrium, Southern Gate, Chichester, West Sussex, PO19 8SQ, UK

For details of our global editorial offices, for customer services, and for information about how to apply for permission to reuse the copyright material in this book please see our website at www.wiley.com/wiley-blackwell.

The right of Skip Dine Young to be identified as the author of this work has been asserted in accordance with the UK Copyright, Designs and Patents Act 1988.

Wiley also publishes its books in a variety of electronic formats. Some content that appears in print may not be available in electronic books.

Designations used by companies to distinguish their products are often claimed as trademarks. All brand names and product names used in this book are trade names, service marks, trademarks or registered trademarks of their respective owners. The publisher is not associated with any product or vendor mentioned in this book. This publication is designed to provide accurate and authoritative information in regard to the subject matter covered. It is sold on the understanding that the publisher is not engaged in rendering professional services. If professional advice or other expert assistance is required, the services of a competent professional should be sought.

*Library of Congress Cataloging-in-Publication Data*

Young, Skip Dine.
    Psychology at the movies / Skip Dine Young.
        p. cm.
    Includes bibliographical references and index.
    ISBN 978-0-470-97177-2 (pbk.)
 1. Motion pictures–Psychological aspects.    2. Psychoanalysis and motion pictures.
 3. Motion picture audiences–Psychology.    4. Psychiatry in motion pictures.
 5. Psychoanalysis in motion pictures.    6. Mental health personnel in motion pictures.
 I. Title.
    PN1995.Y63 2012
    791.43′6561–dc23

                                                                    2011042656

A catalogue record for this book is available from the British Library.

Wiley also publishes its books in a variety of electronic formats. Some content that appears in print may not be available in electronic books.

Set in 10.5/13pt Minion by Aptara Inc., New Delhi, India

1    2012

*To My Family*

# Contents

# List of Illustrations and Figures

**Illustrations**

## Figures

# Acknowledgments

I would especially like to thank Lindsay Marsh and Mary Ryan. Without their help I would never have been able to finish this book (at least not in the current decade). As my research assistant, Lindsay's patience and attention to detail allowed me to focus and work around my own limitations. Mary's invaluable editing and commentary made the manuscript infinitely more readable and helped me (begin) to unlearn decades of bad writing habits.

I appreciate the feedback I received on drafts of the manuscript from my colleagues Bill Altermatt, John Krantz, Ellen Altermatt, Mark Fearnow, Bill Bettler, Jared Bates and Ron Smith. Their comments helped me make adjustments and gave me perspective when I needed it. I am lucky to be a part of a vital faculty that is a tribute to the liberal arts.

Hanover College has been a great support to this project. The grant I received from the Faculty Development Committee and the sabbatical leave from the Board of Trustees provided me with the funding and time I needed. In addition the staff at Duggan Library (especially Patricia Lawrence, Mary Royalty, Ken Gibson and Lela Bradshaw) were extremely accommodating in my attempts to acquire the materials I needed for my own little psychology and film library. I would also like to thank whoever made the decision for the College to mow the lawns on campus housing. That was one distraction I didn't have to worry about that might otherwise have pushed me over the edge.

I am grateful to the many students I have worked with, particularly those who have taken "The Psychology of Film" over the past 15 years. I have found that having students is the only way professors can figure out what is really important.

I thank the faculty at Clark University, particularly my mentors Bernie Kaplan and Lenny Cirillo. Most of the ideas in this book first came to me in graduate school, and I am eternally grateful for the unique intellectual environment at Clark that nurtured so many different thoughts and convinced me that psychoanalytic interpretations of movies and psychological experiments belong in the same universe.

The publication team at Wiley-Blackwell (Andy Peart, Karen Shield and Tori Halliday) gently guided me through a process that was new to me. I appreciate the opportunity.

Special thanks to Alfred Hitchcock, Martin Scorsese, Woody Allen, George Lucas, and the many other filmmakers who inspired my passion for film in the first place.

Finally, I'd like to express my gratitude to my family for accommodating my distraction and diminished energy. I hope to spend more time with them now, playing and maybe watching a few movies (instead of just writing about them).

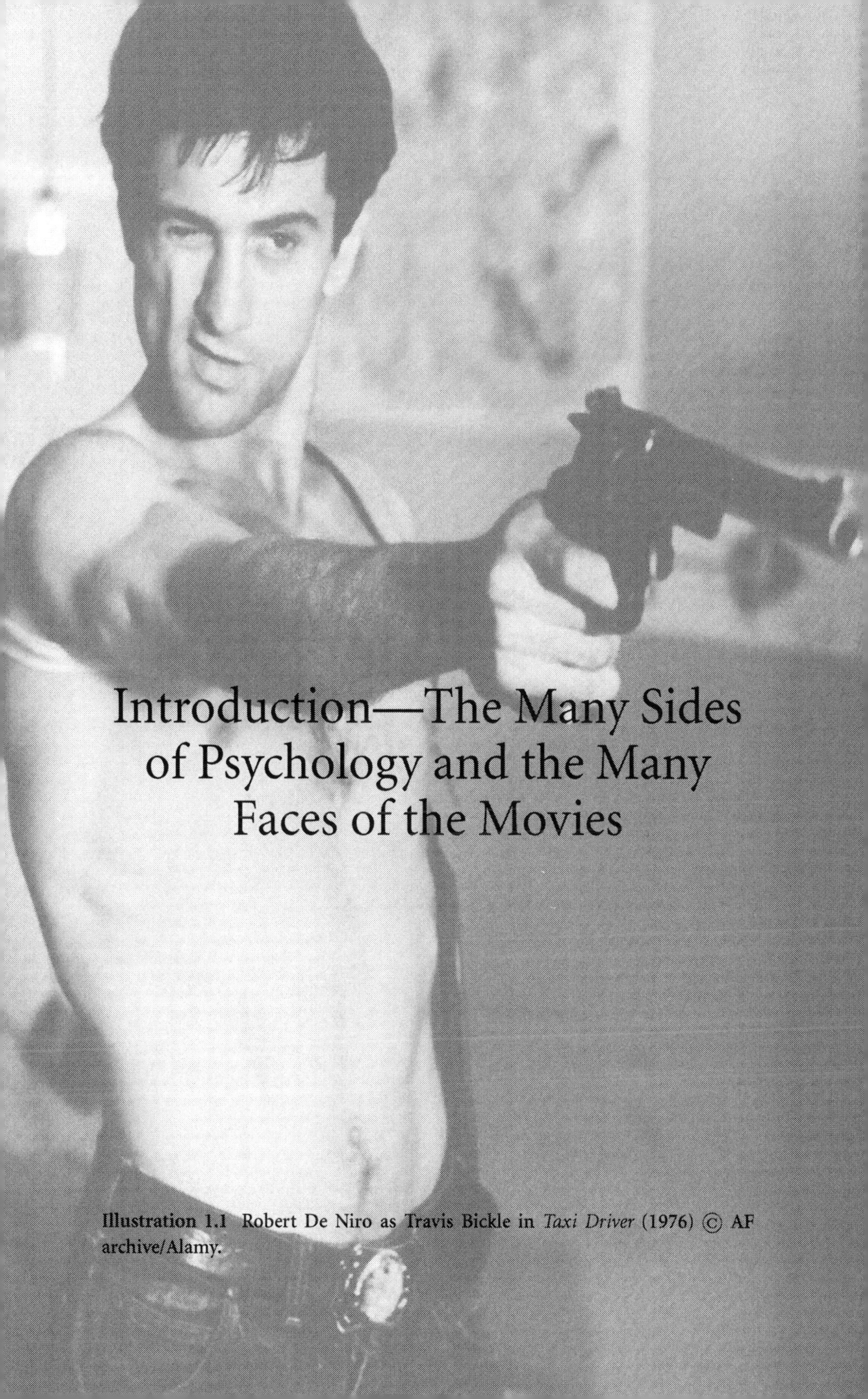

# Introduction—The Many Sides of Psychology and the Many Faces of the Movies

Illustration 1.1  Robert De Niro as Travis Bickle in *Taxi Driver* (1976) © AF archive/Alamy.

# Chapter 1

# Introduction—The Many Sides of Psychology and the Many Faces of the Movies

Like all art, movies are saturated with the human mind—they are created by humans, they depict human action, and they are viewed by a human audience. Movies are a particularly vivid art form, making use of striking moving images and vibrant sounds to connect filmmakers to the audience through celluloid and the senses.

Consider the following story[1]: Martin Scorsese was born in Flushing, New York in 1942 and grew up in the tough Little Italy section of lower Manhattan. Because of an asthmatic condition he could not play like the other children and spent much his time indoors watching movies, where he was partially protected from the mean streets of New York City, yet felt lonely and isolated. He was deeply immersed in Catholicism and briefly attended a seminary before enrolling in NYU's film school.

By the mid-70s, Scorsese was one of the young, ambitious directors (along with Arthur Penn, Francis Ford Coppola, Steven Spielberg and others) who were revolutionizing Hollywood. In 1976, he made *Taxi Driver* about an emotionally unstable cabbie, Travis Bickle, who is trapped by the haunted streets of New York City. Actor Robert De Niro starred in the film and invested Travis's intrapsychic struggles with a terrifying realism.

*Taxi Driver* was a tour-de-force of raw language, disturbing imagery, and innovative cinematic techniques. In one famous sequence, an elaborate,

*Psychology at the Movies*, First Edition. Skip Dine Young.
© 2012 John Wiley & Sons, Ltd. Published 2012 by John Wiley & Sons, Ltd.

Illustration 1.2   Director Martin Scorsese holds a gun on the set of *Taxi Driver*
© Steve Schapiro/Corbis.

Illustration 1.3   John Hinckley Jr, who attempted to assassinate Ronald Reagan
in 1981, poses in front of the White House. © Bettmann/Corbis.

slow-motion overhead tracking shot surveys the carnage that has resulted from Travis's convoluted attempt to rescue a child prostitute (Jodie Foster). That scene in particular was considered so violent that the Motion Picture Association of America insisted that Scorsese alter the hue of the blood in order to avoid an X rating.

Despite its less than commercial subject matter, *Taxi Driver* was highly successful and audiences lined up. Reactions among audience members were polarized. Some viewers proclaimed it to be not only technically brilliant but also a cathartic descent into the scarred psyche of an individual character and of America itself. Other viewers found the film to be exploitative and morally misguided. A scene in which Travis, shirtless but outfitted with multiple guns and holsters, looks into the mirror and asks threateningly, "You talkin' to me?" became a part of the common lexicon.

In 1981, one viewer, John Hinckley, Jr, watched the movie 15 times in a retro theater. He was inspired to assassinate President Reagan in order to gain the attention of Jodie Foster with whom Hinckley was romantically obsessed. The assassination failed, but Reagan was shot and several people were seriously wounded, including Reagan's Press Secretary, James Brady, who was paralyzed for life. Hinckley was diagnosed with paranoid schizophrenia and found not guilty by reason of insanity. The incident became part of the cultural debate on the insanity defense, gun control, and the role of media in society.

Over 30 years later, *Taxi Driver* is still used frequently by pundits and college professors to make points about all manner of things—the cultural zeitgeist of the 1970s; the distortion in media representations; the nature of paranoid thinking; and so on.

Where is the psychology in this story? Obviously, it is everywhere. Scorsese's personal background in a difficult social environment becomes melded with his individual talents and obsessions. These themes of sin, hardship, aggression and redemption appear in films like *Taxi Driver*, not only in the stories but in the choice of camera angles and color schemes. Aware that art has a relationship to the world outside of the theater, some viewers laud the film for its insightful portrayal of insanity and cultural rot while others find the film disturbing and worry about the message it sends. One psychotic viewer takes the movie as a usable model for assassinating the president. One can easily imagine an entire book on *The Psychology of Taxi Driver*.

Perhaps a more revealing question is: What is not psychological about this story? There are elements that could be divorced from the realm of psychology—perhaps the *technical* use of tracking shots or the *historical* aspects of America in the 1970s. But these distinctions break down if you think about them too much. After all, a camera shot forms the basis for the audience's perceptual experience. And the history of the 1970s is embodied in characters like Travis, artists like Scorsese, and audience members like Hinckley. Once you start looking for it, you can't escape psychology in the movies. There may be ways of talking about movies without highlighting psychological elements, but as a psychologist, I am not sure why anybody would want to.

## Goals of *Psychology at the Movies*

The basic premise of this book is that all movies are psychologically alive, exploding with human drama. This drama has been looked at from many different angles. It is significant that both laboratory psychology and clinical psychoanalysis emerged at almost the same historical point as motion pictures—the end of the nineteenth century.[2] The cultural impact of both psychology and film over that next century-plus has obviously been enormous. All along this historical path, there have been many occasions when psychologists have looked at movies as well as many times when movies have looked at psychologists. This book creates a snapshot of the fascinating interweaving between psychology and the movies.

There is no way to even summarize all of the work that has been done on the psychology of movies in one book. The body of available studies, analyses, and commentaries is truly vast—worthy not of a single book but of a library. One prominent early psychologist (and still the psychologist with the best name), Hugo Munsterberg, wrote a book, *The Photoplay: A Psychological Study* in 1916, and the scholarship has been expanding for a century. The present book can be thought of as a kind of directory for the mythical "International Library of Psychology and Film," identifying different sections of the library and calling attention to some of the most interesting works.

The scope of fields I cover is far-reaching. As far as I am aware, no other book has attempted to bring so many diverse approaches together under one cover. It considers everything from Freudian psychoanalysis of Hitchcock films to the uncanny popularity of certain movies to children's film-inspired aggression toward a Bobo doll. As the research on film has become more abundant, it has also become more fractured; most recent books addressing issues related to psychology and film are likely to cover only one or two of the chapters contained here. Throughout this book, I hope to distinguish different approaches, concisely describe fundamental issues, and provide evocative cinematic examples. In every case, my overviews are not meant to be definitive; instead they are meant to provide clues for further exploration.

The primary intended readers for this book are students and non-professionals who have a love of movies and/or psychology. Therefore it is relatively jargon-free, and when I do use technical terms, I pause to explain them. All of the research traditions discussed in this book are grounded in essential film-related human phenomena about which many people are curious; my task is to reveal those kernels of widespread fascination to a broad audience. In addition, the book may be useful to individuals already familiar with certain areas of the psychology of film. By drawing connections between diverse areas of study, alternative avenues of exploration are suggested that may be instructive even for experts. Ultimately, my goal is to help as many people as possible more fully appreciate the movies in our midst.

My personal and professional background has prepared me well for this undertaking. Most importantly, I am a movie fan. Ever since biweekly trips to the grimy movie theater on the American Army post in Germany on which I grew up, I have loved the movies. When I returned to the US in my 'tweens, I discovered the wonders of an ever-expanding cable revolution that made many movies easily available. In my teens, trips to the movie theater and VHS rentals were a critical part of both my social life and my alone time. I learned to like all kinds of movies—American and foreign, popular and arty, old and new—but I developed a particular fondness for Hitchcock, suspense movies in general, and dark, satirical comedies.

It was this passion for movies that led to several educational choices when I got to college. As an undergraduate at Miami University (Ohio), I majored in psychology and minored in film studies. I wrote movie reviews for the school newspaper. I did my senior honors thesis on college men's experiences of watching violence in film using the then-current *Blue Velvet* as my primary stimulus.

I subsequently chose to do my graduate work at Clark University in Worcester, Massachusetts. Clark holds a unique place in the history of American psychology: It was co-founded by the prominent early American psychologist, G. Stanley Hall, and it has the honor of being the only place in America where Freud ever spoke.[3] Clark's intellectual flavor was strongly influenced when developmental psychologist Heinz Werner settled there after fleeing Nazi Germany. Werner considered "development" to be a guiding *concept* that considers what it means for humans to progress toward some imagined end point (e.g., maturity, transcendence, enlightenment, happiness, etc.). His approach was more open to interdisciplinary thinking than much of mainstream American psychology, and Werner's work naturally integrated child development, anthropology, clinical psychology, and philosophy.[4] This unrestricted spirit thrived at Clark in the 1990s when I was in graduate school. I was trained as a clinical psychologist, but I was also immersed in other dimensions of psychology (including developmental psychology, cultural psychology, narrative psychology, and neuropsychology) and was exposed to cross-disciplinary influences such as interpretive philosophy and literary studies.[5] I ended up receiving an almost classical liberal graduate education. In this rich environment, I continued to pursue my interests in the psychology of film.

When it came time to pursue my career, I naturally gravitated toward liberal arts colleges. These kinds of (usually small) colleges take a holistic, interdisciplinary approach to education and strive to teach students fundamental intellectual skills such as writing, critical thinking, and the ability to engage in rational dialogue. I am currently a professor in the Psychology Department at Hanover College in Indiana where I have taught for 15 years. I teach clinically oriented classes like Behavior Disorders and Counseling and Psychotherapy, as well as pet courses like The Psychology of Film. I am also a licensed clinical psychologist.

Teaching at a liberal arts college has helped prepare me for writing this text. I have spent thousands of hours in close proximity to students, giving lectures to small groups, discussing ideas in seminars, and sitting with students working on independent projects. I have frequently used movies, music, and other symbolic media as teaching tools. My students are typically bright, curious individuals, but they do not often share the same language as their professors. This can be a good thing; if one spends too much time around other "experts," it is easy to get lost in jargon and technicalities and to forget the fundamental assumptions of a field. Undergraduate students, on the other hand, tend to ask the basic questions, and far from being naïve, these often get to the heart of the matter. I want *Psychology at the Movies* to focus on the heart of the matter as well.

The type of scholarship that is expected at a liberal arts college is also an advantage in writing this book. Liberal arts colleges are sometimes referred to as "teaching colleges," indicating the high value these institutions place on teaching and student learning. Professors at most liberal arts colleges do not function with the "publish or perish" mentality that characterizes much of modern higher education. I have published in the area of psychology and the movies, but I have also had the freedom to do research on student retention and even on the music of Bob Dylan.[6]

In contrast, much of modern academics has become so specialized that researchers often work in sub-subfields that allow for minimal contact with individuals outside of their specialty, even when they are in the same discipline. The liberal arts philosophy applied to scholarship requires an integrative, interdisciplinary approach. *Psychology at the Movies* casts a wide net designed to fall across many current intellectual divides and, because of this, it will hopefully be stimulating to readers who have an open-minded interest in all things *psychological* and all things *cinematic*.

## Story, Entertainment and Art in the Movies

This book is about "movies," a term everybody understands intuitively. However, there is some fuzziness around the margins that may occasionally be confusing. So in order to limit the scope of the book, I will focus on *narrative, theatrical films created for entertainment/artistic purposes*. A few of these terms are worth exploring:

Narrative: Most of the films that are discussed tell stories that have a beginning, a middle, and an end. Some of the stories are simple, some of them are complex. Some of the stories are told in a very straightforward manner while others make use of flashbacks (e.g., *Titanic*), intentional ambiguity (*Donnie Darko*) or mixed-up time sequences (e.g., *Pulp Fiction*). Occasionally, an experimental film like *Koyaanisqatsi*, which eliminates story almost entirely in favor of a concentration on abstract movement, shape, and color, will find an audience, but this is rare. In general I make the assumption that there is something special about narrative structure that people find especially compelling.

Most commercial films tell fictional stories; they do not claim to represent events as they actually happened. Even biopics that strive for historical accuracy are understood to be *recreations* of past events. Documentary films are the exception because they do purport to present real people and events. Still, in most cases documentaries are organized so that they tell a story about a person, event, or phenomenon. The documentary approach has expanded beyond television news programs and the History Channel to include highly successful films like *Fahrenheit 9/11*, *March of the Penguins*, and *Waiting for Superman*. Documentary stories have somewhat different psychological characteristics, but fictional films are the focus of this book. In particular, commercial feature-length films are my primary concern since most people are not exposed to short or amateur films on a regular basis.[7]

*Theatrical*: Before the 1950s, virtually all movies were meant to be exhibited on a theater screen to a mass audience. Since then, movies intended for theaters have been distributed in numerous formats—on television, VHS, DVD, Blu-Ray, home computer, and so on. These days many visual narratives are created for media other than a theater screen (e.g., a TV sit-com or a "straight-to-video" DVD). There are many similar psychological characteristics shared by film and other visual media. Therefore, some scholars define their subjects of study as "media," not "film" or "television." Yet theatrical movies have a special history and prestige compared with other visual media that contributes unique psychological characteristics. While I occasionally refer to TV and other forms of popular culture, I favor examples from theatrical films.

*Entertainment/Artistic*: All forms of entertainment have artistic qualities, and all art has qualities of entertainment. The term "entertainment" tends to imply that people seek it out because it is pleasurable. People also presumably get enjoyment from their artistic experiences, or they probably wouldn't seek them out repeatedly. Viewers who claim they watch films *only* for their aesthetic value and not because they enjoy them are engaged in a masochistic ritual that is far from the visible passion of fans of either Adam Sandler or Ingmar Bergman (of course, Freud would argue that the masochistic aesthetes are deriving unconscious pleasure out from their sacrificial viewing anyway).

*Psychology at the Movies* is interested in the broad range of movies—high art movies, low culture trash, and everything in between. "Art" tends to imply that an object has some sort of special quality that stimulates a meaningful, reflective experience. Yet this quality may be true of Hollywood's most entertaining movies—*Star Wars, Casablanca, The Wizard of Oz*. The issue of whether a given movie is art (thought-provoking) versus entertainment (pleasurable) is a matter of degree that can vary in reference to the intentions of the film makers, the formal qualities of the film, and/or the attitude and viewing context of the audience. Some films may be more sophisticated, wide-ranging and powerful in their artistic potential, but such claims are about good art versus bad art, not whether something *is* or *is not* art.

## A Liberal Use of Psychology

Many people who have never taken an academic course in psychology tend to associate "psychology" with the ideas of Sigmund Freud (e.g., dreams and the unconscious) or with clinical psychology more generally (e.g., counseling and psychological disorders). These associations are relevant but narrow, since psychology also covers neuropsychology (the chemical activity of the brain), social psychology (people's behavior in crowds), sensation and perception (the workings of the inner eye), learning (modeling the actions of others), cognition (memory) and many other areas and subspecialties. Moreover, psychology overlaps other disciplines in the social sciences such as sociology, anthropology, and communication. Since people are biological beings, there is a strong historical connection between psychology and biology. Finally, psychologists are often interested in the same topics—social relationships, products of the imagination, and human nature—as scholars in humanities such as philosophy and literary criticism.

Psychology is undeniably a broad field, and I treat it even more broadly than most psychologists: I think of it simply as the study of thought and action, with a focus on humans. This definition is not so different from those found in most intro psych textbooks.[8] However, textbooks typically follow with caveats about how the study of thought and action must be done in a certain way in order to qualify as psychology—*particular methods must be followed*.[9] This attention to *method* is important to the textbook writers in distinguishing "real" psychology from what is often referred to as "pseudo-psychology" or "pop-psychology." It is also used to distinguish psychology from related academic disciplines in the social sciences and the humanities.

*Psychology at the Movies* takes a *liberal* (as in "the liberal arts") approach to what is meant by psychology. In these pages, experimental psychology, cultural psychology, Freudian psychoanalysis, mass communication and film/literary criticism (not to mention bits of philosophy, neuroscience and pop-psych) coexist and intermingle. One of my models is Malcolm Gladwell and his best-selling books *Blink* (2005) and *Outliers* (2008). I find Gladwell to be among the most interesting commentators on social psychological phenomena in the past decade. Gladwell's background as a journalist frees him from strict disciplinary loyalty and allows him to freely mix neuroscience, experiments, demographics, and good old-fashioned case studies as he develops his ideas.[10]

In response to the compartmentalizing tendencies of modern academics, Robert Sternberg and his collaborators have called for a "unified psychology" that integrates various related disciplines and subdisciplines by focusing on particular *phenomena of interest* and not simply drawing lines based on different methods and historical traditions.[11] *Psychology at the Movies* is written in this unifying spirit: people *in* movies, people *making* movies, and people *watching* movies are the phenomena of interest. If there are research traditions out there that have been interested in these phenomena, I have attempted to address them, at least cursorily. Unfortunately, many of these approaches have developed in relative isolation from each other over an extended period of time. When there has been contact, it has sometimes been hostile. By making interconnections, I hope I can facilitate overdue conversations between these previously divorced perspectives and methods.

All methods are not the same nor equal in achieving particular ends. Some may be based on nonsense and lead to nothing. However, one can safely assume that any of the methods that have been used by intelligent, thoughtful scholars over a period of many years have a basis in reason. That doesn't mean they never lead to mistakes, but it does strongly suggest there is likely some compelling rationale for the "method in their madness."

Every method allows us to see some things, but it also keeps us from seeing other things. I like the example of an astronomer looking through a powerful telescope allowing him to see faraway galaxies that are invisible to the naked eye, thereby making enormous contributions to knowledge. However, by using a single method, there are many parts of reality of which the scientist may be unaware: he is not only blind to parts of the galaxy where the telescope is not aimed at a given moment, but even to actions occurring in the room, such as his wife walking up behind him. If he wants to see and understand her, he would be advised to use a different method.[12]

Therefore, I will consider all established methodological approaches which claim to shed light on the relationship between movies and human actions. These include methods that lie at the core of psychology as a scientific discipline (e.g., a laboratory-based experiment in which factors are carefully controlled and varied), but also methods that are closer to psychology as a clinical discipline (e.g., a case study of film being used in insight-oriented psychotherapy) and the humanities (e.g., interpretation of a film based on feminist relational theory). Each method is discussed in terms of its advantages (what it tells us) and limitations (what it does *not* tell us). What might at first appear to be different disciplines reaching contradictory conclusions could turn out to be different disciplines looking at different aspects of reality. This approach to method is at once inclusive yet discriminating.

## A Symbolic Framework for the Psychology of Film

The psychology of film can be unified by thinking of movies as symbols. Movies are symbols that have meaning; these symbols are created by filmmakers, and they are received by audiences. The four components of this framework are outlined in Figure 1.1:[13]

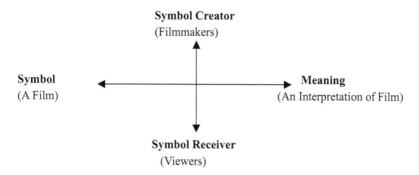

**Figure 1.1** Symbolic activity in film.

Symbols always have physical properties; films are made up of images and sounds projected onto a screen. They are not random but have the potential to be comprehended. A blue neon tube of light accompanied by a humming sound in *Star Wars* is understood to be a light saber (as opposed to a random stream of blue light bouncing around the screen). Symbolic meanings usually build upon one another as individual images are related to other images. As viewers begin to grasp the *Star Wars* universe, they recognize that the person holding a light saber is a member of the Jedi order. Most movies combine symbols into coherent narrative wholes in which a cast of characters participate in events that take place over space and time.[14]

The meaning of symbols can be extended beyond the *story world* and understood as representations of people, places, and ideas that have relevance to the *real world*; that is, viewers can interpret the Jedi's weapon as a symbol of heroism. This theme can in turn be used to interpret *Star Wars* as a film about the triumph of good over evil.

Symbols can be interpreted in many ways, some of which may be contradictory.[15] A Freudian psychoanalyst might look at the long blue beam of light and interpret it as a phallic symbol (it symbolizes erotic yearning). A feminist critic might spin this interpretation and argue that the light saber is actually symbolic of displaced masculine hostility. (This kind of thing can go back and forth for a while.)

Symbols never spring from a void—somebody has to give them life. Symbols are created by symbol-makers. Graphic artists, novelists, sculptors, even the writers of technical manuals on how to shingle a roof, all rely on symbols to communicate their meaning. Moviemakers are another type of symbol-maker. Directors, writers, actors and other artists collaborate to produce the particular symbolic objects shown in multiplexes. Filmmakers inevitably bring aspects of themselves—their deep inner passions, their habitual behavioral patterns, their self-conscious values, their unexamined cultural biases—to the symbols they create.

Finally, symbols are received by other people. They are sensed (seen, heard, felt, smelled and/or tasted) and processed by those who are exposed to them. The potential audience for the cinematic symbols is enormous. Blockbusters like *Avatar* or *Lord of the Rings* are seen by billions of people worldwide.[16] The processing that happens before, during and after viewing a movie is of core psychological interest. Why do viewers decide to spend a Friday evening watching a particular film (whether it's *Saw XVII* or Woody Allen's latest bittersweet comedy)? What is going on inside (both physiologically and psychically) viewers as they watch? And what are the consequences for viewers after seeing a movie and reemerging into their everyday lives?

Every example presented in this book can be seen as a "symbolic event." If a film is said to have meaning, it is symbolic. If the personal characteristics of the filmmakers impacted their artistic choices, it is symbolic. If an audience member responds to a film in a certain way, it is symbolic.[17]

## Organization of *Psychology at the Movies*

Figure 1.2 outlines the structure of the book, with filmmakers on the top, the process of meaning making in the middle, and movie viewers on the bottom.

Chapters 2 and 3 consider representations of human action that may be found *in* the movies. Chapter 2 looks at a variety of human behaviors represented in movies, focusing on interpretive approaches (e.g., Freudian psychoanalysis) that hunt for deeper meanings that many not necessarily be obvious to the average viewer. Chapter 3 narrows the scope to offer an intensive view of activities associated with psychology in the public imagination as they are portrayed in movies: psychological disorders (schizophrenia, alcoholism, narcissism, etc.) and psychological interventions (psychotherapy).

Chapter 4 moves away from movies as objects and considers the people who create movies. What do these filmmakers bring to movies, and in what

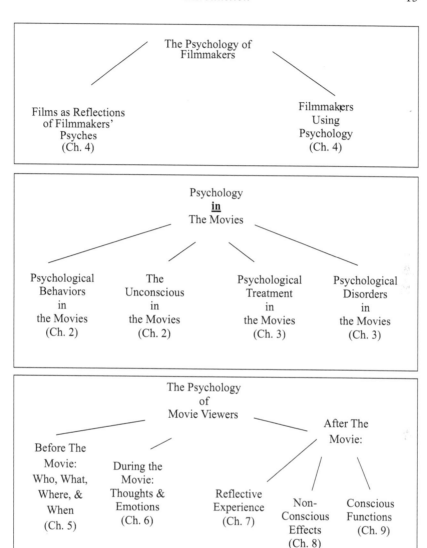

**Figure 1.2** The many faces of *Psychology at the Movies.*

ways do they infuse aspects of themselves into their creations? While it is probable that everyone who works on a movie brings something of him or herself to the activity, I focus on those artists whose individuality is in the foreground—the directors (who make the final choices about how a movie looks and sounds) and the actors (whose visual likeness is so vividly captured on the screen).

Chapters 5 through 9 focus on the other end of the symbolic spectrum—the viewers who interact with the film's images and sounds. Chapter 5 takes a broad view of the audience to consider such psychosocial questions as: What kinds of movies do people watch? Who watches movies? Where and when do people watch movies? Chapter 6 looks at *the cinematic moment*—what is happening *inside* people as they watch a movie. Viewers must perceive images and comprehend them in order to figure out what the story is about. Simultaneously, watching a movie involves a great deal of emotion and can provoke intense feelings of fear, delight, and sadness.

Chapter 7 picks up after the movie has stopped playing yet continues to *live* in the memories and ongoing reflective processes of the viewers. After leaving the theater, viewers often evaluate their experience—good versus bad; enjoyable versus not enjoyable; depressing versus uplifting. Also viewers sometimes take the time to interpret a movie more thoroughly, reflecting on its themes or how it reflects the real world.

Chapters 8 and 9 focus on the consequences of watching movies: Do movies change the thoughts and behavior of the audience? Chapter 8 considers the evidence that movies can affect the behavior and thinking of some people some of the time, even though they may not be aware that film is having an effect on them. Chapter 9 highlights the ways in which movies function as "equipment for living"—those situations in which people *self-consciously* use movies to promote education, healing, and identity development.

Finally, Chapter 10 puts all the pieces together to consider how the many approaches to the psychology of film interact with each other. The combined panorama of perspectives offers a rich, dynamic portrait of the role of film in society and individual lives.

## Further Reading

Munsterberg, H. (1970) *The Film: A Psychological Study*. Dover, New York, NY.
Sternberg, R.J. and Grigorenko, E.L. (2001) Unified psychology. *American Psychologist*, 56 (12), 1069–1079.
Werner, H. and Kaplan, B. (1984) *Symbol Formation*. Lawrence Erlbaum, Hillsdale, NJ.

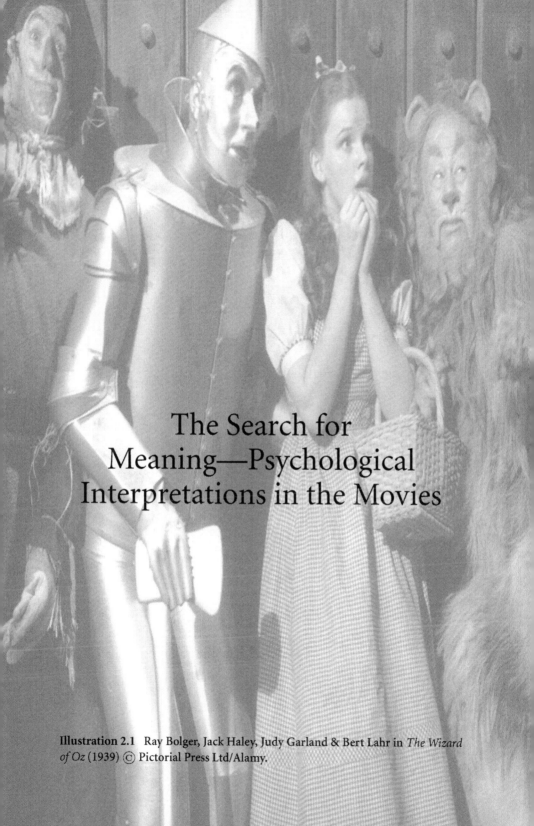

# The Search for Meaning—Psychological Interpretations in the Movies

**Illustration 2.1**   Ray Bolger, Jack Haley, Judy Garland & Bert Lahr in *The Wizard of Oz* (1939) © Pictorial Press Ltd/Alamy.

# Chapter 2

# The Search for Meaning—Psychological Interpretations in the Movies

What is the meaning of *The Wizard of Oz*?

This question upsets some people. They stare at you, squint and declare, "What do you mean, 'What does it mean?' It's a kids' movie. It doesn't *mean* anything." This type of person is going to hate this chapter.

Then there is another type who loves questions like this. Their eyes light up when they hear phrases like "hidden meaning" and "deeper significance." These people are going to love this chapter.

Like it or not, over the years *The Wizard of Oz* has been the object of much high- and low-minded speculation. Because the film has always had a particular fascination for me, I have kept a mental record of the different things people have said about it. One of the first commentaries about *Oz* came in junior high when the phrase, "There's no place like home" was presented as an example of a theme or moral. That made sense, but when I thought about it, I began to wonder if that was the *real* message. I remember thinking that the movie's case for the superiority of "home" was kind of weak. Kansas is presented in dull sepia tones as a barren place of drudgery, while Oz bursts with Technicolor, fantasy and adventure; the choice of which was the better place seemed obvious to me.

The search for meaning didn't stop with these casual musings. In high school, I learned that in his book, L.L. Baum used the Yellow Brick Road

*Psychology at the Movies*, First Edition. Skip Dine Young

as a symbolic defense of the gold standard. I didn't understand (and hardly cared) about turn-of-the-century economic politics, but the interpretation did bring home the possibility of metaphor appearing where I didn't expect it. A few years later, I was exposed to the persistent rumor that if *Oz* was synced with Pink Floyd's classic album *Dark Side of the Moon*, all sorts of cross-references would appear (e.g., a heartbeat heard at the end of "Eclipse," just as Dorothy puts her hand on the Tin Man's chest). What this actually suggests about the *meaning of Oz* is unclear, but this mystical synchronicity did drive the film even deeper into the realm of the profound.

Critics have also spent time interpreting *The Wizard of Oz*. One analyst interprets Dorothy's journey in the film as a metaphor for the feminine transition to adolescence.[1] Another writer extends this analysis to the cultural domain to argue that the film represents a puberty rite.[2] The gender focus is shifted to argue that Dorothy's experience captures gay male individuation, including the coming-out experience.[3] Yet another observer has argued that the characters of the Scarecrow, Tin Man, and Cowardly Lion represent Dorothy's attempt to achieve balance by integrating masculine characteristics.[4] Finally, a psychotherapist argues that the plot systematically captures qualities associated with therapeutic healing (the establishment of interpersonal bonds and the development of perceived mastery).[5]

This chapter takes the perspective that films are *windows* or *mirrors* into the world of human behavior, the workings of the mind, and human nature itself. Contained *in* movies, we can see individual development taking place—the operation of unconscious defense mechanisms, social-psychological processes, and so on. Here, film is a landscape on which psychological entities are projected.

Through a process of *reading* or *interpreting* film as one type of symbolic *text* (other types include novels, poems, photographs, statues, etc.),[6] it is possible to gain greater insight into individuals and society. This interpretive approach has been very popular when it comes to films, not only for the field of academic film studies, but for scholars in other disciplines, film critics who write for newspapers and magazines, and movie buffs who enjoy getting their hands dirty with deeper meanings.

While theorists periodically attempt to laud film for its realism, there has been a long running tendency among film commentators to view films as dreams.[7] Movies have a mysterious quality that suggests their surfaces are not what they appear to be and therefore beg for a more satisfactory explanation than literalism can provide.

If a shared impulse compels people to understand what a movie means, there are few universally shared beliefs about how one should go about interpreting a movie. This is where *theory* comes in; when interpreters approach a movie, they typically have pre-established ideas about the essence of film, society or human nature that directs them as they go about their meaning-making business.[8] The history of film studies is characterized by dozens of more or less distinct theoretical approaches involving textual interpretation.[9]

If we focus on the fact that human minds create films (people make choices about costumes, lightning, dialogue, etc.), all films may be seen as reflections of the human mind. Thus, movies can't be discussed unless they are watched by thinking, feeling human beings. When we analyze a film, we are, at least in part, analyzing the mind *through* film. In this chapter I focus on several approaches to film interpretation *explicitly* grounded in psychosocial theories of human nature and embodied in phrases like "behavioral patterns," "repressed desires" and "mental apparatus."

## Human Behavior in the Movies

While there are infinite realms of human behavior that could be depicted in the plots, characters and setting of films, not all of these behaviors require sophisticated theories to understand. Social scientists have taken a magnifying glass to many behavioral domains shown in the movies including sex, violence, politics, gambling, gender, motherhood, smoking, drinking, sports, college, crime, juvenile delinquency, dreams, poverty, wealth, romance, anger, domestic violence, old age, psychotherapy, and mental illness.[10] Usually studies that zero in on particular types of behavior or people are interested in trends across multiple movies. While these cinematic depictions do not necessarily portray objective reality accurately, we can assume that they capture widespread perceptions of particular behaviors and even viewers' attitudes toward these behaviors.[11]

One approach to classifying behavior exhibited in film is relatively intuitive. An analyst simply defines a particular behavior pattern and then identifies select films, characters, and genres that exemplify these trends. It has become common for movie critics in publications like *Time* and *Entertainment Weekly* to refer to the "man-child" phenomenon in the comedies of the 1990s and 2000s—emotionally stunted characters often played by Adam Sandler, Will Farrell, or Seth Rogen who reflect the hesitancy of Generations X and Y to "man-up" and accept their responsibilities. Intuitive approaches also appear in scholarly journals; one article examines films since

1970 that routinely portray evangelical Christians as hypocritical, naïve, or psychotic.[12]

Content analysis is a more systematic approach to studying human behaviors in media; it can be applied to written (novels and poetry), aural (music), or visual (magazine advertising and film) forms.[13] This approach has two defining components: systematically generating a *sample* of films to be analyzed, while consistently applying an explicit *coding scheme* to each film in the sample. Content analysis represents an alliance between mainstream social scientific approaches and textual/interpretive approaches. Since the coding scheme is designed to be applied by anyone and yield the same results, a demonstrable degree of "reliability" is established (the observations of one observer are shared by other observers). Thus, a carefully conducted content analysis is able to assert that a particular analysis is not just the idiosyncratic fantasies of one clever critic.[14]

Just like rock and roll, the most common topics of interest for film content analysis have been violence, sex, and drugs (and other unhealthy behaviors).[15] In regards to violence, a widely cited national study documented that children's programs were significantly more violent than adult programming, with up to 30 acts of violence per hour.[16] Many of these incidents were less graphic and more humorous than adult violence, however. It is likely that this pattern holds for children's movies as well. While some believe that unrealistic violence is less disturbing to children, the authors point out that such depictions can be relatively more influential on children's behavior because the negative *consequences* of violence are downplayed.

Researchers have also focused on "relational aggression"—indirect but harmful actions such as spreading rumors, exclusion, and the silent treatment captured in *Mean Girls*.[17] Animated Disney films were found to represent indirect aggression nine times per hour.[18] Interestingly, both "good" and "bad" Disney characters engaged in relational aggression. However, the good characters' actions tended to be lightly aggressive (e.g., a defiant gesture or a dirty look) while the bad characters' actions were more harmful to others (e.g., pressuring, casting harmful spells, or scheming, such as Gaston's plotting against the Beast in *Beauty and the Beast*).

Sex in the media has also received a great deal of attention, not just in mainstream film, but in women's magazines, television, and pornography. The practical reality of how these studies are conducted is a bit surreal: graduate students in austere laboratories, surrounded by stacks of porn, watch people have sex while they hold clipboards in their laps and take notes on the variations in sexual partners and positions. The results of this odd activity sometimes confirm what most people would intuitively guess, but occasionally the results challenge assumptions.[19] By watching a sample of R-rated films from the 1980s, researchers found that sex between unmarried couples was more commonly depicted than sex between married couples. While this may not be shocking in itself, the strength of the pattern was surprising: 32 unmarried sex acts to one married sex act. Either Hollywood believes that married people do not have sex, or marital sex just isn't that interesting to screenwriters.

Analyses of pornographic videos/movies tend to focus on tabulating gender-pairings and types of sex acts.[20] Such studies provide a picture of the kinds of pervasive images that are part the cultural environment. One finding from a large-scale analysis of 443 sexually explicit videos from the 1980s looked at *power relationships* in the depiction of sex acts.[21] It found that only a third of the sex scenes clearly indicated that both partners were equally motivated. Instead, the majority of sex acts were initiated by the physical domination (usually by the male) or manipulation (e.g., an employer exploiting a worker) of one partner over the other.

The combination of sex *and* violence in the movies has proven to be an irresistible research topic. In the mid-90s an unlikely scholarly debate broke out between two factions of social scientists arguing about the gender-ratio of violent deaths in so-called "slasher" films (horror films in which a homicidal maniac stalks and kills a series of victims).[22] One group of researchers contended that movie slashers were equal opportunity killers when it came to gender, while the other group emphasized the frequency of violence against women and the degree to which the female characters' sexual activity was related to their ultimate demise. The pattern that "good girls" survive while "bad girls" are killed is recognized outside academia; characters in the blockbuster *Scream* self-consciously muse about the fate of other characters based on their sexual behavior. The most recent analysis of this issue confirmed that, indeed, sexualized females characters are less likely to survive slasher films and that their death scenes are likely to be extended.[23] This is a good example of how social science research can overlap observations made by attentive fans and critics.

Health-related behaviors (or, more typically, *unhealthy* behaviors) in film such as alcohol/substance use, condom use and exercise are frequent topics of content analysis. This interest corresponds to the recent expansion of health psychology, an applied subfield dedicated to helping prevent and treat health problems through the application of psychological techniques.[24] As one of the crucial applications of health psych is on smoking prevention and cessation, it is not surprising that smoking in movies has been an area of interest.

The glamorous black and white images of classical Hollywood stars like Humphrey Bogart and Lauren Bacall seductively puffing on cigarettes as wisps of smoke twirl around them is imprinted in the public imagination. Given the change in social attitudes, one might assume that smoking behavior has decreased in movies. Yet several content analyses indicate that this is not the case; the incidence of smoking in movies was the same in 2002 as it was in 1950, despite a dramatic drop in the proportion of the US population that smokes.[25] The same studies do reveal significant differences in *how* smoking is portrayed. In recent years, *minor* characters smoked more often than stars, and smoking is presented in a more negative context (e.g., associated with hostility or tension reduction).[26] This is an interesting example of how Hollywood wants to have its cake/cigarettes (continue to portray a visually dramatic behavior) and eat/smoke it too (sympathetically reflect current values).

## Unconscious Conflict in the Movies

To some critics, content analysis as simply a way of scratching the surface of movies. In order to really understand the psychological implications of movies, the analyst has to consider *the deeper significance; the subtext; the implicit meaning; the hidden message; the underlying symbolism,* and so on. Paul Ricoeur's definition of a symbol is any object with both a "direct, primary, literal" meaning *and* an "indirect, secondary and figurative" meaning.[27] If film is understood to be inherently symbolic, with multiple levels of meaning, movies take on a magical quality in which they are "pregnant" with significance at the same time their meaning is uncertain. According to Ricoeur, twentieth-century thinking about human nature was strongly influenced by three scholars—Marx, Nietzsche, and Freud—whom he called "protagonists [philosophers] of suspicion."[28] Each of these theorists found that the major domains of human motivation (money, power, and sex, respectively) occurred on at least two levels—the obvious and the unobservable. Forces at the unobservable level have an enormous impact on the activities of daily life, yet by their nature, they resist easy understanding. Such theories have a high degree of "suspiciousness" built into them that does not trust the surface; truth is always buried and elusive.

Of these so-called suspicious philosophers, Freud has had the greatest influence on film theory.[29] Freudian theory (psychoanalysis) is extremely complicated; it uses a lot of jargon and has a fractured history, with many branches (like an extended family tree or the history of the Protestant church). Freud has always been a controversial figure, and serious criticism can be made of his methods and conclusion. As a result, when people first encounter psychoanalysis, they are often confused and sometimes tend to dismiss it based on a first impression of its most outlandish features. Yet many psychologists (myself included) still believe that many of Freud's core contentions are on target, and that even those ideas that seem off the mark are interesting.[30]

In my undergraduate teaching, I have sought to teach Freud in a manner that is accessible yet true to his ideas. The core of Freudian thought can be understood by grasping a few essential assumptions about human nature,[31] all of which have significant implications for how movies are interpreted.

1. From birth, human beings are *motivated* by selfish desires (such as hunger, sex, aggression) to please themselves and avoid suffering. *Self-centered pleasure seeking is commonly found in movies.*
2. We are born with basic motivations, our primordial life energies (the id). The harsh realities of life teach us that all of our desires cannot be fully satisfied, and we learn to negotiate the necessary compromises of everyday life (the ego). We eventually gain an internalized sense of right and wrong from our parents (the super-ego). If this internal organization does not *develop* properly, people run into problems. *Movies often share the belief in the importance of early development by employing life-spanning plots, flashbacks, or references to critical childhood events in dialogue.*
3. Because the id, ego, and super-ego all want different things, these three psychic structures are in an endless *conflict* with each other. Freud locates the center of the war zone in the ego; "a poor creature owing service to three masters and consequently menaced by three dangers; from the external world, from the libido of the id, and from the severity of the super-ego."[32] *All film narratives are grounded in conflict of one sort or another.*
4. Much of our psychic conflict is *unconscious*. Our consciousness feels the pain of our internal war, but the intricate attacks and counter-maneuvers themselves (defense mechanisms) are largely invisible. While unconsciousness is never revealed in its pure form, we can catch glimpses and shadows through *symbols. Since films are symbolic, they parallel the processes* (e.g., dream interpretation) *crucial to psychoanalytic therapy. The significance of a movie which is captured in a plot summary is only the surface; symbolic probing takes us into the hidden realms.*

Many viewers will acknowledge that the complex, hallucinatory master-pieces of a Hitchcock, Lynch, or Aronofsky explore basic human motivations and conflicts, but from a psychodynamic perspective,[33] *all films* (indeed, all stories) are reflections of our unconscious. Bruno Bettelheim's *The Uses of Enchantment* (1975) suggests that children's fairytales reveal universal unconscious conflicts. From his perspective, *Hansel and Gretel* is not just a fanciful tale; it has symbolic qualities that resonate with the desires and fears of children's young psyches. Hansel and Gretel's ravenous consump-tion of the gingerbread house represents the impulse toward ultimate oral gratification. Their imprisonment reflects the fears associated with acting on that desire. The witch is symbolic of the "bad mother," a child's anxiety that his or her mother may be not only inadequate, but dangerous.

Movies have their own fairy tales and wicked witches. A representa-tive Freudian reading of *The Wizard of Oz* takes Dorothy's adventure as a metaphor for the adolescent journey, the last distinct stage in Freudian developmental theory.[34] In terms of sexuality, adolescence is referred to as the "genital stage" in which the individual's erotic interests are focused on achieving intercourse. The social dimension of this shift is that before a girl can develop a sufficiently strong sense of herself as an individual worthy of a love partner, she has to recognize her parents' limitations. This possi-bility is initially so terrifying that "half-buried conflicts of childhood [are] resurrected to be resolved or haunt us forever."[35] Dorothy's first response is to rebel against her caring but imperfect guardians by retreating into fan-tasy. In her fantasy world, parental figures are polarized in their goodness (Glinda the *Good* Witch and Oz the *Powerful and Mighty*) and badness (the *Wicked* Witch). Dorothy must first face and conquer the Wicked Witch, the oppressive fantasy of parenthood that she fears. But she must also unmask the omnipotent Wizard in order to realize the power to go home is located in her. By the time she returns to Kansas, she has achieved the ego-state of a young adult who is ready to confront the realities of her everyday sepia-toned world.

The tradition of psychoanalytic film interpretation is not limited to children's movies. Wolfenstein and Leites' *The Movies: A Psychological Study* from the 1950s was one of the first attempts to articulate psycho-logically relevant themes in mainstream American movies using psycho-dynamic assumptions. One such theme—unjust attacks on an innocent hero—is captured in the *noir* classic *The Big Sleep*. Private eye Phillip Mar-lowe (Humphrey Bogart) is so regularly assaulted and threatened that he drolly remarks that everyone he meets seems to be pulling a gun on him. Since psychoanalysis assumes that all people are driven by selfish, impure impulses, the very idea of "innocence" is called into question. The aggression to which Marlowe is subjected is interpreted as a projection of his own aggressive impulses against the external world. Believing that the world is hostile can make it a scary place, but according to Freudian reasoning, this possibility is easier than accepting responsibility and guilt for our own aggression.

Psychodynamic analyses of movies can be maddening in their attention to seemingly unimportant details, and fascinating in their attempts to explain mysterious phenomena. Years ago my attention was drawn to an analysis of Kubrick's adaptation of *The Shining* in a psychoanalytic journal.[36] I have always found the movie uniquely creepy and mesmerizing. Freud would call my reaction to the film an example of the uncanny—the unnerving, chilling feeling of unexpectedly encountering some seemingly ordinary stimulus that nevertheless resonates on a deeper level. Freud of course has an explanation—it is what happens when we are unconsciously reminded of something we have repressed (held in the dark recesses of our minds). This repressed material is revealed for a fleeting moment, and we are left feeling uncomfortable yet intrigued.

Psychoanalysis suggests that the reason I have such a notable reaction is that, through subtle clues and hidden symbols, *The Shining* evokes the impulse toward genocide in Western masculinity. Freud argues that all people have a death instinct, and when it grows too strong and threatens the self, it is directed to other people. Genocide is an extreme variation of this death impulse. The film draws the connection to genocide, particularly Nazi-era Germany, through subtle clues and hidden symbols: the doomed writer, Jack Torrence (Jack Nicholson), drives to the isolated hotel in a Volkswagen; the yellow car (and other prominent yellow objects later in the film) is similar to the Star of David that Jews were forced to wear during World War II; Jack types his demented memoirs on a Nazi-era German typewriter; variations of the number 39 (as in 1939, the start of the war) can be seen on boxes in the food locker scene, and so on.

Numerous criticisms may be lodged against an analysis like this. First, it seems unlikely that these symbols were intended by the filmmakers; indeed, there is no evidence that this was the case.[37] However, the *conscious intentions* of writers and directors do not limit psychodynamic interpretations; it is always possible that *unconscious associations* are having an influence on artistic creation. Skeptics may also object that interpreting insignificant minutiae like the numbers on boxes strains credibility. However, for classical psychoanalysis, nothing is unimportant, as the unconscious mind perceives and associates to symbolic details of which we are consciously unaware.[38] It is hard to prove these kinds of claims, but once people start seeing movies this way, it can be hard to stop.

## Archetypes in the Movies

Carl Jung's archetypal theory is another psychological approach that has contributed a great deal to film interpretation.[39] Jung's theory is also centered on notions of symbolism and the unconscious, yet it diverges from Freud in notable ways.[40] In particular, Jung's understanding of the unconscious is that it is more than just primal impulses and unresolved personal complexes. Jung studied the images and stories of cultures from around the globe and across history and concluded that there are *universal* themes and patterns. He posited that the unconscious has a sphere called "the collective unconscious"—a psychic realm that is shared by all human beings. He argued that the collective unconscious is populated by universal themes (or forms of thought) he called archetypes. Archetypes manifest themselves as familiar characters, such as the Mother, the Father, the Wise Man, the Hero, and so on. [41]

While the archetypes in their pure form are inaccessible, people experience and understand these archetypes through symbols. We are surrounded by all sorts of symbols (touched by archetypes) in the course of day-to-day life—in dreams, on T-shirts, in novels, on billboard images, and of course in movies. When we are really paying attention, these archetypal symbols are emotionally resonant or even luminous. Thus, Jung asserts that symbols of motherhood are more than simple presentations of the reality of childbirth; instead, maternal symbols help people understand what it means to nurture and care for other human beings. Symbols are not just about understanding ourselves as individuals, or even our culture. They connect us to a bigger world, a world that is beyond us, a world of psychic "others."

We can choose to explore symbols or we can ignore them (or at least *try* to ignore—some symbols, like some movies, seem to haunt us). Symbols are not just a means of uncovering disturbing material from our unconscious; instead, they are full of possibility for personal growth and greater understanding of the cosmos. Analyzing films from this perspective can have a more playful quality than the dead-serious detective work often found in Freudian analysis. This is not to claim that a Jungian analysis of movies will always lead to positive feelings. The archetypes are not our friends, in that they do not necessarily have our best intentions in mind. Instead, archetypes present an unknown possibility between polar opposites. For example, nurturance is not the only side of the Mother archetype; the other pole is devouring, where the Mother threatens to overwhelm and suffocate her children. We can cite movies with saintly mothers such as *Lorenzo's Oil*, but *also* movies that present frightening mothers, like *Mommie Dearest*. The exploration of archetypal symbols in movies may be delightful at times, but the journey will be occasionally be scary and horrific.

*Star Wars* has probably received more attention from archetype-minded interpreters than any other film.[42] Listing its characters is like a stockpiling of archetypal personalities: Obi-Wan Kenobi (the Wise-Man); Luke Skywalker (the Hero); Han Solo (the Rogue); Princess Leia (the Damsel in Distress); Darth Vader (the Shadow), and so on. An obvious use of Jungian symbols occurs in a scene in *The Empire Strikes Back* where Luke is training with Yoda. In a mysterious, misty cave, Luke comes face-to-face with Darth Vader. In a brief light-saber battle, Luke seems to slay Vader. But when Luke opens the front of Vader's mask, he sees his own face. This scene calls to mind Jung's notion of the Persona, the mask we wear in public that stands in contrast to who we really are. More than that, Luke realizes that he shares part of his identity with Vader, his dark-side or "Shadow." He has seen the enemy, and it is himself.

The use of archetypal characters in *Star Wars* has been developed beyond the presence of familiar characters and particular scenes. Luke's journey though Episodes IV-VI can be viewed as an extended narrative centered on his confrontations with a series of father figures.[43] At the beginning of the films, Luke is seemingly fatherless, without a guide. His well-meaning Uncle Ben comes close to a father substitute, but in attempting to deny Luke's wish to fight in the galactic rebellion, he is preventing Luke from pursuing his individual destiny. Obi-Wan Kenobi soon becomes a replacement father. He facilitates Luke's journey in discovering The Force (a symbol for the realization of transcendent selfhood). Even in death, Obi-Wan becomes an internalized guide for Luke. At the same time, Obi-Wan does not have all the answers, and even lies to Luke about his origins.

Luke confronts another father figure in Yoda, whose small, strange appearance and goofy behavior seems at first very unfatherly. However, he is eventually revealed as one of the wisest and most powerful of the Jedi Knights, an order that assumes a paternal role toward the galaxy. Yoda is not able to help Luke either, but as he passes away, he reveals the truth that Darth Vader is Luke's biological father. Vader's evil nature (hunger for power, inability to love) at first makes this revelation seem like a cruel twist of fate. However, in a climactic confrontation with the Emperor, Luke refuses to give into his impulses of rage and revenge toward Vader. Luke's mercy triggers the buried compassion in his father, and Vader sacrifices himself to save Luke. Vader perishes, but this final fatherly act allows Luke to individuate and transcend in his journey toward selfhood. Self-development always comes at a cost.

While fantasy movies advertise their mythic origins, and therefore welcome Jungian analysis, the theory asserts that all stories come from the same place: the collective unconscious. Even a topical movie like *The Graduate*, usually analyzed as a reflection of the cultural revolution of the 1960s, may be analyzed through Jungian eyes to reveal other dimensions.[44] Specifically, Mrs Robinson (Anne Bancroft) can be seen as a variation on the Mother archetype, with a strong emphasis on the terrible, destructive side of motherhood. Jung notes how many ancient cultural symbols feature female goddesses (Kali in Indian myth, Hecate in Greek myth) who embody a femininity that is not caring and nurturing but powerful, insatiable, and destructive. Mrs Robinson is never even given a first name; the emphasis being placed on the "Mrs." This connotation is both ironic and revealing as she seduces Benjamin (Dustin Hoffman), the inexperienced college graduate. She wears clothes that prominently feature black, and in one key scene, even wears a leopard-skin coat, connecting her to a feline predator and the legend of "The Lady of the Beasts." The crucial Jungian insight is that what appears to be modern is actually rooted in ancient, primordial symbols.

## Ideology in the Movies

Along with Freud, Paul Ricoeur singles out Karl Marx as one of his "suspicious" philosophers.[45] This quality can be seen in Marx's central notion of ideology, the cultural forces that prevent individuals within a society (especially a capitalist society) from seeing the truth of their own circumstances. Under the distorting gauze of ideology, the true meaning of social products like movies are by no means self-evident; in fact, the obvious and accepted meanings that may be reflexively attributed to a film are merely the party line, effectively blinding the masses with false consciousness.

While this kind of language is often associated with Marxist interpretations, not all ideological analyses need be so condescending. Ideology can be defined as simply "a system . . . of representations (images, myths, ideas, or concepts, depending on the case) endowed with a historical existence and role within a given society."[46] The problem is that while the members of a society are immersed in these representations, the social codes themselves are not explicitly stated and therefore may be invisible in daily life. This process can be understood as a form of social unconscious; instead of coming from within (Freudian), the distorting forces that prevent us from seeing reality come from without. Ideological analyses thus promise to unravel these codes and provide a path to another kind of hidden meaning in film.

Marx is usually classified as an economist and social philosopher. However, the line between the social and the psychological is by no means clear. While sociologists are interested in broad social phenomena and patterns, such patterns manifest themselves in the thinking, actions, and experience of individuals. Cultural psychology (sometimes called sociocultural psychology) is a branch of psychology that aims its gaze directly at the overlap between sociology and psychology.[47] Most cultural psychologists are interested in the actions of individuals, but assume these actions are constructed by the social conditions that surround them. Cultural studies, including ideological interpretations in film studies, is an interdisciplinary field of scholarship that uses textual interpretations of cultural products to gain insight into what is really going on in a society at a particular historical moment (its values, attitudes, anxieties, and so forth).[48]

The analysis of products of popular culture as richly symbolic forms of art and entertainment has been a critical part of cultural studies.[49] From the perspective of cultural psychology, these textual analyses are one way of revealing the social dimensions of human life. Examples of readings that use film to understand people through their social conditions are common and come from many different directions.

One classic psychosocial study of film is *From Caligari to Hitler* (1947), in which Siegfried Kracauer attempts to understand the German psyche prior to the rise of Hitler by analyzing movies of that time period. In the early 1930s, certain German movies emphasized an anti-authoritarian attitude but did not provide a constructive social alternative. In contrast, other movies presented a singular hero exhibiting strength, leadership and determination, all of which appealed to a nation wounded by defeat in World War I. For Kracauer, *The Cabinet of Dr. Caligari* was a particularly defining movie in which the plot involving a hypnotist who mesmerizes a young man into committing murder because it is the perfect metaphor for Hitler's spell on his fellow Nazis.

Wolfenstein and Leites' *Movies: A Psychological Study* provides another example of cultural psychological analysis of film. In addition to their psychoanalytic angle, the authors offer a cross-cultural analysis of American, British and French films made shortly after World War II. They consider themes contained in these films as reflections of the national character of their respective countries.

Compared to American detective films such as *The Big Sleep* in which the hero is portrayed as an innocent who projects his own aggression onto external threats, British films of the time were more concerned with the *danger* of aggression arising from within. These heroes struggle with self-doubt even when they were innocent (such as in *I Became a Criminal*). Postwar French films were characterized as having an ironic attitude toward violence, in which justice is not always done and the universe is random; the authors interpret this attitude as a reflection of the helpless feelings experienced as a result of Nazi Occupation during the war.

*From Reverence to Rape* is a psychosocial critique of movies in which Molly Haskell traces the representation of women in mainstream Hollywood film through the early 1970s. She argues that the epistemological assumptions of Western civilization are characterized by "the big lie"—the inferiority of women to men. She believes this lie creeps into all cultural products, including the movies. More often than not, this falsehood is not expressed explicitly but a distorted notion of feminine inferiority manifests itself below the surface. Thus, representations of women as creatures (objects) to be placed on a pedestal are common in Hollywood. Classic Hollywood stars like Ingrid Bergman are presented as goddesses, with lighting techniques that make them literally glow with radiance and beauty. Other actresses are presented reverentially as noble earth mothers, such as Dallas (Claire Trevor), the prostitute with a heart of gold in the archetypal western, *Stagecoach*.

Many reverential treatments of women occurred during an epoch when it was widely accepted that women had fewer choices than men. In this mindset, it was assumed that men were needed to raise women onto the pedestal since it wasn't something they could do themselves. According to Haskell, this formula was reversed in the movies of the 1960s and 1970s, as the Women's Movement gained ground. Hollywood shifted from portraying women as innocent, motherly and/or glamorous to graphically flawed—whores, quasi-whores, jilted mistresses, emotional cripples, drunks, daffy ingénues, Lolitas, kooks, sex-starved spinsters, psychotics, icebergs, zombies, and ball-breakers.[50] Haskell sees film rape (such as the infamous scene in Sam Peckinpah's *Straw Dogs*) as an extreme expression of the impulse to keep women in their place despite changing cultural tides.

Most of the examples I have presented of ideological interpretations of movies started with representations of certain types of characters and then drew conclusions about national character. Is this perhaps the way Hollywood wants it? Such an approach puts the impetus on individual character, and as Robert Ray has argued, one of the most culturally and psychologically revealing aspects of Hollywood cinema is that it favors the myth of unbounded individualism at all costs: "[Hollywood's] underlying premise dictated the conversion of all political, sociological and economic dilemmas into personal melodramas."[51] For example, America's anxiety about intervening in World War II is contained in Rick's (Humphrey Bogart) reluctance to help Victor Lazlo (Paul Henreid) in Casablanca. Virtually all American movies must be built around a small number of individual stars that determine the action of the entire film.

While it is difficult for many Americans to imagine any alternative to this formula, early Russian films like Eisenstein's *Battleship Potemkin*, which builds its plot around a historical event and not particular characters, provide a counterpoint. When the film was shown in my undergraduate survey class, it was so strikingly different from other films we had seen, there was nearly a revolt among the students. Not because they were offended by the Soviet politics, but because they found the lack of a protagonist almost intolerable.

## Spectators in the Movies

While film has interested scholars from the beginning of the technology, the first 50 years of film scholarship were produced by individuals trained in other disciplines (e.g., literature, psychology, aesthetic philosophy, etc.) who decided to focus their attention on movies as a particular topic of study. This tendency of scholars to "moonlight" with movies continues today; many of the examples of interpretations presented above come from psychologists, psychoanalysts, or cultural critics outside academia. In contrast, the scholarly field of film studies has arisen in which film comes first.[52] Many critics use Andre Bazin's founding of the influential journal *Cahiers du Cinema* in the 1950s as a marker for the birth of a separate film studies discipline. As can be seen in the title of Bazin's most famous work, *What is Cinema?* film scholars initially found it critical to distinguish the nature of film from other art forms. The significance of movies is not just found in what they are about (their content); instead, the ways in which movies are filmed (framing, camera movement, editing, etc.), produced, and distributed are just as important.

When I started taking film studies courses as an undergraduate, I struggled to understand the filmcentric orientation. As an aspiring psychologist,

I wanted to talk about the characters and what they did. If I paid attention to stylistic aspects of a film, it was usually how character behavior was colored by elements of the *mis-en-scene* (the things in front of the camera such as actors, costumes, make-up, sets, and lighting). My professors, however, were interested in other things—the way a camera panned from one side of a room to another, or a quick edit between day and night. Curiously, when aspects of *mis-en-scene* were emphasized, they tended to be items like a mirror, a window frame, or a pair of binoculars. I frequently had the experience of watching a movie filled with scenes of human passion, and the only thing the professor seemed excited about was a two-second shot of a character glancing into a hand mirror. I eventually realized that for them, objects like mirrors, frames and binoculars captured the fundamental formal qualities of film—"Movies mirror reality," "Film frames our world," "Cinema is a tool for seeing."

My naïve approach was a type of *objectivity*—I was treating movies as objects that I could analyze. My professors, on the other hand, following decades of scholarly precedent, were using a more *subjective* approach in which they were trying to "get inside" the movie to identify the reflexive process by which the film was functioning. I eventually realized these kinds of analyses were attempts to connect the stylistic components of film with the viewing experience itself, thereby bringing film studies closer to psychology, but in a way I didn't recognize at first. I finally asked my film studies advisor about the connection between psychology and film. The first word out of his mouth was "Lacan."

Jacques Lacan is a French psychoanalyst whose postmodern spin on Freudian theory has had an enormous impact on film studies since the 1970s. Led by Christian Metz, many film scholars have integrated Lacanian psychoanalysis, along with ideological approaches, feminism, and semiotics (the study of signs), into the theories of film interpretation that have dominated film studies for decades.[53] While there is much variation among these theories, they all use careful textual interpretation to gain a better understanding of the experience of viewers. Such approaches clearly have a psychological dimension and are collectively labeled "theories of spectatorship."

The work on spectatorship in film studies has a curious relationship to the interpretive approaches presented in this chapter. Film studies' reliance on Lacan for its psychological theorizing creates a chasm compared with the traditional psychoanalytic approaches to analyzing film. Most American psychotherapists have never even heard of him.[54] As a result, they have a tendency to find modern film theory difficult to grasp.[55] On the other side, film studies appears to have little awareness of what is going on in modern American psychotherapy. I recall a film studies professor's surprise when I told him that the Freudian concepts of penis envy and castration anxiety were not a central part of modern psychology (or even psychodynamic therapy), given how often they appear in psychoanalytic film interpretations.

Perhaps the defining aspect of spectatorship theories derived from Lacan is its focus on uncertainty. The theories of Freud and Marx can be seen as questioning *obvious* reality, but these theorists offer their psychoanalytic and ideological analyses *as replacements* for the naive view of reality. Lacan and other postmodern theories take this skepticism a step further by essentially giving up on a reliable ground for reality.[56] Interpretations in this tradition can thus be either delightfully playful or maddeningly noncommittal, depending on the reader's mood.

Despite the complexities of spectatorship studies, many of its key psychological components can be found in four proposed processes that constitute the ways in which viewers relate to a film:

*Identification*: Film viewers identify with certain elements (usually a character) of a film and experience the film world as though they were inside it; on another level, they know they are not a part of the film, and that the film is unaware of them.

*Voyeurism*: Because viewers are simultaneously participating in a film at the same time they are separate from it, a distance is created between viewers and film that is both frustrating (because it is incomplete) and pleasurable (because it is contained and safe).

*Fetishism*: The technical qualities of film (a beautifully photographed sunset, or a sweeping pan shot) become cherished objects even though ultimately we cannot possess that which is only being *re*-presented (the sunset itself).[57]

*Suture*: Films present a series of physical spaces that are incomplete in one way or another (the edges to the screen suggest a larger reality to which the viewer is not privy). In order to identify with a film, viewers have to accept its incomplete narrative reality as their reality by "suturing" over the elements that are missing in order to create a unified experience when there is none (e.g., remaining engaged in a film after an edit that abruptly moves the action from California to New York). Some films try to make suturing easier while others, like *Psycho*, challenge the audience by frequently changing character perspective and refusing to answer questions the film appears to be asking.[58]

The concepts of voyeurism, identification, fetishism, and suture are all components of a favorite trope of academic film analysis, "the gaze" or "look." The gaze refers to the fact that when a film camera captures an image, it does so from a particular perspective or vantage point. This perspective is necessarily that of the audience members as they watch the screen. Therefore, viewers must adopt the gaze which becomes a stand in for the totality of their visual experience. The importance of the gaze is highlighted in films that use camera shots representing the point-of-view of a particular character (jiggling the camera when a character is running; cross-cuts between a close-up on an object and an exaggerated facial reaction). In this way, the audience's identification with those characters who control the gaze is heightened.

This process happens in a twilight zone of consciousness in which viewers feel they understand the experience of the hero, at the same time that they "know" they are not in the exotic land in which the movie occurs. The viewer's experience is further heightened by the voyeuristic pleasure of being able to look into the private lives of others. This pleasure can only be achieved through suspending disbelief by suturing together the various gaps in the narrative. When the fleeting experience of a time-limited movie isn't enough, the viewer can attempt to *freeze* the look by claiming the object through fetishistic adoration (movie posters) or ritualistic reviewing (a task made easier by modern digital technology).

The complicated, sometimes confused relationship between viewer and film is captured in the song *Brownsville Girl*, cowritten by Bob Dylan (who has starred, written and/or directed a number of films) and playwright, screenwriter and actor Sam Shepard:

> Something about that movie though, well I just can't get it out of my head
> But I can't remember why I was in it or what part I was supposed to play
> All I remember about it was Gregory Peck and the way people moved
> And a lot of them seemed to be lookin' my way.
> Brownsville Girl, Written by Bob Dylan, Copyright © 1986 by
> Special Rider Music. All rights reserved. International
> copyright secured. Reprinted by permission.

The gaze has proven to be a powerful analytical tool, and one of its primary applications has been in feminist criticism. An influential essay by Laura Mulvey argues that Hollywood has typically used the gaze in a gender-biased manner—it is male characters who control the gaze and subsequently control the narrative of the film[59] while female characters are primarily there to be looked at by the male characters. Therefore, viewer identification is located in a masculine perspective. Mulvey uses Freud's notion of castration anxiety to argue that staring at a woman is anxiety-provoking; for a woman viewer, the female star is a reminder of what she has lost, and to a man, what he could lose (literally, the penis; figuratively, power). Mainstream cinema copes with this voyeuristic anxiety by either punishing the woman ("bad girls" and "bitches") or fetishizing her, making her into an untouchable superstar.[60]

Mulvey exemplifies her argument by considering several Hitchcock films that express both sadism toward women and fetishism. In *Vertigo*, the first half of the film is dedicated to Scotty's (Jimmy Stewart) trailing of the graceful and sophisticated Madeleine (Kim Novak). Hitchcock uses long tracking shots that lovingly capture the beauty of both the perfect blonde and the city of San Francisco. The second half of the film explores Scotty's sadistic attempts to transform the unsophisticated lookalike Judy (also played by Novak) into Madeleine. Given the pleasure that the audience receives from Hitchcock's manipulation of the gaze, Mulvey argues that the purpose of her essay is to "destroy pleasure" by revealing the underlying sexist ideology behind the movie.[61]

## Closing Shots: The Boons and Banes of Interpretation

This chapter has focused on interpreting movies as texts, symbolic containers that can be unpacked and found to contain meaning. Some critics have argued it is a mistake to focus on anything other than the text—that focusing on filmmakers risks limiting interpretation to what they might have intended, which is largely inaccessible and sometimes inane and inarticulate (the intentional fallacy). On the other hand, focusing on viewers risks getting caught up in momentary emotional experience that takes the analyst away from the real truth contained in the text (the emotional fallacy).[62]

Very few, if any, of the interpretations presented in this chapter succeed in completely excluding filmmakers and viewers. Some refer to the motives (particularly the unconscious sort) of filmmakers. And many interpretations, especially in the spectatorship section, discuss the experience of the viewer. Even when there are no explicit references to viewers, the use of language associated with psychology suggests an *implied viewer*.[63] If critics refers to a film as "disturbing" it is reasonable to assume that they were disturbed or that they believe that the film is likely to disturb at least some members of the audience. *Everything* on the screen can potentially be taken as a reflection of the movie-makers and/or the audience.

Despite the potential for psychological interpretations, the whole process of psychological interpretation is considered suspect by some psychologists, because it is not an empirical method—textual interpretations do not study human behavior because they do not involve gathering data about physical reality. This is a narrow and indefensible notion of empiricism however. Films are physical products of social activity; the interpretation of film involves closely observing and analyzing a human product.

There are a number of legitimate differences between film analysis and the methods used in mainstream psychological/social science research (e.g., experimentation): (1) the relevant *data* (movies) were not carefully collected in a controlled atmosphere (rather, they came into existence as part of a loose collaborative artistic process with no clearly defined rules); (2) the critic is usually analyzing a small number of films and thus there are questions about how *generalizable* results are (perhaps the critic's analysis is only relevant to a particular movie and has nothing to do with any other aspect of reality); and (3) there are questions about how *reliable* critics are (the possibility or likelihood of multiple interpretations of any given movie hovers over the activity of assigning meaning to film[64]). The ideal goal of learning *the* meaning of a movie and thereby gaining a single truth about the world is placed in jeopardy.[65]

The ambiguity inherent in interpretive approaches to movies is not, however, a sufficient reason to ignore them. Psychologists like Jerome Bruner have argued that it is not possible to escape meaning-making in the social sciences, and alternative approaches to experimental methods are necessary.[66] For Bruner, psychology should seek "to discover and describe formally the meanings that human beings created out of their encounters with the world" and be focused on "the symbolic activities that human beings employed in constructing and in making sense not only of the world, but of themselves."[67] He argues that while the *logical* methods of mathematics and the natural sciences certainly play a role in this meaning-making process, so do the *narrative* methods of the humanities. Logic and storytelling are both reflections of the human mind.[68] It is often necessary for people to make sense of particular observations, in particular settings, with particular actors. This is exactly what psychotherapists do when they sit down with clients and try to understand what is going on in their lives; it is also exactly what film critics do when they attempt to understand a particular film. The subject matter of the social sciences and the humanities is essentially the same, and the two orientations would benefit from moving toward each other.

A full psychological understanding of the movies cannot be accomplished without embracing interpretive/symbolic approaches.

At same time, textual interpretation would benefit from considering the insights of the social sciences. The specific challenge to film studies is to take seriously the actual experience of the audience and the filmmakers. The move between interpreting the film and interpreting the audience is done too quickly and seamlessly. The obvious limitation (at least to anyone with training in the social sciences) of relying on an implied viewer is that film scholars rarely reference the experience of an actual person (viewer, projectionist, director, actor or even an actual critic).

I contend that knowledge gained from interpreting a text overlaps knowledge gained from studies that look directly at audience members. Both sources of knowledge would be enriched if they purposely interacted with each other, allowing textual and participant-based approaches to inform the other's questions and answers.

## Further Reading

Casetti, F. (1999) *Theories of Cinema: 1945–1995.* University of Texas Press, Austin, TX.

Greenberg, H.R. (1993) *Screen Memories: Hollywood Cinema on the Psychoanalytic Couch.* Columbia University Press, New York, NY.

Iaccino, J.F. (1998) *Jungian Reflections Within the Cinema: A Psychological Analysis of Sci-Fi and Fantasy Archetypes.* Praeger, Westport, CT.

Metz, C. (1982) *The Imaginary Signifier: Psychoanalysis and the Cinema.* Indiana University Press, Bloomington, IN.

Mulvey, L. (1986) Visual pleasure and narrative cinema, in, *Narrative, apparatus, ideology,* P. Rosen (ed.). Columbia University Press, New York, NY, pp. 198–209.

Wolfenstein, M. and Leites, N. (1971) *Movies: A Psychological Study.* Hafner, New York, NY.

# Psychopathology, Psychotherapy and *Psycho*—Psychologists and Their Patients in the Movies

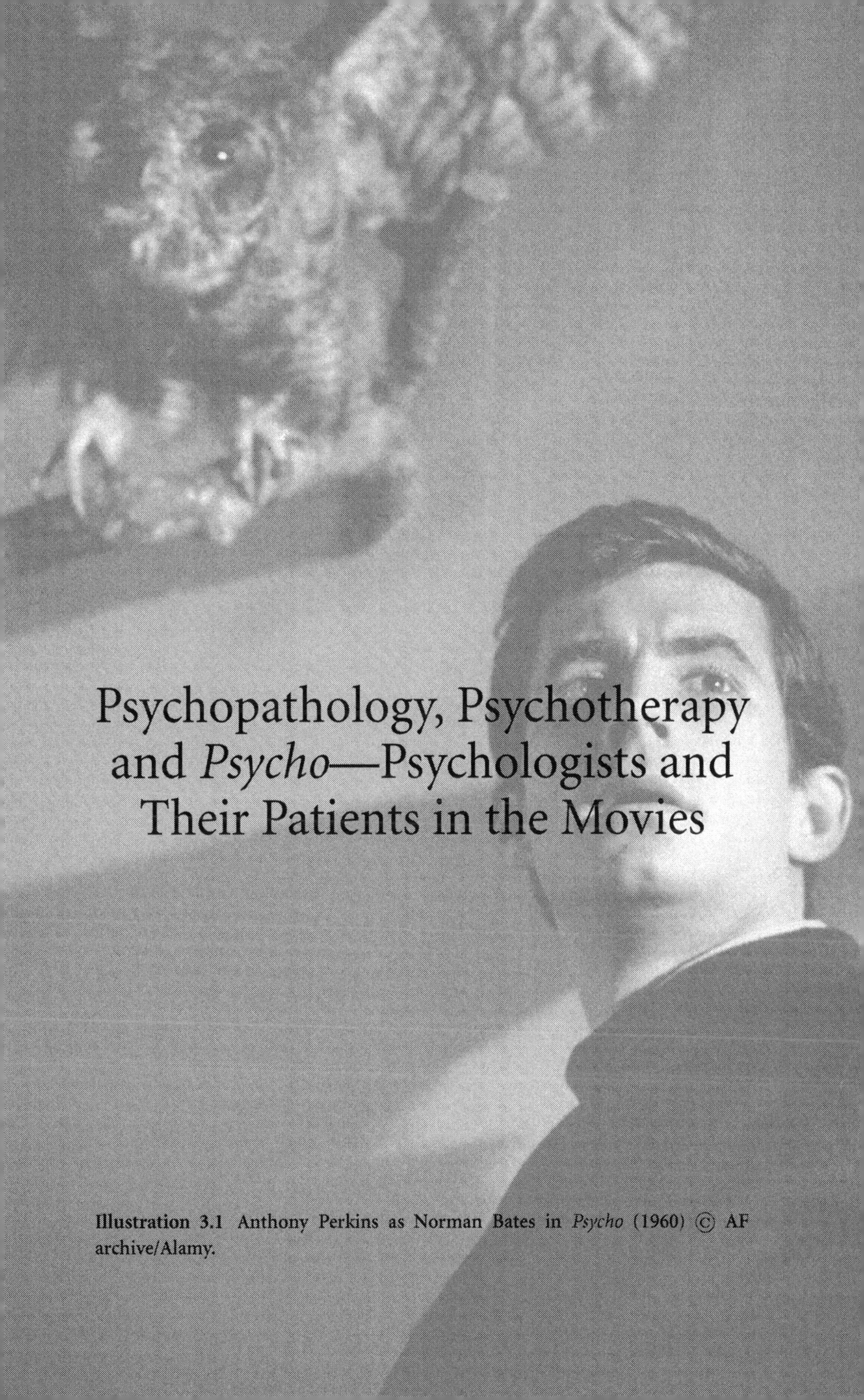

Illustration 3.1 Anthony Perkins as Norman Bates in *Psycho* (1960) © AF archive/Alamy.

# Chapter 3

# Psychopathology, Psychotherapy and *Psycho*—Psychologists and Their Patients in the Movies

*When you hear the term "psychological disorder," what is the first image that pops into your mind?*

Maybe you thought of a friend who's struggled with anxiety. Or perhaps you have worked in a hospital where some of the patients were depressed. I wouldn't bet on these kinds of responses, however. More likely, the first image you had was Anthony Perkins as Norman Bates in *Psycho*, his dark eyes darting back and forth nervously. Or you may have envisioned Jack Nicholson's character Melvin Udall in *As Good as It Gets*, selecting an individually wrapped bar of soap, meticulously washing his hands once, and then dropping the soap in the trash. Or you might have pictured Russell Crowe as the mathematician John Nash in *A Beautiful Mind* as he weeps on the floor of his bathroom after nearly drowning his infant child.

*When you hear the term "psychologist," what do you immediately think of?*

Perhaps you remembered a counselor who helped you during a difficult time or a professor who taught psychology when you were in college. Again, these associations are possible, but it is more likely that you thought of the blowhard psychiatrist who appears at the end of *Psycho*, to explain once and for all what really happened at the Bates Motel. Or you might have pictured Robin Williams as Dr Sean Maguire in *Good Will Hunting*, a therapist so brutally honest and expressive he thinks nothing of choking his delinquent

*Psychology at the Movies*, First Edition. Skip Dine Young
© 2012 John Wiley & Sons, Ltd. Published 2012 by John Wiley & Sons, Ltd.

**Illustration 3.2** Robin Williams & Matt Damon as Sean & Will in *Good Will Hunting* (1997) © Moviestore Collection Ltd/Alamy.

client if it means gaining the young punk's respect. Or maybe you called to mind the image of Ben Kingsley as Dr John Cawley in *Shutter Island*, the director of a mental hospital who presents himself as caring and progressive but who appears to be hiding a more menacing side.

This chapter continues our look at psychology *in* the movies, particularly those aspects of psychology that are foremost in the public imagination—psychotherapy and psychological disorders. The preceding thought experiment provides compelling evidence of the potential for movies to shape the ways that people see these aspects of psychology. Years ago, when I was working on a project exploring the representation of mental health professionals in film, I saw it as a curious but somewhat marginal topic for clinical psychology—pretty much an excuse to combine my interests in film and clinical work, and watch a lot of movies in the process. I have since become convinced that the representation of psychology in the media is actually quite important, given its impact on how a significant portion of the general public understands psychology, for better and worse.

## Representations of Psychological Disorders

Imagining psychological disorders brings us to the scary edge of human functioning, where people act "wrong," do not behave as other people want them to, and/or don't behave as they themselves think they should. The realm of psychological disorders or "madness" is the inevitable dark side of the mental health field—if it weren't for the possibility of disorder, a field dedicated to health would not be necessary.

Madness is certainly a realm in which filmmakers seem to delight, and film is an excellent medium for vividly depicting this realm. The character of the Joker in *The Dark Knight* is an excellent example.[1] Actor Heath Ledger (who won a posthumous Best Supporting Actor Oscar for the role after his tragic death), director Christopher Nolan, and the other filmmakers marshal a host of technical and symbolic resources at their disposal to depict the Joker's madness. To begin with, other characters in the movie refer to him that way, using terms like "freak," "madman," "murdering psychopath," and "agent of chaos." His physical appearance is bizarre (stringy, unkempt green hair, bright purple suit, white face paint, and smeared red lipstick around his scarred lips), and it is highlighted by close-ups and strange camera angles. Discordant music often accompanies the Joker's appearance. The chaos of the Joker is also enhanced in the confusing, rapid editing that is often used in the scenes in which he appears. The Joker's craziness is "over-determined"—that is, it is impossible for anyone to miss the point.

There is no question that the depiction of the Joker in *The Dark Knight* is mesmerizing and makes for good cinema. The highlight of one of the highest grossing movies ever, the Joker was witnessed by hundreds of millions of viewers across the world. Of course, the Joker is not the only cinematic portrayal of lunacy available for public consumption: These depictions have been of great interest to psychologists and psychiatrists. Otto Wahl's *Media Madness: Public Images of Mental Illness* identifies over 400 feature films explicitly advertised to the public as being about mental illness.[2]

Mental illness itself is an issue of much contention: What is it? Who has the authority to diagnose it? How should it be treated? And what should it even be called?[3] It is therefore not surprising that there is a great deal of controversy with regard to how mental illness is dramatized in the movies and other media. Psychiatrists, psychologists, and other mental health professionals have long been concerned that these kinds of portrayals are exaggerated, inconsistent, inaccurate and potentially damaging to those experiencing real psychological problems, not to mention counterproductive when it comes to attempts by mental health professionals to treat people diagnosed with such disorders. With the Joker's violent, erratic actions and distorted face having entered the public consciousness, mental health professionals worry that this image is now a "resource for other stigmatizing portrayals."[4]

Moviemakers like to play fast and loose with the behaviors associated with mental illness. They are in the business of being dramatic and selling theater tickets. They know that most audience members aren't psychologists, and therefore aren't going to quibble about inaccuracies. Any psychologists in the audience, however, have tended to be very concerned about inaccuracies and distortions.

You don't have to go very far to find examples of films that take liberties with reality when it comes to mental illness. Broad, vulgar comedies such as *Me, Myself and Irene* are eager to make fun of any human weakness, while horror movies are eager to exploit all human fears. This is true of the Joker as well. I have never seen or heard of a patient like him, and I am fairly confident that there are no cases in the psychological literature of a criminal mastermind who dresses like a clown to conduct his business.[5]

Inaccurate portrayals of mental illness apply even to acknowledged movie icons like Norman Bates. The American Film Institute ranked *Psycho* as the fourteenth best film ever (see Appendix B), and it is my favorite movie.[6] By no stretch of the imagination, however, does the movie realistically portray a known form of mental illness. This assertion runs counter to the impression given at the end, when psychiatrist Fred Richman (Simon Oakland) appears out of nowhere to "merely explain" Norman's behavior to a presumably perplexed audience. Dr Richman establishes the case that Norman is suffering from what was called multiple-personality disorder at the time and is now called dissociative identity disorder (DID).[7] According to Dr Richman, Norman embodies both his own personality and the personality of his dead mother. After killing his mother and her lover in a jealous rage, Norman dug up the mother's body and embalmed her. He then began to engage in conversations with the corpse, alternating between his own voice and an imitation of his mother's voice. It's all quite understandable, according to Dr Richman (although his caricatured pomposity is an indication that he should be taken with a grain of salt).

In fact, Norman Bates's behavior doesn't match psychiatric criteria for DID in several crucial ways: (1) people with DID do *not* mimic the personalities of specific individuals they know; they may adopt various personalities but not of someone who already exists; (2) different personalities do not dialogue with each other (in fact, the basic idea of dissociation is that different parts are split off from one another and avoid interaction, in some cases not even sharing memories); and (3) people with DID are typically not psychotic (do not have major breaks with reality) and would be unlikely to believe that an embalmed body is alive.[8]

Hitchcock did not seem particularly concerned with accuracy at numerous levels of reality—psychiatric diagnostic criteria; the events in the life of the film's real-life inspiration;[9] or even the routines of late night motel clerks.[10] Therefore, judged against these aspects of reality, *Psycho* could be considered a failure. However, based on Hitchcock's stated goal (to play the audience "like an organ"[11]), the film is a huge success (albeit in a sadistic kind of way). In movies like *Psycho* there is a trade-off. While these films heighten the *dramatic* reality of psychological disorders, they distort *physical* reality.

Certain distortions of actual mental illness have been used by filmmakers so often, they can be categorized into character types:[12]

> *The Homicidal Maniac*: Norman Bates is often presented as the prototype of the homicidal maniac in modern film, but this character reached its simplified zenith in the character of Michael Meyers, an escaped mental patient who kills for fairly random reasons, in *Halloween*. This slasher film exploits the fear that other people pose a potential threat, even when we haven't done anything to them. Yet it contrasts with the fact that most psychiatric patients are not violent, and those who do behave aggressively typically act out toward their caregivers (family, nurses, etc.); not random strangers.
>
> *The Enlightened Free Spirit*: In some ways the opposite of depicting the mentally ill as evil, another cinematic stereotype presents the mentally ill as superior to "normal" people, in that they are freer, more creative, and more fully alive. This type can be seen in abundance in the French classic *King of Hearts* and in American films such as *One Flew Over the Cuckoo's Nest* and *Patch Adams*. While there is something admirable about the attempt to show virtue where others see pathology, the "free spirit" characterization can seem naïve. Anyone who has spent even a small amount of time with people diagnosed with mental illness can recognize the degree to which they are truly suffering.
>
> *The Seductress*: This type refers to the the nymphomaniac[13] female psychiatric patient who, along with whatever other problems she might have, flaunts her sexuality to everyone around her, including her caregivers. As *Lilith*, Jean Seberg plays a seductress who ruins the career of a young doctor played by Warren Beatty. More recently, Angelina Jolie won an Academy Award for her portrayal of Lisa, an erotically charged agent of chaos in *Girl, Interrupted*. These portrayals seem to blur the line between the distress associated with mental illness and our cultural anxiety with overt sexuality.
>
> *The Narcissistic Parasite*: In cinematic depictions, patients in outpatient psychotherapy often don't have any genuine problems other than a self-indulgent need for attention. This type is played for laughs in Woody Allen's *Annie Hall* and *Manhattan* in which the lead characters,

while highly functioning in many ways, still regularly attend therapy to whine about their unsatisfying love lives. In this way, psychological problems are presented as nothing more than mild character deficits.

In contrast to these distorted and overly dramatized depictions, there are films that get it almost right with regard to diagnostic accuracy.[14] In *Reel Psychiatry: Movie Portrayals of Psychiatric Conditions*,[15] David Robinson (2009) developed a rating scale and a list of 100 films he believes show relatively accurate (though not necessarily perfect) diagnoses using official diagnostic criteria[16].

> *Amphetamine-Induced Psychotic Disorder*: *Requiem for a Dream* features realistic and disturbing depictions of substance abuse by four main characters. The dangers and degradations associated with heroin use are captured in the younger characters, but Sara Goldfarb (Ellen Burstyn), the mother of one of the addicts, is particularly notable. Sara gets hooked on speed (in the form of diet pills) so that she can fit into a tight dress for an upcoming game show appearance. Her increasing reliance on the pills has devastating consequences on her physical and mental health. Her downward spiral of addiction is vividly captured in a scene in which the appliances in her home come to horrific life and attack her.

> *Borderline Personality Disorder*: *Fatal Attraction*, a major box office hit, has been criticized for the film's presentation of a double standard with regard to extramarital affairs. The cheating husband is portrayed sympathetically while the "other woman" is depicted as a crazed, vengeful bunny killer. Yet Glenn Close's performance captures the volatility and contradictions of the Alex Forrest character and is a notable example of the extremes of Borderline Personality Disorder (suicidality, promiscuity, angry outbursts, etc.). Alex's unstable perception of self is reflected in her unstable relations with other people, particularly Michael Douglas's cheating husband. There is some accuracy in how Alex's behavior alternates between cool distance and extreme clinging, first expressing devotion and then exploding in rage.

> *Dissociate Fugue*: *Paris, Texas* opens with Travis Henderson (Harry Dean Stanton) walking out of the Texas desert, with apparently little idea of who he is and no memory of what he's done for the past decade. While Travis tries to reconnect with his life, particularly his young son, who has been living with his brother and sister-in-law, the audience doesn't learn much about what happened to Travis during his "fugue" state (a period of aimless travel accompanied by memory loss). We do

learn that the episode was triggered by an incident in which his younger wife set fire to their trailer in response to his abusive and pathologically jealous behavior. This persistent and troubling gap in Travis's memory, his difficulty in emotionally connecting to his present circumstances, and the traumatic initiating event are all characteristic of this rare but fascinating disorder.

I would personally add the schizophrenic symptoms of John Nash (Russell Crowe) in *A Beautiful Mind* to the list of compelling psychological depictions. While legitimate criticisms have been raised about the way the film handles Nash's psychiatric treatment,[17] it succeeds in capturing the symptoms of delusions and hallucinations remarkably well, both through Crowe's acting and the way the film is structured. The first time I saw the film (I had not read the book), I felt annoyed as Nash began to get involved in undercover espionage. I knew that the film was based on a real-life account, so the car chases and shootouts struck me as unrealistic. I figured the film-makers were throwing in some action sequences because simply presenting the plight of someone with schizophrenia wasn't dramatic enough. When the big plot twist was revealed, I realized that like the rest of the audience, I too had been fooled into believing that the whole espionage plot was real. I had not recognized that it was a part of Nash's delusional system.

The reason I was fooled was because the events (which turned out to be imaginary delusions) appeared as perceptually convincing as they would if they were real. This is exactly the way delusions (false beliefs) and hallucinations (false perceptions) appear and feel to people with schizophrenia—perceptually, they have the same physical qualities as real events and images. Imagine if someone was holding a carnation and a rose, and insisting that one was real but the other was a figment of your imagination—how could you possibly decide which was which? *A Beautiful Mind* manipulates the perceptual qualities of cinema to evoke an experience that is vivid yet unreliable in a manner that is parallel to the experience of people with schizophrenia.[18]

## Representations of Psychologists and Psychological Treatment

Gabbard and Gabbard's *Psychiatry in the Cinema* (1999) is a comprehensive examination of the many ways that psychiatry, psychology, and psychoanalysis have interacted with film.[19] Their index lists over 450 feature films, from

1906 (the amusingly titled *Dr. Dippy's Sanitarium*) to 1998, representing mental health treatment providers.[20] Clearly Hollywood has a fascination with psychotherapy and psychotherapists.[21]

Gabbard and Gabbard's historical analysis of the representation of cinematic mental health professionals highlights how attitudes change over time. In the early days of film up through World War II, psychiatrists were portrayed in a blatantly unrealistic manner. Often they were depicted as quacks, using satire to deflate medical pompousness (as in the silent *Dr. Dippy's Sanitarium* and the classic screwball comedy *Bringing Up Baby*). In the 1940s and 1950s, films became increasingly serious in their treatment of psychoanalysis, culminating with the late 1950s and early 1960s, referred to as the Golden Age of psychiatry in the movies. In films from this period (*Fear Strikes Out*, *The Three Faces of Eve*, *David and Lisa*, the biopic *Freud*), psychiatrists and psychologists are treated as competent, compassionate, and even likable. In *David and Lisa* (1960) Dr Swinford (Howard Da Silva) is shown as wise and caring, yet vulnerable and human, as he treats the hospitalized young patients.

The Golden Age didn't last long. In the 1960s and 1970s, mental health professionals were subjected to the skepticism that was applied to all established institutions. The portrayal of the quack returned, this time with a harsher edge, and more serious criticisms of basic psychiatric motives were advanced in films like the Oscar-winning *One Flew Over the Cuckoo's Nest*.[22]

Another way to understand how Hollywood looks at psychologists is through patterns, not only within time periods but in the types of characters presented over time. A triad of cinematic shrink stereotypes has been described:[23]

> *Dr Dippy*: This type is primarily characterized by comic foolishness. These characters are meant to be laughed at or dismissed as inept. Dr Montague (Harvey Korman) in Mel Brooks's *High Anxiety* and Dr Marvin (Richard Dreyfuss) in *What About Bob?* are classic examples.
> *Dr Evil*: This stereotype reflects psychologists who use their knowledge of the human mind to abuse, manipulate, or otherwise harm patients for personal gain. The murdering, cannibalistic Hannibal Lecter (Anthony Hopkins) in *The Silence of the Lambs* has become the iconic example of Dr Evil in modern cinema. Nurse Ratched (Louise Fletcher) in *One Flew Over the Cuckoo's Nest* may not seem quite as evil, but the movie emphasizes her domineering motivations. Dr Cawley in *Shutter Island*, director of a menacing 1950s insane asylum, appears to be a Dr Evil despite his claims of progressiveness. Compared

to the Dr Dippy subtype, such mental health professionals seem quite formidable, even though their moral compasses are decidedly off kilter.

*Dr Wonderful*: These characters are competent, caring, and effective in their treatment. There seem to be no limits to what they will do to help their patients. While prevalent during the Golden Age, these noble characters did not disappear completely. Dr Berger (Judd Hirsch) in *Ordinary People* is a reference point for this kind of therapist: the good doctor thinks nothing of coming to his client's house to do emergency, and ultimately transforming, counseling.

Other types have been added to the list. Over the past 20 years movies have seen many depictions of "the Wounded Healers"[24]—professionals who may share many characteristics of Dr Wonderful but have psychological issues of their own that interfere with their work. In *Good Will Hunting* Dr Sean Maguire is a wounded healer who valiantly attempts to treat Will (Matt Damon) while struggling with grief over the death of his wife. Such movies may seek to deflate grandiose notions about the perceived superiority of mental health practitioners by portraying them as flawed (or human) individuals.

Another prominent characteristic of movie shrinks is an unusually common tendency to engage in sexual relationships with their patients; this type could be labeled Dr Sexy[25] or Dr Line-Crosser.[26] In psychological thrillers, therapists who have sex with their patients share an element of Dr Evil in that they are coldly exploitative,[27] but in many mainstream movies, such therapists typically fall in love with their patients.[28] Many movies have featured female therapists are who young, sexualized (in how they dress), and lonely. These characters experience personal transformation when they fall in love with their male clients.[29] Hitchcock's *Spellbound* is a classic example of this pattern, while *The Prince of Tides* offers an updated variation—therapist Dr Lowenstein (Barbara Streisand) falls in love with her patient's brother and then engages him in treatment.[30] Clearly, whatever fascination filmmakers have with the profession of psychology, it is trumped by their fascination with desirable and desirous women.

As with mental illness, a deeper understanding of the representations of psychotherapy can be gained by considering the underlying dramatic truths that capture the imagination of filmmakers. One way of accomplishing this is by looking at *character motivations*. What appears to be driving these characters? Are there ways in which the motivations of fictional therapists relate to those of real therapists?

In a systematic study of mental health professionals in the movies, colleagues and I looked at the top 20 US box-office films for each year from 1990–1999.[31] We identified 34 films (17% of the films we sampled) featuring mental health professionals. Of these, 58 individual characters were identified (see Appendix A). We then considered whether each character seemed driven by the following: money/prestige; power; love/lust; self-healing; or concern for others. Such representations tended to both distort and reflect reality.

> *Money/prestige* (motivating 52% of characters): In the comic farce *What About Bob?*, the egotistical Dr Marvin (Richard Dreyfuss) worries excessively about television publicity for his latest pop-psych book while displaying little concern for the neurotic Bob (Bill Murray). Like many professions with relatively high prestige and compensation, mental health professionals are vulnerable to being represented as greedy. In fact, many real mental health providers feel they have a calling to contribute to the common good. From this perspective, Dr Marvin is not a humorous caricature but rather a therapist's nightmarish alter ego.
>
> That said, mental health practice is a profession, one which requires a great deal of training and commitment, and most practitioners want to be well-compensated. At the same time, it has been argued that the failure of some therapists to treat their work as a business can actually undermine treatment by failing to create clearly defined boundaries. While Dr Marvin's callousness is open to disdain, do his nicely appointed office and vacation home by themselves contradict the ambitions of the professional helper?
>
> *Power* (a motivator of 62% of characters): A deadly three-way power struggle is portrayed in *The Silence of the Lambs* between Dr Chilton, the scheming director of a maximum security psychiatric hospital, Dr Hannibal Lecter, a brilliant psychiatrist imprisoned for murder and cannibalism, and Clarice Starling, a young FBI agent trying to negotiate between both men to catch a serial killer. Lecter's character is particularly disturbing because he taps into the widespread suspicion that mental health professionals have special "powers" over the human mind.
>
> At the same time, such professionals have power in that they are representatives of socially sanctioned institutions. The most common areas of medical malpractice in treatment settings relate to violations of power.[32] From a didactic standpoint, Drs Chilton and Lecter may

be understood not simply as libelous to decent psychiatrists, but as exaggerated warnings to mental health professionals everywhere.

*Love/lust* (which motivates 24% of characters): The quasi-pornographic fantasy *Basic Instinct* features the provocatively dressed and ethically challenged police psychologist Dr Garner (Jeanne Tripplehorn) who proclaims her love for a detective she has been treating even after he sexually assaults her. Mental health professionals tend to be outraged by these depictions since sexual relationships between practitioners and clients are clearly prohibited by the ethical codes of all the major disciplines.

Nevertheless, psychoanalysis was founded on Freud's observation that sexuality is a primary motive for human behavior. While most modern treatment approaches have decentralized sexuality, mental health treatment remains an intimate experience. Most psychologists report having been sexually attracted to at least one client (although only a small percentage act on this attraction).[33] As the psychoanalyst Marshall Edelson has pointed out, it is difficult to forget the importance of erotic feelings in human relationships if one watches many movies.[34]

*Self-healing* (a motivator for 26% of the characters): In *The Sixth Sense*, Dr Malcolm is a successful child psychologist who becomes so depressed and guilt-ridden after one of his patients commits suicide that his marriage is threatened. This variation on the wounded healer motif also emphasizes psychotherapeutic failure.

Real mental health professionals are imperfect. The idea of professionals having preexisting psychological and emotional issues that determine how they engage in their work has been normalized in such concepts as counter-transference. Successful mental health providers must find ways to resolve, bypass, or even constructively use their emotional issues to become better professionals. *The Sixth Sense*, driven by a surprise ending that forces Dr Malcolm to radically reevaluate his place in the world, dramatizes the real struggles and fears of therapists.

*Concern for others* (a motivator for 66% of characters): In the comedy *Analyze This*, Dr Sobel (Billy Crystal) is initially reluctant to treat his Mafioso client, but becomes so committed that he risks his life to help the mobster heal his abusive past. While concern for others appears to be more positive than the other motivations, it is equally open to distortion. The almost unbelievable benevolence and self-sacrifice of some movie professionals establishes selflessness as a requirement of the profession.

At the same time, concern for others is perhaps the one necessary (although not sufficient) requirement for mental health professionals. The importance of empathy is widely understood to be a critical component of successful therapy.[35] To an extent, even Hollywood movies recognize this. Despite the prevalence of concern for others as a motivation in Hollywood therapists, the depiction of a superhuman professional (aka Dr Wonderful) was actually quite rare in our sample. The combination of concern for others with a desire for self-improvement may not be an inherently bad combination, an insight that can be witnessed in many movies (even if it requires viewers to look past such dramatic liberties as a breakthrough counseling session conducted in the midst of a gun battle).

Most of our attention to psychological treatment in the movies has focused on psychotherapy. In part, this is because the privacy and intimacy of psychotherapy allows for the revelation of a darker side of humanity, one that is open to either sensitive or salacious treatment. Other treatment modalities don't offer that dramatic flair. For example, the prescription of psychoactive medication—antidepressants like Prozac and antipsychotics like Risperdal—is probably *the* dominant mental health treatment of the modern age. Yet 1997's *As Good as It Gets* was the first major movie to depict the effective management of mental health symptoms (obsessive-compulsive disorder) through medication in an outpatient setting.[36]

When aspects of psychology and psychological treatment other than therapy *are* presented, they generally capture institutional oppression. Thus, when the use of psychiatric medications in an inpatient setting is depicted, emphasis is exclusively placed on their sedating effects (e.g., *Girl, Interrupted*). The application of electro-convulsive (or "shock") therapy pops up occasionally, but these cinematic representations are always brutal (see *One Flew Over the Cuckoo's Nest*).[37] The other explicitly psychological activity which is regularly presented in the media is that of criminal profiler, which emphasizes the ability to understand the mind of serial killers and other criminals.[38]

The appeal of psychotherapy in film goes beyond its ability to explore provocative topics that preoccupy filmmakers and film audiences. Psychotherapy and narrative film share many qualities—storytelling that is grounded in emotional experience, personal discovery, and, in many cases, striving toward an improved life. It is not surprising, then, that psychotherapy and film have found each other so often.

## Closing Shots: The Impact of Representations of Psychology

Representations of psychological disorders and psychological treatment would not attract so much attention from psychologists were it not for concerns about the impact such depictions might have on real-world attitudes toward psychology and whether they may do more harm than good.[39] In the cinema of pure fantasy, verisimilitude is rarely a concern (few people worry whether the Orcs in *Lord of the Rings* are being accurately portrayed). But unlike fantasy monsters, psychology *is* real, so there is the possibility that the public will take such dramatic representations as the truth.

Representations of people with mental illness are particularly concerning. Surveys have indicated that for many members of the public, most of their knowledge about mental illness comes from the media.[40] Otto Wahl is concerned that movies and other media have promulgated a view that the mentally ill are objects of ridicule, violent and dangerous, and fundamentally different from other people.[41]

I have personally witnessed the public's attitudes toward mental illness in my own undergraduate students. Most are savvy enough to recognize that movies, particularly comedies, exaggerate symptoms, yet their attention to certain phenomena has definitely been heightened by media accounts. When I lecture on schizophrenia, I discuss subtypes, the relatively late onset of the disease, responses to antipsychotic medication, and so on. But inevitably students will blow past these facts and start asking about psychokillers. For some students, the connection between schizophrenia and murder is so strong, they are stunned to learn that many people who carry the diagnosis are able to go about their day-to-day lives quite normally. While students are typically receptive to altering their beliefs, I sometimes wonder how long their enlightenment will last when they are once again faced with the onslaught of popular culture.

The negative impact of depictions of mental illness can also be seen in individuals with psychological disorders. An honors graduate in film studies who was diagnosed with schizophrenia recounted the impact of film representations on her life. Not surprisingly, she is often hesitant to share her diagnosis for fear of being perceived as a "homicidal maniac." Negative media depictions can be so powerful, she admitted she even occasionally wondered about herself after watching movies, even though she knew better.[42]

When large-scale studies of the impact of media on perceptions of mental illness have been conducted, the results confirm that both fictional and non-fiction media can have an effect on how viewers perceive mental illness.[43] One group of researchers found that when people get most of their information from electronic media, they tend to develop authoritarian attitudes (that is, they believe that people with mental illness should not be treated in the general community).[44] When another researcher interviewed groups of individuals about their attitudes toward mental illness, movies like *Silence of the Lambs* and *Psycho* were often referenced in association with negative beliefs.[45] In yet another study, student attitudes toward mental illness became more negative after viewing *One Flew Over the Cuckoo's Nest*.[46]

As we have seen, psychologists and filmmakers approach the cinematic representations of madness in very different ways. According to Fleming and Manvell, "For the psychologist madness is primarily something to be quantitatively understood and then cured. For the film artist madness is principally a subject whose depiction provides the darkest and most hidden side of our being."[47] To the extent that distorted depictions of the mentally ill *do* impact the public perception of mental illness, the appeal for positive and accurate portrayals is understandable.

Still, mental health professionals should not be naïve; we are not in the same business as filmmakers. A psychologist may object to a character's being labeled "manic-depressive" instead of the more modern "bipolar disorder," while a filmmaker is likely to think that "bipolar" sounds like some kind of geographical term, and prefer the more dramatic "manic-depressive."

Furthermore, movies do not have to accurately capture diagnostic reality in order to effectively ruminate on the nature of madness. Films capture the behaviors of people that both threaten and fascinate us. At the same time, these representations evoke the possibility of behaviors within ourselves that we fear and/or desire. Psychiatrist Harry Stack Sullivan has stated that "everyone is much more simply human than otherwise."[48] Sullivan's statement is useful when considering any aspect of human diversity, [49] but the appeal for unity is particularly relevant for psychological disorders where examples of diversity are so vivid. The symptoms of these disorders strike many people as bizarre and odd and very different from ourselves. Sullivan's adage can help mitigate the tendency to alienate the afflicted by emphasizing the things that all people share (the desire for friendship, the capacity for love, curiosity about other people, etc.).

Films that are sympathetic toward mentally disordered characters can have a potentially humanizing effect. In *A Beautiful Mind*, John Nash is presented as having positive qualities that invite the audience to like or even identify with his struggle, despite his sometimes erratic behavior. Films can also encourage viewers to reflect on how they may share some of the characteristics of so-called madness (i.e., psychological symptoms). For example, normal nightly dreams may appear similar to hallucinations (both of which feature unreal sensory perceptions), and both are similar to surreal movies. The tendency to see similarities between various domains of human experience (including such everyday phenomena as dreams and symptoms of mental illness like hallucinations) forms what has been termed a "formal parallel."[50]

When we look at cinematic depictions of mental illness in this light, even extreme characterizations such as Norman Bates or the Joker are potentially revealing. Why do these characters fascinate us? Could it be that they are not only *different* from the average person, but that we also recognize something about them that is uncomfortably *familiar*? I don't view Norman Bates as a realistic patient, yet as a film character, he arouses deep anxiety and sympathy and speaks to my fears about a loss of rationality, self-control, and meaning. And while the Joker is an atrociously inaccurate depiction of mental illness, there is nevertheless something we can learn from him about the appeal of chaos.

Attention has also been given to the impact of film representations of psychologists and other mental health professionals. There is, however, one important distinction between this group and the mentally ill—we belong to a professional guild and we make a decent living. Thus, an argument could be made that health professionals need to be more thick-skinned and be prepared to put up with uncomplimentary depictions (the price of having social prestige and power).

Media representations of psychologists have actually been debated among psychologists themselves. In the late 1990s, the monthly newsletter for the American Psychological Association announced the formation of MediaWatch, a subcommittee devoted to monitoring and engaging in public relations issues around media representations of psychologists. The inappropriate behavior of movie psychologists in *The Prince of Tides* and *Good Will Hunting* were cited.[51] A few months later, a practicing psychologist responded with a letter entitled "Political Correctness Run Amok." He argued that MediaWatch was an indication of psychology's "continuing insecurity as a profession."[52] As a lover of such "psychologically incorrect" films as *Psycho* and *One Flew Over the Cuckoo's Nest*, I partly agreed with the letter writer. Yet having joined MediaWatch, I thought the group had a legitimate purpose. While psychologists certainly need to criticize/laugh at themselves, exaggerated depictions pose a danger to public perceptions of the profession.

Psychological treatment, particularly psychotherapy, is particularly vulnerable to misrepresentation. Psychotherapy sometimes has a mysterious aura, in part related to doctor-patient confidentiality, one of the bedrocks of competent counseling. Without the promise of confidentiality, clients would justifiably worry that their therapists might reveal their private thoughts, leading to a reluctance to share sensitive information. One of the unintended consequences of psychological confidentiality, however, is that it prevents most people from directly witnessing the counseling process. Movies and other media thus become the only way that the general public can get a glimpse into the private domain of psychotherapy. Even sophisticated viewers who are wise enough not to believe everything they see may find their understanding is affected in the absence of any other picture of therapy.

Even seemingly positive depictions of mental health treatment can be problematic. Several authors have pointed out the prevalence of the cathartic cure in cinematic psychotherapy—a dramatic moment of blinding insight when "the secret" is revealed, and the client, no matter how disturbed, is suddenly relieved of his or her suffering.[53] I was awed by this phenomenon when I first saw *The Three Faces of Eve* in my high school psychology class; in the climactic scene, Eve (Joanne Woodward) is cured of multiple personality disorder through the revelation that her symptoms began when she was forced to kiss her grandmother's corpse at the wake. Other cathartic cures are featured in *The Prince of Tides*, *Ordinary People*, and *Good Will Hunting*. These catharses are dramatically satisfying as they symbolically pull together various threads and wrap them up in a gratifying conclusion. Unfortunately, that is not the way therapy generally works. Instantaneous cures of severe problems are almost nonexistent. Therapeutic progress is usually slow and much less dramatic.

Such inaccuracies raise the possibility that people may avoid treatment altogether. One study demonstrated that adolescents who were "vulnerable" (experiencing depressive or suicidal symptoms) were more likely to believe that treatment would be ineffective after seeing films like *The Virgin Suicides*, *Girl, Interrupted*, and *A Beautiful Mind*. This finding is particularly concerning since these films are at least marginally sympathetic to psychological treatment and certainly not the worst depictions of mental health treatment available.[54]

Another study compared the perspectives of people who had seen a particular film to those of people who had not. The film was *Lovesick*, a 1980s romantic comedy starring Dudley Moore as Dr Saul Benjamin, a psychiatrist who decides to pursue a relationship with one of his patients. This romantic decision liberates him and inspires him to give up his lucrative psychoanalytic practice in order to help the poor. Participants who saw the film were found to be more accepting of a sexual relationship between a therapist and a client than participants who did not see it. As a romantic comedy, the narrative success of the film depends on convincing the audience that true love trumps all other considerations, including professional ethics. However, spreading the attitude that a romantic relationship is possible between therapist and client is not in the public good. Potential clients could either be horrified by this possibility and avoid therapy, or be enticed to seek out therapy for all the wrong reasons.[55]

Psychology and cinema grew up together during the twentieth century, and psychology and psychotherapy are, like Hollywood, well-established institutions. Because psychology doesn't have as good a publicity machine, it has ended up relying on Hollywood for promotion. In the 1990s, one out of six blockbusters featured mental health professionals engaged in a variety of treatments including individual psychotherapy, marital counseling, substance abuse counseling, and psychological assessment.[56] These practices have become commonplace within US culture, to an extent film may be simply reflecting reality. But it is also possible that the high level of therapeutic exposure in the movies has played a role in facilitating cultural acceptance (as well as considerable ambivalence).

Movie psychologists have encouraged some viewers to pursue a career in psychology or related fields. Marshall Edelson, a psychologist and psychiatrist at Yale, commented that Ingrid Bergman's performance as a psychoanalyst in Hitchcock's *Spellbound* had such an effect on him.[57] Based on my conversations with colleagues, it appears that many therapists of my generation (born between 1960–1975) were inspired by Judd Hirsch's Dr Berger in *Ordinary People*. Skeptics may worry that Dr Berger's selflessness sets impossible standards for budding therapists, but the established counselors I've talked to weren't so blindly idealistic. Instead, they focus on some of Berger's characteristics (compassion, patience, sensitivity) that continue to inspire them.

Other commentators have found good therapeutic models in the movies. Though a supernatural ghost story, *The Sixth Sense* has been lauded as an example of the difficulty therapists can have accepting the subjective realities of their patients. In the beginning Dr Crowe can't accept the reality of his young patient, Cole, who declares, "I see dead people." It is only when Dr Crowe does accept Cole's perceptions as the truth of his subjective world that he is able to help Cole cope with the ghosts that haunt him.[58] Dr Crowe's lack of awareness of his own issues initially leads him to react defensively when confronted with Cole's belief system. By refusing to believe and pulling away, he avoids confronting his own failures and limitations.[59] Despite the supernatural twist of *The Sixth Sense*, we can see how a movie can reveal truths about successful psychotherapy, and successful interpersonal relationships in general.[60]

# Further Reading

Dine Young, S. *et al.* (2008) Character motivation in the representations of mental health professionals in popular film. *Mass Communication and Society*, **11** (1), 82–99.

Gabbard, G.O. and Gabbard, K. (1999) *Psychiatry and the Cinema*. American Psychiatric Press, Washington, DC.

Hyler, S.E., Gabbard, G.O., and Schneider, I. (1991) Homicidal maniacs and narcissistic parasites: Stigmatization of mental ill persons in the movies. *Hospital and Community Psychiatry*, **42** (10), 1044–1048.

Pirkis, J. *et al.* (2006) On-screen portrayals of mental illness: Extent, nature, and impacts. *Journal of Health Communication*, **11** (5), 523–541.

Robinson, D.J. (2003) *Reel Psychiatry: Movie Portrayals of Psychiatric Conditions*. Rapid Psychler Press, Port Huron, MI.

Wahl, O. (1995) *Media Madness: Public Images of Mental Illness*. Rutgers University Press, New Brunswick, NJ.

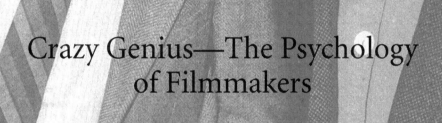

# Crazy Genius—The Psychology of Filmmakers

Illustration 4.1  Woody Allen and Mia Farrow in New York City. March 1986.
© Trinity Mirror/Mirrorpix/Alamy.

# Chapter 4

# Crazy Genius—The Psychology of Filmmakers

In Woody Allen's *Husbands & Wives*, Gabe (Allen) and Judy (Mia Farrow) are New York intellectuals. From the outside, their marriage appears to be a model modern, urban relationship. The couple pursues successful professional careers while entertaining friends at dinner parties and going to restaurants and plays. However, a deep malaise has set in, and Gabe, a college professor and writer, finds himself drawn to one of his students, precocious 20-year-old Rain (Juliette Lewis). But after flirting with Rain and joking about years of psychotherapy dialing 911, he decides against pursuing her in order to break a pattern of doomed relationships.

In the early 1990s, Woody Allen and Mia Farrow's own relationship was widely viewed as a model modern, urban relationship. Though not married, and maintaining separate apartments, they made a dozen movies together, and in public, appeared to be a loving, committed couple with several adopted children and one biological child. In 1992, a month before the release of *Husbands & Wives*, news broke that Allen had been having an affair with Farrow's 19-year-old daughter, Soon-Yi (adopted during Farrow's marriage to Andre Previn).[1] Allen claimed that he was in love with Soon-Yi, that he had never been a father figure to Soon-Yi and that for some time his relationship with Farrow had been platonic and emotionally disengaged.[2]

*Psychology at the Movies*, First Edition. Skip Dine Young
© 2012 John Wiley & Sons, Ltd. Published 2012 by John Wiley & Sons, Ltd.

**Illustration 4.2**  Mia Farrow & Woody Allen as Judy & Gabe in *Husbands and Wives* (1992) © AF archive/Alamy.

The parallels between film and reality—an older man falling for a younger woman in the midst a dreary relationship hidden behind a public façade—were striking. Could they be "just a coincidence"?

Woody Allen downplays the significance of the connection between life and art. While acknowledging that artists borrow elements from what they see in their environment, he claims that *Husbands & Wives,* like all his movies, is a fictional story, concocted out of his imagination.[3] Admittedly, the parallels are not perfect (Gabe and Judy are childless; Gabe decides not to pursue a relationship with Rain). Nevertheless, most people find Allen's assertion that *Husbands & Wives* is pure fiction disingenuous. It is evident to many that, in this example, art imitates the artist and vice versa.

## Psychobiography and Filmmakers

This chapter shifts the focus from movies to moviemakers. Movies are not just about people, they are made *by* people—brilliant, egocentric, passionate, and maybe a little crazy. Any scan of the bookstore biography section or grocery tabloids will make it clear that, from Orson Welles to Lindsay Lohan, the public is passionately interested in the lives of people who make movies. This chapter considers how the experiences, personalities, values, and unconscious motivations of filmmakers are reflected in their work.

Psychobiography is the study of human lives across the lifespan.[4] Like a regular biographer, the psychobiographer compiles details from a person's life and makes a case for which events are important. However, in psychobiography, the personality dimensions underlying the subject's overt behaviors are highlighted. Often there is an attempt to explain these patterns using a particular theory of human development. For example, Erik Erikson used his developmental theory (often referred to as the Eight Stages of Man) to analyze Martin Luther, placing emphasis on his identity development in adolescence and young adulthood.[5]

Biographies are generally about people who have lived in the public eye (politicians and prominent intellectuals). This is true of psychobiographies as well, and there is a preference for artists and writers as subjects, resulting in analyses of Vincent Van Gogh, Sylvia Plath, and Elvis Presley.[6] Not surprisingly, the first psychobiography was Freud's analysis of Leonardo da Vinci's life and creative work.[7] One reason da Vinci provided such a fruitful subject was that he left behind a large body of paintings and notebooks (symbolic products) which shed light on his inner life. In psychobiography, an artist's creations are treated like life-long versions of the projective tests used in psychological assessment (in which subject's drawings and stories are taken to be reflections of their inner selves).[8]

When applied to film, psychobiography assumes that all the symbolic elements (dialogue, costumes, even camera movements) represent the psychological makeup of the people who created them. Psychobiographers go beyond the "what" of a filmmaker's career to ask "why?" Why do Hitchcock's films embody so much anxiety? Why does Jack Nicholson always play rebels? While there have been few psychobiographies of filmmakers by trained psychologists,[9] the technique of making connections between the personal aspects of a filmmaker's life and his or her art is widespread.

## Auteurs: Profiles of Directors

One of the important developments in film studies was the emergence in the 1950s of auteur theory, when French film critics argued that their focus should be directors who imbued their work with a personal vision exhibiting both stylistic and thematic consistency.[10] The original auteur criticism championed particular directors as exemplars, but more than that, it meant that films, like novels, poems, and plays, could now have "authors."

One of the unintended consequences of the theory was that directors became ripe for biographical analysis. If one believes films are the reflections of an individual's personal vision, then movies themselves open up a director's life for study.

## Alfred Hitchcock

Hitchcock's presence, as a personality as well as an artist, hangs prominently over his movies. Witness the audience fascination with his brief cameos in many of his films.[11] Biographer Donald Spoto believes there is a close connection between Hitchcock's own complex and paradoxical character and his movies: "Hitchcock's films [are] his notebooks and journals . . . his almost maniacal secrecy was a deliberate means of deflecting attention away from what those films really are: astonishingly personal documents."[12] Outwardly, this doesn't seem to be the case. None of Hitchcock's movies are about a droll, corpulent Englishman leading a comfortable life in southern California. But Spoto asserts that if you look into Hitchcock's life and movies, you will find a man of stark contradictions. The public persona of a simple family man who just loved to make movies contrasts with a darker inner life of guilt, anxiety, and anger—hence the title of Spoto's biography, *The Dark Side of Genius* (1983).

One of Hitchcock's favorite boyhood anecdotes was about the time he committed a minor offense and his father William asked a policeman friend to lock Alfred in jail for a brief time to teach him a lesson. Hitchcock used this story to explain his lifelong fear of imprisonment and the police.[13] His father comes off as an emotionally detached disciplinarian, a picture consistent with what little is known about him. Spoto speculates that his death when Hitchcock was 15 might have caused him guilt based on the hostile feelings (perhaps even a death wish) that he harbored for his stern father.[14] Presentations of authority as unreliable, oppressive, and potentially dangerous are everywhere in Hitchcock films: the spy bosses in *Notorious* who callously throw Alicia (Ingrid Bergman) into harm's way; the menacing motorcycle cop in *Psycho*; the flawed judicial system condemning an innocent man (Henry Fonda) in *The Wrong Man*; and so on.

While Hitchcock seemed to view the childhood jailing incident as a macabre joke, it demonstrates at least a sliver of awareness of the connection between his life and art. There may have been other connections Hitchcock was not so willing to publicly discuss. He was infamous for his unflattering portrayals of maternal figures. This is exaggerated in the character of Madame Sebastien (Leopoldine Konstantin) in *Notorious*, especially the scene where she lights a cigarette, glares menacingly, and contemplates how to extricate her wimpy Nazi son, Alexander (Claude Rains) from his marriage to an American spy. *Psycho, Marnie, North by Northwest* and others offer examples of mothers who are controlling or twisted. Spoto suggests that these mothers may mirror Hitchcock's ambivalence about his own mother, with whom he lived until his marriage to Alma Reville in his late twenties. He was reportedly very close to her, although he may have felt resentful when she became despondent after his father's death and required significant care.[15]

Spoto believes Hitchcock's anxiety about mothers and mothering continued into his relationship with Alma. She had an enormous influence over Hitchcock's life and work, but Spoto characterizes the majority of their private relationship as platonic.[16] Again, this tension can be found in Hitchcock's movies. In *Vertigo* (1958) Midge (Barbara Bel Geddes) is attractive, intelligent, and committed to the protagonist, Scotty (Jimmy Stewart). Theirs is a close friendship dating back to their college days when they were engaged. Yet Scotty takes Midge for granted, at one point dismissing her concern with the remark, "That's awful motherly of you."

According to Spoto, Hitchcock's insecurity about his physical unattractiveness led to obsessive relationships with his lead actresses. The Hitchcock "type" (blonde, sophisticated, cool, and unattainable) appeared in his films from the 1940s through the 1960s (e.g., Ingrid Bergman, Tippi Hedren, Grace Kelly, Kim Novak). Hitchcock had notoriously intense relationships with these actresses. He could be attentive and adoring; Kelly affectionately described how Hitchcock sought her opinions about her wardrobe in *Dial "M" for Murder*.[17] He could also be perversely controlling and maintained extraordinarily unrealistic standards. He was outraged when Vera Miles had to drop out of *Vertigo* when she became pregnant with her third child. He told her that "one child was expected, two was sufficient, but that three was obscene."[18]

Spoto sees *Vertigo* as the quintessential example of Hitchcock's psychic obsessions. During the first half of the film, Scotty trails mysterious, ghostly Madeleine (Novak), the wife of a rich college chum, through an equally mysterious and ghostly San Francisco. At first, she is idealized and out of reach. But as soon as Scotty initiates an affair, she falls to a death from which he, crippled by a fear of heights, was incapable of saving her. In the second half, Scotty tries to make over Judy (also Novak), a dark-haired, vulgar Madeleine look-alike. He is relentless, meticulous and thoughtless as he transforms Judy into his memory of Madeleine. Eventually he discovers that Madeleine and Judy are the same person, hired to take part in a murder conspiracy.

As he drags Judy up the stairs of a mission bell tower, Scotty chokes out the following dialogue:

> He [the murderer] made you over, didn't he? He made you over just like I made you over—only better. Not only the clothes and the hair, but the looks and the manner and the words . . . And then what did he do? Did he train you? Did he rehearse you? Did he tell you exactly what to do and say?

Spoto believes this speech is not simply a description of the characters' actions in *Vertigo*, but also describes Hitchcock's own attitude and treatment of his leading ladies.

### Martin Scorsese

For an industry that is often accused of being secular and agnostic, it is interesting how many great directors are preoccupied with religious and spiritual themes. When Martin Scorsese made *The Last Temptation of Christ* in 1988, he brought his religious preoccupations to the foreground, but these themes were evident in all of his previous movies—including Travis's (Robert De Niro) pseudo-Biblical speeches in *Taxi Driver* about the coming rain that will cleanse the filthy city streets, and the religious preoccupations of Charlie (Harvey Keitel) in *Mean Streets*.

Biographer Vincent LoBrutto argues that much of Scorsese's visual flare and aesthetic sensibility come from the rituals and sacraments of the Catholic Church—the focus on blood and the body, intense myths, a rich color palette reminiscent of stained glass. These images overlap the cinematic themes found in the gladiator movies, historical epics, and religious spectacles that were popular when Scorsese was growing up in the 1950s.[19]

Of course, these images and themes are not unique to the Catholic Church but are also related to pagan influences that go even further back in Scorsese's Sicilian heritage.[20] While Catholicism was important to Scorsese's family while he was growing up, there was always suspicion of the Church and nobody else in his family was especially devout. LoBrutto concludes that ultimately cinema was Scorsese's true religion and that Catholicism was important mostly for its visuals.[21] However, Scorsese apparently internalized the morals and dogma of the church more than his family; he was briefly in seminary and intended to enter the priesthood. The movies won out, but the religious themes of guilt and redemption form the backbone of his work. While LoBrutto emphasizes the sexual guilt in Scorsese's early preoccupations, a broader sense of being inadequate as a human being still haunts Scorsese: "I took the Gospel very seriously. I wondered then and I still wonder whether I should quit everything and help the poor. But I wasn't, and I'm still not, strong enough."[22] Consistent with this lack of resolution, many of his characters struggle for redemption, but rarely find it. In *Taxi Driver*, Travis Bickle's redemption in the eyes of the press and the law is demonstrated to be ironic and false. It is only the character of Jesus in *The Last Temptation of Christ* who is strong enough to unequivocally make the right choice.

### Akira Kurosawa

Psychobiographers, like many developmental psychologists since Freud, tend to pay special attention to events in childhood—including the relationship to parents, socioeconomic hardships, and traumatic experiences. While childhood is important, its influence may be overstated. The developmental aspects of adulthood have not been given equal attention.

A lifespan approach to the career of the Japanese director Akira Kurosawa provides one alternative.[23] Kurosawa's most famous and critically hailed films such *The Seven Samurai* and *Rashomon* were made in the 1950s when Kurosawa was already in his forties; he lived to be 88 and made films into the 1990s, though for the most part, these are not as celebrated as his earlier work. It may be that the evaluation of Kurosawa's later films is based on a developmental misunderstanding—critics considering the older style of an experienced artist from a middle-aged analytical perspective.

Like many artists, Kurosawa turned more inward as he aged. After a great deal of personal turmoil and a suicide attempt, starting in the mid-70s he consciously decided to make films that were more autobiographical yet also less realistic. Some critics see this shift as a loss of artistic focus and control. Yet, by loosening the story and abandoning a youthful cinematic propensity for action, Kurosawa's later films capture the reflective stillness of a contemplative life. *Dreams* (eight vignettes that embody Kurosawa's own dreams) is an attempt to create "biographical space" for the resolution of previously competing life forces.[24] This artistic accomplishment was only possible by an accumulation of life experiences both in and outside the cinema.

## Star-Gazing: Profiles of Actors

Most movie stars have an instantly recognizable public persona—qualities that are attractive and intriguing. This public perception is often exaggerated as stars tend to play variations of the same character over and over. Even at public venues like the Academy Awards, they present a stylized version of themselves. Such appearances effectively become yet another role that contributes to their star quality. In the end, it is this stardom that outshines both their acting roles and the reality of their daily lives. Their fans come to feel that they know these stars. In some ways, they seem to have normal human qualities and are relatable. Yet, in other ways, movie stars are not like other people at all. They are in fact "bigger than life" and somehow purer.[25]

Star power is so potent that, for many Hollywood movies, an argument can be made that the stars are the real auteurs. A John Wayne movie or a Will Smith movie defines what the characteristics of the movie should be and how it needs to look. It is the job of the other filmmakers, including the directors and screenwriters, to construct such a movie around its star.

The psychobiography of movie stars explores how an actor's roles, public persona, and private life intermingle. Movies are unlikely to be transparent replicas of an actor's underlying personality, but they may act as distorted prisms for his or her psychological reality.

## Jack Nicholson

Nicholson's body of work is impressive, particularly the films he made in the 1970s, from *Five Easy Pieces* to *The Shining*. While these films were directed by renowned filmmakers, critics believe it is Nicholson's performance that defines them. As an actor Nicholson projects the intensity and psychological complexity of post-Brando movie acting, yet he is also a throwback to an older Hollywood in the sense that no one would ever say he "disappears" into his roles. Whatever the character, part of his appeal is that he is always "Jack being Jack," a characteristic that invites psychobiographical analysis.

Patrick McGilligan's *Jack's Life* (1994) explores a variety of psychobiographical themes, but it is Nicholson's parentage that stands out as most unusual. His mother June gave birth to Jack when she was 18. The father of the baby is unclear. In order to allow her daughter to pursue a show business career, Jack's grandmother Ethel May took over the role of raising Jack, telling him that she was his mother and that June was his sister. Jack's grandfather and nominal father, John J., moved out when Jack was a baby, though they continued to have sporadic contact as Jack grew up.[26] Nicholson did not find out the true circumstances of his birth until he was contacted by a reporter from *Time* just as *Chinatown* was being released in 1974. This revelation reportedly had a strong emotional impact on Nicholson and he tearfully told the story to various confidantes.[27]

Starting with Bobby Dupee's infamous "chicken salad" tirade in *Five Easy Pieces*, Nicholson's acting has become associated with intense emotional outbursts. Often these eruptions have a strong air of righteousness about them. In *One Flew Over the Cuckoo's Nest*, McMurphy is the noble truth teller in the oppressive environment of a mental ward. In early interviews, Nicholson emphasized the importance his family always placed on honesty.[28] Biographer McGilligan claims that Nicholson's cinematic tantrums were perfected when the young Jack wanted attention from the women in his grandmother's beauty parlor.[29] This behavior, combined with the fact that major secrets were being kept from him, might lead one to reinterpret the grown-up tantrums of Bobby, McMurtry, and other Nicholson characters. Seen in this light, such outbursts take on a frantic, searching quality, where truth is not something that has been found, but something for which the characters, like Nicholson, are desperately striving.

*Angelina Jolie*

Angelina Jolie is perhaps the preeminent young female star of the modern age. Since winning Best Supporting Actress in 2000 for *Girl, Interrupted*, Jolie has been a regular media presence, either because of her movie roles, her personal life, or her humanitarian efforts. One constant feature of her public persona is her sexuality. Even in a movie that has minimal explicit sexual content such as *Lara Croft: Tomb Raider*, her hyper-toned body is nearly fetishized. What makes Jolie particularly modern is her openness about her sexuality, particularly practices like bondage, bisexuality, and tattooing that are generally associated with alternative lifestyles. Freud's observations about the motivating power of sexuality are clear in terms of Jolie's celebrity but you could hardly say it is treated as a buried secret.

Jolie's only major biography this far, *Angelina: An Unauthorized Biography* by Andrew Morton, devotes substantial attention to her racy image. Its index includes bisexuality, S&M fetish, and romantic relationships with various famous people, as well as such pathologized topics as cutting, drug use, eating disorders and "knife fascination." Childhood and humanitarian work are also included, but curiously, there are no entries for acting and other professional topics typically prominent in the biographies of filmmakers. Passages like the following are sprinkled liberally throughout the book: "While there was sexual hesitancy on film, among the actors and crew [of *Foxfire*] there was no such inhibition, the eight-week shoot turning into one long and decadent sorority trip."[30]

Morton attempts to explain Jolie's sexuality as the results of her childhood and parenting. A lesbian relationship in her early twenties is interpreted as an attempt to seek revenge on her father, actor Jon Voight, because she knew he would not approve. Morton bolsters his analysis of Jolie's bisexuality by soliciting the perspectives of a psychoanalyst—"Bisexuality is part of being lost. . . If you don't understand yourself and what you need, you are going to experiment"—and a psychologist (in reference to Jolie allegedly being left unattended in her crib)—"If you are [a woman] starved for intimacy, if you have been abandoned, you feel like nothing. If you have an attraction to a woman, it is going to end up sexual."[31]

Such opinions, particularly the causal connection between newborn attachment and bisexuality, are not accepted by most mental health professionals, and their truth is dubious. They do, however, succeed in providing explanations that are more lurid and provocative than the behaviors they are attempting to explain. Instead of her simply being involved in a lesbian relationship, readers form a picture of Angelina Jolie as a wild, lost little girl running around Los Angeles, desperately searching for her mother by doing a lot of "experimenting." It's the kind of thing that gives psychobiographies a bad name.

## Cast Psychology

Despite the inordinate attention given to movie stars and star directors, movies are not made by individuals. No matter how charismatic an actor or how visionary a director, filmmakers don't work alone. Movies are the reflection of many people working together on a shared purpose over a lengthy period of time. More than the sum of these individual experiences, the pieces fit together in unique ways. The famous aphorism, "the whole is greater than the sum of its parts,"[32] can be readily applied to psychobiography.

Italian director Bernardo Bertolucci had a revelation about the interdependence of cast and crew on the set of his vast historical epic *1900*:

> For a long time, I thought that a movie was the expression of one person. That's why I started making movies when I was very young. I was coming right from the experience of being a poet. [Eventually] I had to accept that the film was also the expression of and the result of a collective creation. Everybody in the crew, everybody on the set, participates in my movies.[33]

The collective psychology of every participant also rubs off on the movie. Bertolucci points out how the use of non-professional shepherds added an air of authenticity to a film about the history of Italy. And actress Fiona Shaw likens the film crew to a family (albeit a peculiar kind, where everyone on the set is avoiding their real families[34]). A darker version of how group psychology can affect the final product is captured in Francis Ford Coppola's comments about *Apocalypse Now*: "It was a little like the Vietnam War, a group of people went into the jungle and went mad."[35] For better or worse, the interactions of many people coming together are what's responsible for the ultimate meanings and feelings contained in a film.

Recently, there has been a trend toward filming epic stories in a multi-movie series (*The Lord of the Rings, Harry Potter*) that requires the cast and crew to work intensely over a period of years, sometimes filming in physically challenging locations. Like all modern blockbusters, these films have plenty of visual effects, but their phenomenal success has just as much to do with the bonds between the characters. The actors involved in these marathon shoots speak movingly about the intense camaraderie that develops among the cast and crew. The friendships formed behind the camera manifest themselves in the movies. *Harry Potter* director David Yates expressed this sentiment regarding one of the final scenes with Harry (Daniel Radcliffe), Hermione (Emma Watson) and Ron (Rupert Grint): "It wasn't just the actors playing the scene, it was the kids reflecting on growing up in this moviemaking world, and I believe a bit of that has ended up on [film]."[36]

## Psychology for Filmmakers: The Case of Woody Allen

Psychology is not just for psychologists. The ideas of Freud and Jung have spread beyond academia and the therapist's office to be adopted by laypeople, including biographers. Some filmmakers have been influenced by psychological concepts in their own lives and art, providing many "how to" hints for the film industry.

One of the most significant developments in twentieth-century theater and film acting was the so-called Method. Based on the work of Stanislavski, it was developed by Lee Strasberg for his Actors Studio and popularized by actors of the 1940s and 1950s including Marlon Brando, James Dean, and Paul Newman. Method acting encourages artists to find the emotions and motivations for their characters inside themselves. This inward turn was part of a post-Freudian *zeitgeist* that emphasized subjective experience and multiple levels of consciousness.[37]

Some psychologists have packaged psychological insights specifically to help actors, directors, and screenwriters develop characters which are psychologically complex and realistic. Writers are encouraged to align their characters with ancient archetypes such as the hero, the wise man, and the fool to forge a more profound connection to the audience.[38] The goal is not just to access parts of an individual's unique self but to connect with those parts of the self that everyone has.

A number of stars, directors, and movie moguls have experienced clinical psychology themselves. In *Hollywood on the Couch*, Stephen Farber and Marc Green (1993) explore the long, intense, and sometimes inappropriate history of moviemakers who fell under the spell of psychology, particularly psychoanalysis. In 1924 Samuel Goldwyn offered Sigmund Freud $100 000 to help fashion a love story with psychoanalytic insights.[39] Freud declined without comment, but many other psychoanalysts were on hand to offer their assistance. Most of their methods did not correspond to modern standards of care. A psychiatrist employed to be Judy Garland's crisis counselor on *The Pirate* assisted the producer and director, Arthur Freed and Vincente Minnelli, with the editing of the film.[40] This type of influence by psychologists continued in Hollywood for decades. In the 1980s and 1990s, pop psychologist John Bradshaw developed a professional relationship with a number of celebrities including Barbra Streisand. He influenced the making of *The Prince of Tides*, both in the characterization of Steisand's Dr Lowenstein and in the plot device based on a cathartic revelation of abuse.[41]

But it is Woody Allen who holds the closest association with psychology in the public imagination. Certainly therapy plays a prominent role in many of his films. In *Husbands and Wives,* a shelf of Freud's books is visible behind Gabe as he conducts self-revealing interviews with an unseen documentarian/quasi-therapist. In *Another Woman* Marion (Gena Rowlands) finds her life altered when she overhears a suicidal patient talking to her analyst. In Allen's films, therapy is presented as part of the New York intellectual lifestyle. In *Annie Hall*, Alvy (Allen) even pays for the analysis of his therapeutically naïve girlfriend, Annie (Diane Keaton). Occasionally, Allen's therapists are harshly satirized, such as when Helen (Demi Moore) in *Deconstructing Harry* repeatedly ends therapy in order to start love affairs with clients, or Mary's (Keaton) therapist in *Manhattan* who Isaac (Allen) ridicules by saying "You don't get suspicious when your analyst calls you at home at three in the morning and weeps into the telephone?"[42]

The presence of therapists in Allen's movies is not surprising. Allen first began therapy in 1959 when he was 24; by the 1990s, he had been in extended psychoanalysis for intermittently periods with five different analysts.[43] Still, beyond acknowledging that he is a long-term psychotherapy client, Allen's biographers have said little about the specific content of his analysis or the role it has played in his life since, beyond the occasional jokes and generalizations, Allen has rarely talked about his own analysis.

Despite this contrast between the public and private Woody Allen, many people assume there is little difference between the two. To his fans, he seems so familiar that we feel comfortable referring to him as "Woody." Few people imagined that Hitchcock's personal life was like something out of his thrillers, yet many people believe that Allen's Manhattan existence parallels the lives portrayed in *Annie Hall*, *Manhattan*, and *Husbands & Wives*. And while Hitchcock's leading men (Cary Grant, Jimmy Stewart, Henry Fonda) bear no physical or personality resemblance to him, Woody often plays the interchangeable protagonists in his films. Even if this sameness is due to his limited acting range, it emphasizes a singular personality. Occasionally in Allen directed films such as *Celebrity*, the male protagonist (Kenneth Brannagh) appears to be doing a Woody Allen impersonation. For all these reasons, most fans assume that the Woody character is much like Allen himself.

Because audience felt they "knew" Allen, the disastrous ending of his relationship with Mia Farrow disturbed many people. When the scandal broke, I was a few years into my clinical training in psychology, and it was a topic of heated conversation. Since Allen was associated with psychology, and many of my peers were fans, the whole affair seemed vaguely embarrassing. Among the people I knew there was an attitude that with all those years of analysis, Allen should have learned it was not a good idea to become involved with your significant other's adopted daughter. Before the affair, the psychotherapy presented in Woody Allen movies could be dismissed as gentle satire. But after the fact, there was an overwhelming impression that psychotherapy was a means for bored intellectuals to indulge themselves.[44]

Perhaps it would be prudent for psychology to simply bury its association with Allen. Yet psychologists and psychiatrists continue to analyze Allen's films for their portrayals of psychotherapy and human relationships in general. Some commentators see them as modeling the essential psychodynamic tenet that self-understanding is an ongoing process of making connections between past, present and future.[45] Personally, I still find *Annie Hall* to be both hilarious and insightful. For better and worse, psychology has served a role in Allen's life while his films have influenced how psychology is understood by psychologists and nonpsychologists alike. And while one may be tempted to separate the art and the artist, in Allen's case it really isn't possible.

## Closing Shots: Evaluating Psychobiography

Asking penetrating questions about the psychological origins of an artist's work doesn't necessarily mean that the answers will be profound—often, such questions open the door to cheap and easy psychoanalysis ("Film-maker X has castration anxiety") or tabloid level muckraking ("Filmmaker Y's mother was a prostitute"). Serious psychobiographers need to develop definite criteria to separate lurid speculation from psychobiography.

A good psychobiography should demonstrate coherence and consistence.[46] All the "facts" of a person's life should fit whatever overarching psychological claim is being made. Facts that run counter to the developing theory mustn't be ignored but rather integrated into a revised theory. In addition, interpretations should not be based on a single instance but con-firmed by multiple observations.[47] Thus, if a filmmaker writes an emotional letter to his mother, this is not in itself evidence of major dependency issues.

Common mistakes in psychobiography include reconstruction in which one speculates about unknown events in order to support an interpretation. Spoto's unsubstantiated conjecture that Hitchcock had a death wish for his stern father would fall into this category.[48] Even Freud made serious errors of omission and forced interpretation in his analysis of Leonardo Da Vinci, errors that say more about Freud's psyche than about his subject.[49]

Another danger in psychobiography is pathography—conceptualizing a person's whole life in terms of a pathology or illness.[50] This type of criticism has been directed at entire theories. Freud began by observing his impaired clients and then built a general theory of the mind to explain their impairments. The examples I have presented (Hitchcock's conflicted relationships with women or Nicholson's family secrets) are also guilty of focusing on pathology. This orientation can lead to a one-sided view of people. The bonds of friendship that appear on screen in *Harry Potter* are an alternative example consistent with positive psychology, a movement toward a more optimistic and constructive orientation for the field.[51]

In the psychobiography of artists, it is difficult to avoid psychopathology however. Shakespeare uses the phrase "strong imagination" in *A Midsummer Night's Dream*, to capture the mental activity shared by both the poet and madmen.[52] Certainly there is anecdotal and demographic evidence that ge-nius and mental illness may be linked. Consider the artists/musicians/writers who experienced periods of psychosis: Kandinsky, Van Gogh, Schumann, Poe, Pound, Woolf, Plath, Hemingway, and Blake.[53] Other lists could be generated for disorders such as depression, anxiety, and mania. The proportion of eminent people, particularly artists and poets, who have experienced significant psychopathology, is much greater than the general population.[54] The relationship between creativity and mental illness is even more pronounced, given how imaginative creations can take on the qualities of dreams and altered states of consciousness. An ideal psychobiography addresses the unhealthy aspects of artists' lives without reducing them to mere clinical diagnosis.

Movies offer filmmakers different types of psychological outlets. Some are autobiographical in how they depict events which are recreations of the filmmaker's past. This may be done for the sake of nostalgia or perhaps as an opportunity to work through the past. Both tendencies can be seen in the films of Woody Allen.

For some filmmakers, their work becomes a stand-in for their fantasies about alternative lives. People create art in order to expand their range of experience, to pretend to be in a different time and place. As a creative medium, movies are particularly good at allowing artists to explore magical worlds (*Harry Potter*), exotic locales (*Vertigo*), or historic events (*1900*).

Filmmakers also tend to make movies about the things they desire. Freud compared creative storytelling to children playing make-believe or adults daydreaming. He contended that all these individuals are indulging in *wish fulfillment*.[55] While reality may prevent people from acquiring unlimited love, wealth and power, these limitations can be overcome in stories. On the other hand, films also contain images of despair, violence, and horror, experiences that most people would not wish upon themselves. In some cases, making a movie is a way for filmmakers to face their fears, psychologically preparing for the worst. The frequent violent confrontations in Scorsese's films are one example; Roman Polanski's are another.

In most cases, the psychological experience of a filmmaker cannot be categorized as purely autobiographical or pure wish fulfillment. Movies represent a range of experiences that can get mixed up together in a single film. While *Vertigo* allowed Hitchcock to vicariously fetishize Madeleine, it also reflects his guilt in requiring that Scotty pay for his weakness. Such multidimensionality can be seen in the audience for movies as well.

## Further Reading

Farber, S. and Green, M. (1993) *Hollywood on the Couch: A Candid Look at the Overheated Love Affair between Psychiatrists and Moviemakers.* William Morrow, New York, NY.

Lax, E. (2000) *Woody Allen: A Biography*. Da Capo Press, Cambridge, MA.

LoBrutto, V. (2008) *Martin Scorsese: A Biography*. Praeger, Westport, CT.

McGilligan, P. (1994) *Jack's Life: A Biography of Jack Nicholson*. W.W. Norton, New York, NY.

Schultz, W.T. (2005) *Handbook of Psychobiography*. Oxford University Press, New York, NY.

Spoto, D. (1983) *The Dark Side of Genius: The Life of Alfred Hitchcock*. Little, Brown, Boston, MA.

# Picturing the Audience—Psychological Profiles of Moviegoers

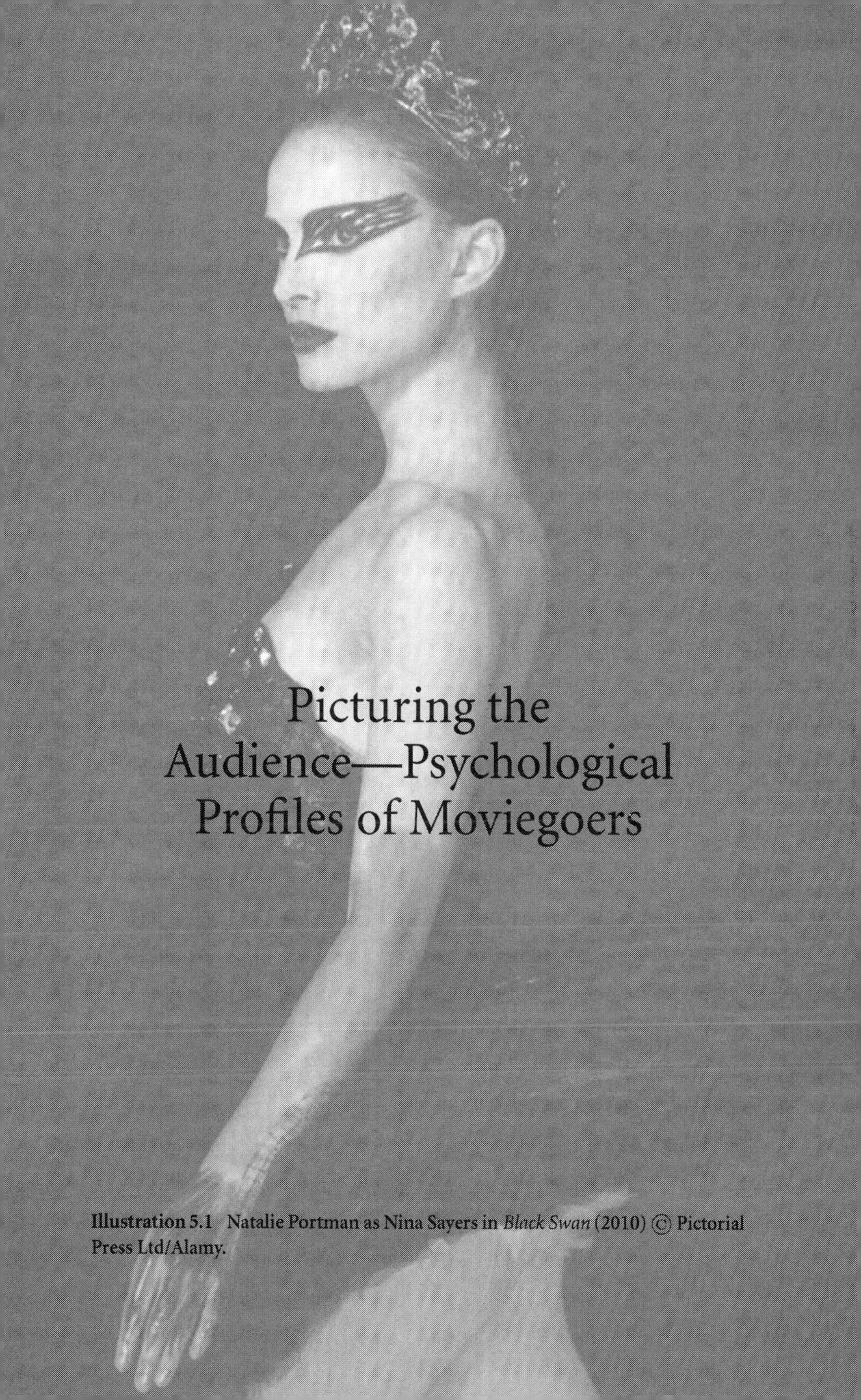

Illustration 5.1   Natalie Portman as Nina Sayers in *Black Swan* (2010) © Pictorial Press Ltd/Alamy.

# Chapter 5

# Picturing the Audience—Psychological Profiles of Moviegoers

A few weeks after it was released, I saw *Black Swan* on a big screen with a state-of-the-art projection and sound system in a theater in Louisville, Kentucky. For years the cinema had been the only art theater in town, but when a nearby multiplex closed, it altered its format to capitalize on a larger audience. While it still showed independent films, it mixed these smaller movies with wide-release titles. *Black Swan* was the perfect film for such a venue. Directed by *wunderkind* Darren Aronofsky, it had artistic credibility, on the way to becoming a box office smash.

I went to an early evening show on an impulse, after doing some errands. I chose *Black Swan* because it had been well-publicized, the ads looked intriguing, and it had gotten some good reviews. It was not a film my wife would want to see; she's not a fan of violent psycho-horror-dramas, even ones set in the world of ballet.

I got my trough of popcorn and bucket of cherry coke and took a seat in the middle aisle, toward the back. The place was soon packed, and I watched people as they came in. The majority were somewhere between college age and thirty-something. Gender was mixed, perhaps skewing a little toward the female. Most of the audience appeared to be upper middle-class; their dress was nondescript Midwestern casual, with a smattering of hip urban styles. The audience was primarily white with a number of Hispanics, Asians

*Psychology at the Movies*, First Edition. Skip Dine Young
© 2012 John Wiley & Sons, Ltd. Published 2012 by John Wiley & Sons, Ltd.

and African-Americans. Most were in groups of two to four, either on dates or out with friends, with younger people sitting in larger packs.

A group of giggling high school girls sat in the front (apparently the R rating was not a prohibition). A well-dressed couple in their twenties sat directly in front of me; judging by the man's comments before the movie started, *Black Swan* was not his choice. A college-age woman and her mother sat next to them; even in the darkened theater, they communicated palpable tension, particularly during the lesbian love scene. A few seats ahead of me, I saw an older man and woman leave soon into the movie, when vulnerable ballerina Nina's (Natalie Portman) self-mutilating hallucinations were just beginning. Down in front, I heard a woman repeatedly threaten to take her pre-school child home if he wouldn't keep quiet (a promise she didn't make good on until about three-fourths through the movie).

A few days later, I got into a discussion of the film with a group of undergraduate students who had all seen *Black Swan.* Their orientations to the film differed widely. One young man, a movie buff who had taken every film course the college offered, had been looking forward to the film ever since the concept was leaked to the media. Two women next to him recalled Natalie Portman from the *Star Wars* prequels and chose *Black Swan* because "there was nothing else on." They agreed that they never would have gone to the movie if they'd known about its grotesque and sexual content (and vowed never to see another Natalie Portman movie). A third woman strongly disagreed; she hadn't known much about the movie and admitted that she "usually doesn't go for scary movies," but qualified her preferences, stating that she likes movies that differ from the "same old thing."

This chapter shifts the focus to viewers of films. The above example presents a snapshot of the audience for a particular movie and highlights the big picture questions about moviegoing behavior: When and where do people watch movies? What kind of movies do people go to see? And what kinds of people go to see which kinds of movies?

Such questions are variants of a phenomenon psychologists call "selective exposure."[1] People have to make choices about which environments and events they are willing to expose themselves to—a library, a city street, an office, a movie theater, and so on. They make these choices based on the degree and type of stimulation that will reward them. In the case of entertainment, the movies we expose ourselves to vary from person to person, yet patterns emerge that reflect historical, cultural and personality trends.

## Movie Audiences through the Years

For over a century, movies have been a pervasive cultural presence, but the cinematic universe continues to expand. In recent years, people have become used to watching movies on planes, in cars, at the doctor's office, and so on. Thanks to digital devices like BlackBerries and iPhones, movies have become even more portable and ubiquitous. With cyber-cinema options like Netflix Online sprouting at a rapid rate, it feels as though all movies are available all the time. The only thing the audience has to do is plug in.

Yet, no matter how flexible viewing options become, people will always enjoy watching movies at a certain time in a certain place. There is a historical and physical quality to movie watching, even if it *feels* as though images are simply being radiated into us.

The context of movie viewing can be important to how a movie is experienced. You may watch *Avatar* on an iPhone and follow the plot, but you won't experience its multidimensional magnificence. You could view *The Social Network* in an empty second-run theater in Kalamazoo, but it won't be the same as seeing it at a packed showing in Harvard Square. *Gone with the Wind* can be checked out on a decaying VHS tape from the local library, but it can't compare with seeing a celluloid print debuted in a grand movie palace.

The history of film exhibition demonstrates how new technological and financial innovations have altered the viewer's experience.[2] By the turn of the twentieth century, moving pictures were a popular form of entertainment. Like travelling theater productions or concert tours, movie exhibitors would transport their equipment from town to town, and at the invitation of local organizations, set up a screen in an opera house, church, or other public space. Initially, films focused on short, exciting spectacles (an approaching locomotive) presented to amazed audiences. By the 1910s, small nickelodeons sprang up in cities and towns. The content of motion pictures moved toward the story-based, star-driven films that defines mainstream filmgoing. Grander, more technically sophisticated films like D.W. Griffith's *Birth of a Nation* and *Intolerance* required opulent palaces that could seat thousands of people. Such cinemas started out in major urban areas, but by the 1920s, movie theaters were found all across the country.

With the emergence of "talkies" in the late 1920s up to the early 1960s, movies were the dominant form of American entertainment. It was known as the Golden Age of Hollywood. Many elements define this period, including a set of stylistic conventions and a mode of production dominated by the major studios. Movies and movie stars saturated popular culture. During this time, a quarter of Americans' recreational budget was spent on movie admissions. Attendance peaked in 1946–48 when the weekly average audience was 90 million (in a population of approximately 140 million).[3] Not quite everyone went, and some people claimed they didn't like them, but no one was unaware of the movies.

The Golden Age began to fade with the development of television. By 1960, almost all American households had a TV,[4] and people preferred to spend more time in front of the tube than the silver screen. TV did not eliminate the audience for film, but it put a hefty dent in it. By 1975 only 4% of recreation expenditure went to movie admissions and theater attendance was down to 20 million.[5] A 1977 Gallup poll indicated that 30% of respondents preferred to spend an evening watching television, compared with 6% for movies.[6]

Television and film were not always in direct competition; Hollywood soon co-opted TV as an alternate means of exhibiting movies. Local stations broadcast older movies during non-network times (during the day and late at night), and the networks advertised "first-time on television" primetime broadcasts of newer box office hits. The availability of uncut movies on cable further changed the landscape, and television continues to be an important medium for seeing movies.

But television was only the first in a series of visual technologies that have challenged movie theaters as the apotheosis of popular culture. Other technological and exhibition trends have significantly expanded the possibilities for film viewing. In the mid-60s, drive-ins accounted for nearly a quarter of all film revenues. As a relative bargain, they attracted teenagers and low- to mid-income families. Drive-ins also encouraged Hollywood to produce a greater range of B-movie genres—family comedies, beach movies, cheap horror films, science fiction, and so on. The social atmosphere for watching a movie was altered now that people could have close contact with a small group of intimates (family, friends, dates, etc.) while at the same time isolate themselves from other moviegoers. Audiences experienced drive-in theaters as more comfortable, private and fun.[7] It was these qualities that, according to the *Saturday Evening Post*, allowed drive-ins to simultaneously serve as "passion pits" to entice teenagers, and havens for families where parents could be entertained without having to pay a babysitter.[8]

Videotape brought movies into the home in a way that gave audiences more control than viewing on broadcast TV. Tapes (and later DVD and Blu-Ray) allowed choice in viewing options. As a result, viewing patterns associated with watching recorded video differed from watching TV. One study indicated that when people watched a video, they made more preparations, engaged in fewer household activities (doing chores, conversing, etc.), and were more attentive and engaged.[9] Choosing to watch a movie on video is seen as an *event* that deserves its own space and attention.

Computer-based media such as videogames, web sites, social networks and a myriad of other technologies now compete for the attention of media consumers. Yet by some measures movies are still thriving. Because of increased ticket prices, 2009 and 2010 were the highest box office grossing years ever.[10] The film industry has found ways to cooperate with new media. Although videogames engage time that could be otherwise spent watching movies, Hollywood has capitalized on audience familiarity by making movies based on TV shows (*Transformers*) and videogames (*Lara Croft: Tomb Raider*). When a new medium like Facebook catches on, the film industry seizes on the technology to create buzz.

So, while movies have learned to share the mass market attention, they have not gone away. They may not be the *dominant* form of entertainment in the 2010s, but they are arguably still the *preeminent* form. They offer a level of demographic-spanning prestige, visibility, and influence unmatched by any other popular media. TV and pop music stars remain more interested in becoming movie stars than vice versa. The ratings for the Oscars are still higher than other awards shows. Academics and critics still take the aesthetic aspects of movies more seriously than they do videogames. Consequently, certain qualities of filmgoers and the film-viewing experience remain distinct.

## The Movies People Watch

Why are people flocking to superhero films and ignoring Westerns? What happened to the popularity of drama? These questions are interesting from a cultural psychology perspective because they seek to identify patterns of behavior that reflect the attitudes and values of a certain group at a given time, rather like interpreting responses to a Rorschach Inkblot Test at the cultural level.[11] Such interpretations are hard to prove or disprove, but they do provide a provocative impression of cultural activity.

Box office and attendance figures are one means of quantifying the kinds of movies that people are watching. Appendix B gives the 50 top-grossing films of all time (adjusted for inflation).[12] This list provides a good picture of the movies that have most permeated American life. Not everyone has seen all of them, but most are at least tangentially familiar to adult

Americans,[13] producing a wealth of shared cultural references. The images and story elements of *Jaws*, *Bambi*, and the *Ten Commandments* are so widely understood, they afford material for allusions and jokes (i.e., ones about skinny dipping, dead mothers, and parting seas).

What makes a film a box office success? So far Hollywood has been unable to figure out a perfect formula, but we can see certain patterns in the list of box office champions. First, they are "democratic" movies, in that they appeal to a wide range of demographics. While some animated films are clearly meant for children, other "child-friendly" (or at least "adolescent-friendly") movies attract adults as well (*Shrek II*). Few of these films were particularly controversial at the time of their release (notable exceptions include *The Graduate*, *The Godfather*, and *The Exorcist*). Instead, these films appear to capture mainstream ideas and sentiments, inhabiting a familiar and comfortable zone for the majority of American society.

To gain a more precise picture of the movies that people are watching, one can use statistical methods to gauge box office success combined with other characteristics of a film or its audience.[14] In recent decades, the most predictive factor has been budget—films with higher budgets tend to do better. The psychological mechanisms at work aren't entirely clear. While bigger budgets may allow movie-makers to give the audience what they want, this situation may also be a case of studios dictating what people want. Through intense advertising and controlling theater distribution, the success of certain films can be gained through constricting audience choices.[15] Still, there are always exceptions to the "big budget = big box office" rule of thumb. A film like *Paranormal Activity*, made for next to nothing, can gross over a $100 million while an expensive film like *Sucker Punch* can bomb.

There are other predictors of box office success, though none of these factors are very strong. Films that take home awards—Oscars in the major categories (Best Film, Best Actor, *et al.*) and the technical categories (Best Visual Effects) tend to do somewhat better. In recent times, genre has become important—comedies, sci-fi, and fantasy films tend to be more profitable than other types of films.[16] Factors that are minimally predictive of success include whether a film is a sequel or a remake, has a longer run-time or a PG-13 rating (although G and PG movies can do well), and features non-gory violence. Films that do poorly may attribute their failure to factors like: being a biopic or literary adaptation, having an R-rating, or featuring graphic sex. These findings are consistent with the theory that blockbusters must target the vast middle of the population—movies with some (but not too much) sex and violence; are familiar and well-made but not too highbrow; and emphasize humor, nonreality and spectacle.[17]

Over the years, the appeal of dramas has diminished while the popularity of fantasy epics has risen. While some dramas do sell tickets and win Oscars (*The King's Speech*), their financial success can't compare to summer blockbusters. One explanation for this is technological. In order to compete with more intimate forms of visual entertainment like television, movies have had to "go big" by maximizing visual effects. Another explanation is sociopolitical, that today's escapist entertainment is an expression of the narcissistic consumerism that took hold in the 1980s and continues to hold sway in America and other first world countries.

Other patterns have been observed regarding movie-going and other cultural and economic conditions. One study found that between 1951–2000, there was more slapstick violence in top-grossing comedies (*Blazing Saddles, Home Alone, Austin Powers: The Spy Who Shagged Me*) made during times of high: unemployment, consumer price index, and suicide/homicide rates.[18] While it is unlikely that *Blazing Saddles* was responsible for the social conditions of the 1970s, it is possible that the film (featuring a corrupt, bungling governor, racist townspeople, and flatulent cowboys) visually captured the frustrations of that period.

What are the kids are watching? The viewing habits of children and teens tend to raise concerns about what how much exposure is appropriate. Young adults and adolescents are a major market for summer blockbusters, since they are most likely to be repeat viewers. Younger children and the family members that accompany them are the driving force behind G and PG-rated films, especially animation (one reason why these films are more successful than R-rated films is simply that they allow more audience members).[19]

Theatrical attendance figures, however, don't accurately reflect what kids are watching because most children, particularly those under the age of eight, watch more recorded videos. Video viewing is difficult to track because once a movie is purchased or rented, it is unclear who watches it; and the same video can be watched many times. The same problems are associated with movies broadcast on cable or over the internet. Even so, large-scale surveys have indicated that when it comes to total media use, kids and teens spend less time watching movies/videos than they do television, videogames, or computers. Still, at the turn of the twenty-first century, the average teen watched an average of two movies/videos a week.[20]

We can assume that kids watch a lot of G/PG-rated movies on video, but this does not mean that films with age-appropriate content are the only things children are seeing. A 2003 survey asked children aged 10–14 how many movies they had seen that featured extremely violent content including gore, sadism and sexualized violence.[21] More than a third (including 20% of the 10 year-olds) reported having watched these R-rated horror films: *Scary Movie* (48%); *I Still Know What You Did Last Summer* (44%); *Blade* (37%); and *Bride of Chucky* (37%). Children's exposure to questionable film content is of interest because it is connected to such social concerns as cultural values, parenting choices and the effects of media.[22]

Scholars curious about social psychological trends aren't the only ones researching what people watch. Hollywood pays for similar research to use in developing, marketing, and advertising movies. While some of this research is publicly available in scholarly journals,[23] most is a closely guarded secret in order to gain advantage over the competition. Marketing research uses even more diverse methods than we have considered—audience responses at test screenings, focus group interviews, and exit surveys.[24] Compared with academic research, commercial researchers are only interested in human nature and cultural conditions as they relate to the bottom line—the profit margin. This data would be a goldmine for social scientific analysis, but it is kept locked away, used to determine which movies get the green light and what alternate ending gets left on the cutting-room floor.

## The Movies People Like

While box office and attendance figures don't exactly lie, they can be misleading when it comes to gauging people's true preferences. Gigantic advertising campaigns and controlled distribution can get people into the theaters, but they can't guarantee audiences will actually like what they see. Films like *Hancock* starring Will Smith, may be a success at the box office yet generate so little excitement that few people remember them after their release. On the other hand, a movie like *Fight Club* may fizzle at the box office, but have such a fervent following, it becomes the subject of many cultural references.

Audience preferences are reflected in such criteria as critical ratings and awards. Appendix B includes a list of the 50 greatest American movies as judged by the American Film Institute in 2007.[25] The AFI list, along with the Oscars and critics' awards, represents the opinions of an exclusive group of people in the movie industry; films that insiders believe represent what is best about the medium and are therefore worthy of praise.

The popular Internet Movie Database (IMDB.com) has a rating system to which any user can contribute, and offers a more democratic measure of film preference. The top 50 *user*-rated films are also included in Appendix B.[26]

Voters on IMDB tend to be film buffs—people who don't work in the industry but have more than a casual interest in film.

Interesting patterns emerge from a side-by-side comparison of these three measures of movie acclaim (box office, AFI, and IMDB). There is relatively little overlap (seven films) between box office totals and the AFI choices. Initial financial success apparently has little to do with lasting acclaim. History has not been kind to several of the films on the box office list; epics like *Independence Day*, *Cleopatra*, and *Airport* would struggle to find viewers who consider them high-quality films (much less among the greatest ever). On the other hand, a number of classics (*Citizen Kane*, *The Wizard of Oz*, and *Casablanca*) under-performed or even flopped upon initial release. Overall, the box office champs tend to be movies everyone can enjoy (witness the high number of children's and animated films) while the AFI list captures distinct artistic and historical qualities.

When the choices of IMDB users were compared with box office totals, only six films (primarily the classics of the special-effects era—two *Star Wars* installments, *Raiders of the Lost Ark*, and *The Dark Knight*) overlapped both lists. In general, most of the feel-good musicals, comedies, romances, and light action movies that dominated the box office list weren't especially well-regarded by film buffs. Their choices were darker, including horror films (*Psycho* and *Silence of the Lambs*), intense crime/suspense films (*The Usual Suspects* and *Pulp Fiction*), and violent dramas (*American History X* and *Taxi Driver*). Even the comedies tended to have a sharp satirical edge (*Dr Strangelove* and *American Beauty*). If IMDB.com users represent the typical modern movie buff, particularly men, their darker tastes may reflect the cultural shifts of the 1960s and beyond (*Toy Story 3* and *Amelie* being the notable, and reassuring, exceptions).

There was considerably more overlap (15 films) between the critical establishment (AFI) and IMDB users. Both groups are more discriminating than everyday moviegoers, who claim to simply want to be entertained. One notable difference was the greater presence of recent films among the film buffs' choices.[27] Twenty-six films on the IMDB list were made after 1990 compared with only two on the AFI list; clearly, AFI members gave greater weight to classics that have stood the test of time. While IMDB voters did not ignore older films (both *Citizen Kane* and *Casablanca* made the list), these films tended to be the exceptions. While IMDB users may overvalue the new (e.g., *Inception* appearing as #8 on the list) and lack historical perspective, the preference for recent films also reflects the visceral impact of immediate experience that gets watered down when films are removed from their original cultural and historical context.

Only two films made all three lists: *The Godfather* and *Star Wars*. Their universal appeal appears rare in a diverse, postmodern society. Made in the 1970s within five years of each other, they represent different poles of the New Hollywood that emerged after the Golden Age. Though technically studio films, both were created by individuals with a strong personal vision who were intentionally manipulating the rules. *The Godfather* is a serious artistic statement while *Star Wars* is a valentine to the wonders of imaginative filmmaking, yet both films have strong connections to film history and were hugely popular. Respectively, they set the standards for dramatic independent filmmaking and high concept fantasy that still resonate with audiences today.

None of the lists in Appendix B were constructed using scientific methods.[28] In order to take more focused look at audience preference patterns, social scientists use surveys that access a representative sample of the population. One study surveyed over a thousand people about their preferences for movie monsters (or villains).[29] Horror movies have been a robust genre throughout movie history, and the monsters are what appeal to the public imagination. Dracula and other vampires proved to be the most popular, for a variety of reasons including their agelessness, their intelligence, their supernatural strength and even their fashion sense and sex appeal.[30] Other favorites included Godzilla, Freddy Krueger, Frankenstein, Chucky, Michael Myers, King Kong, and Hannibal Lecter. The reasons these monsters were popular echoed the popularity of vampires: intelligence, superhuman powers, and the ability to reveal the dark side of human nature.

When it came to monster preference, there were marked differences between the generations. The "slashers" (i.e., homicidal humans) of *Halloween*, *Friday the 13th*, and *A Nightmare on Elm Street* series were popular with younger respondents (under 25 years of age) but not appreciated by older respondents (over 50). In part, this seemed due to an exposure effect (motion picture homicidal killers have been more frequent in recent decades). There were also differences in the rationale behind the preferences. The fans of Jason, Michael and Freddy tended to focus more of their admiration on negative and pathological qualities ("pure evil," and "serious psychological problems") and killing proficiency. Preferring monsters for the degree of their murderousness may have disturbing moral implications, but it could also reflect an honest ability to appreciate qualities that lie at the very core of being an effective monster.

Other research has focused on the preferences of subgroups of movie viewers. For example, sensation-seeking is a personality characteristic that refers to seeking out novel and risky experiences that provide sensory stimulation (fast driving, gambling, skydiving). Individuals who measure high in sensation-seeking tend to like films with a great deal of violence, horror, action, and rapid editing. Given that men have higher sensation-seeking tendencies than women, this factor may partially explain men's greater preference for action, horror, and sci-fi genres. [31]

The popularity of movie stars is another reflection of audience attitudes and preferences. Many observers have noted that actors have longer and more successful (in terms of number of roles) than actresses. One study systematically assessed the careers of hundreds of Hollywood stars between 1926–1999.[32] It confirmed that as women aged, they had fewer starring roles and total roles than actors of the same age. In recent years, the number of roles for older actresses has increased, but the availability of lead parts remains well below those for older men. These results may be interpreted as a reflection of a cultural perception that older women are less attractive. They also raise concerns that this pattern perpetuates the devaluation of older women by effectively removing them from the media spotlight.

## Closing Shots: The Viewers behind the Numbers

Behind the box office numbers, demographic trends, and aggregate statistical analyses lie the experiences of real people. John Movie Fan spends hours online getting pumped for the latest superhero blockbuster and contributes a small part to the film's record-breaking box office when he attends the midnight opening. Jane Movie Fan, a teenager dreading/anticipating a date to see the latest horror film, is part of a trend of adolescent girls watching more horror movies. Joe Movie Fan, a middle-aged man who daydreams about speeding off into the median while stuck in rush hour traffic, reflects the fact that men love movie car chases.

We have looked at the "where" and "when" of movie viewing, and have considered characteristics (age, gender, personality) that predict what people are likely to watch which movies. But what happens when people actually watch a movie? And what happens after they watch the movie?[33] Box office grosses and demographics can't answer these questions by themselves, buy they set the scene for our continued attention to movie audiences.

## Further Reading

Austin, B.A. (1989) *Immediate Seating: A Look at Movie Audiences.* Wadsworth, Belmont, CA.

Pritzker, S.R. (2009) Marketing movies: An introduction to the special issue. *Psychology & Marketing*, **26** (5), 397–399.

Roberts, D.F. and Foehr, U.G. (2004) *Kids and Media in America*. Cambridge University Press, Cambridge.

Simonton, D.K. (2011) *Great Flicks: Scientific Studies of Cinematic Creativity and Aesthetics*. Oxford University Press, New York, NY.

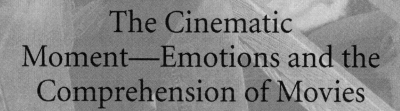

# The Cinematic
## Moment—Emotions and the
## Comprehension of Movies

**Illustration 6.1** Jim Carrey & Kate Winslet as Joel Barish & Clementine Kruczynski in *Eternal Sunshine of the Spotless Mind* (2004) © AF archive/Alamy.

# Chapter 6

# The Cinematic Moment—Emotions and the Comprehension of Movies

When *Eternal Sunshine of the Spotless Mind* opens, it is Valentine's Day. Joel (Jim Carrey) impulsively skips work to take a train from New York City to Montauk Beach on Long Island. Coming back, he meets Clementine (Kate Winslet). Joel is mopey and withdrawn, while Clementine is outgoing and outrageous. Quirky, likable oddballs, the couple hit it off.

Up to this point, around 10 minutes in, a first-time viewer would have no difficulty following the plot. In fact, most viewers would have a strong intuition for where things are heading: the characters' lighthearted, slightly neurotic chemistry would indicate we are in the land of romantic comedy. Joel and Clementine will fall in love; there will be complications due to their personality quirks; but in the end, they will wind up happily ever after.

And while the predicted story arc (boy finds girl, boy loses girl, boy regains girl) is fairly accurate, the viewer's journey through this strange film is anything but typical. The first 10 minutes actually represents the *second* time that Joel and Clementine meet on the train from Montauk. In between the two train trips, they have lived together, broken up, and had their memories erased. The movie flashes back to the fateful night that Joel's memories were deleted using a computer-assisted neurophysiological gadget.

*Psychology at the Movies*, First Edition. Skip Dine Young
© 2012 John Wiley & Sons, Ltd. Published 2012 by John Wiley & Sons, Ltd.

Within this larger flashback, we get other flashbacks of Joel's relationship with Clementine, but not in sequential order. Many of the memories feature physical environments that are literally falling apart, a visual representation of how memories can be destroyed. To make things more difficult, some of the memories of Joel's childhood are transformed by Clementine's intrusion.

*Eternal Sunshine of the Spotless Mind* is a challenging intellectual puzzle. It takes effort to figure out what is happening. Yet, for many people, it also evokes strong emotions of longing, regret and emotional courage. To watch it, one has to think and feel, usually at the same time. This is true of any movie, but in an unusual film like *Eternal Sunshine*, we become more aware of what is going on in our heads and our hearts. This chapter isolates the "cinematic moment" when cognitive and emotional processes occur as viewers sit in their seats, gaze at the screen, and try to make sense out of their immediate experience.

## Cognitive Psychology and the Movies

Our minds are very active when we watch movies. On the most fundamental level, we perceive the sights and sounds of the movie. The characters in *Eternal Sunshine* are really just two-dimensional projections of alternating light patterns, yet our visual system makes them appear to be moving human bodies. Furthermore, our hearing system contributes additional information by recognizing voices and separating out background noise.

Along with perception, we must be able to comprehend the story we are watching. We are able to identify the distinct characters of Joel and Clementine. We develop opinions about their personalities. We realize that they are on a train and that they are attracted to each other.

The interrelated mental activities of perception and comprehension are represented in Figure 6.1.[1]

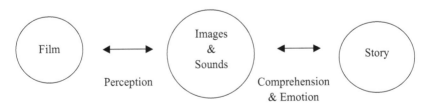

**Figure 6.1** Symbolic activity in film viewing: Comprehension, emotion and perception.

The process of perceiving and comprehending movies is so familiar it is sometimes not even obvious when it is occurring. This is especially true for viewers who have grown up with movies. Classical Hollywood production (clear establishing shots, seamless edits, smooth camera movements, etc.) intentionally tries to make storytelling invisible.[2] From this stylistic perspective, a good movie flows so smoothly that we forget we are watching a movie, and it feels effortless. The answers to questions like "Who is who?" and "What is what?" are so evident, it never occurs to most people to ask them.

A closer consideration of the way that movies work reveals a different story. Watching the first 10 minutes of *Eternal Sunshine*, we must focus on the screen and not the person in front of us. Also we must remember that when Joel starts talking to Clementine, he came to the beach alone. We have to be aware that Joel and Clementine are on the same train, even though the camera only shows one character's face at a time. When the movie moves into its elaborate flashback structure, audience members realize they must piece together the chronology of Joel and Clementine's relationship to make sense of the story.

Perception and comprehension are important topics in the domains of cognitive psychology, cognitive science and neuroscience.[3] These fields study various processes that constitute human thinking including sensation, perception, attention, memory, organization, problem solving, and so on. In recent years, cognitive science has had a significant impact on aesthetic criticism. In film studies, David Bordwell has led a movement to extend the precision of cognitive concepts and apply these concepts to narrative comprehension.[4] Recently it has become common for film scholars to use vocabulary like "schema," "long-term memory," "emotions" and "associative networks" when discussing film techniques or genres. Cognitive concepts such as these have been used to construct new theories of film viewing, narrative comprehension and emotional experience.[5] The confluence of film studies and cognitive science is part of an exciting intellectual trend combining scientific methods (experimental and laboratory observations) with the humanities (textual analysis) to help understand not only the perception and comprehension of film, but the human mind itself.

## The Perception of Movies

To understand a movie, you must first see it and hear it. Everything we know about visual perception (color, depth, movement) and auditory perception (loudness, pitch, sound localization) is conceivably relevant to experiencing motion pictures. While a thorough explication of the *The Godfather* in terms of its perceptual components is beyond modern science, film technology is an area where film studies and perception research have historically overlapped.[6]

One problem in understanding perception and motion pictures is that film images don't really move. A series of 24 successive still images a second are captured by a movie camera and then, at the same rate, projected on a screen by an ultra-bright projector. Each image is briefly frozen before the film advances to the next frame. The actual movement of the film through the camera has to be disguised by the light temporarily flickering between frames (otherwise, the moving image would appear as a blur). Therefore, the viewer sees no real movement while watching a movie—this experienced motion is referred to as "apparent motion." This technology was figured out by experimental perception researchers and commercial scientists (cameramen and projectionists) in the first decades after movies were invented. Through trial and error (the basis for the scientific method), these scientists and technicians discovered the speed at which film had to move through the camera in order to approximate the perception of real movement.

Later, academics studying visual perception were able to explain the phenomenon of apparent motion in psychological terms; apparent motion was stimulating the same cognitive and physiological pathways as real motion. When the static, pictorial differences between two successive frames of film are so small, the mind can't tell that they're different. Instead, it is fooled into thinking that there is physical continuity (like the way an object moves in the real world) even though such continuity is only an optical illusion.[7]

Over the years, film directors and cinematographers have developed rules of thumb for editing films in a manner that will orient viewers. Researchers have confirmed that these rules are grounded in the basic realities of human perception. One example is match-action editing, where one shot of a character engaged in some activity is followed by with another shot of the same character from a slightly different perspective. If these cuts are done the wrong way, they disorient the viewers (these are called jump cuts). However, when edits are done right, the audience never notices them.

Imagine a character stooping to pick up a diamond necklace that has been thrown to the ground. The audience first sees this action from approximately 20 feet. After a sudden edit, we see the action from the same angle, at a distance of five feet. It appears the character has jumped toward us, which will strike most viewers as unrealistic. Rules of continuity editing suggest that if a director is going to match action, the second shot must be from an angle at least 30° from the first shot. (A sudden edit from 20 to five feet at a significantly different angle will appear natural to the audience and will not be disorienting.)

When we know that we are moving through space (a phenomenon called proprioception, a perception of stimuli coming from the body itself), our visual system integrates multiple perspectives. In crossing a room, we see different objects from many different angles; this is not jarring because we know we are moving. After a 30°+ cut, the focal object appears sufficiently different that we assume we must have moved. However, in a jump cut where there is no discernible difference in the angle of the shots, the only aspect that changes is an object's size. In these situations our perceptual system does not receive the expected cues that we have moved through space, and we therefore assume that the object must have jumped. Since we rationally know this is impossible, the perception is disconcerting.[8]

Perceptual mechanisms are essential to everyday movie-going enjoyment. Most viewers know little about motion detection, but everyone knows the jarring sensation caused by choppy editing (or avante garde filmmaking such as in Goddard's *Breathless*). The science of perception is also important to the technological advancements which have made modern fantasy/sci-fi films possible. Although the Oscars for technical achievement are often ignored by the average viewer, such innovations as a new type of lens can alter the audience experience for billions of people.

Julian Hochberg, a vision researcher who has studied film perception, claims that perceptual processes should get more attention from film scholars.[9] He believes that the foundations of perceptual processing are hardwired into human biology; they are universal and not determined by cultural variations (such as whether the film is a product of a capitalist society). While Hochberg does not consider culture irrelevant to the production, interpretation and reception of movies, he argues that certain aspects of the film experience do not vary significantly from culture to culture or from person to person.[10] Perceptual processes can place certain parameters on how viewers understand a film. The philosophical meaning of *Citizen Kane* is open to debate, but what is unequivocal is the visual starkness of the black and white photography which allows a greater range of shadings than color film.

## The Narrative Comprehension of Movies

Movies tell stories. The perceptual details of a film combine to create an overall structure, and in most films, that structure is narrative. Thus, when viewers try to understand a film, they must look at how the pieces of the story fit together. Bordwell argues that narrative comprehension is an ideal focus for film scholars because it is accessible to concepts of cognitive science and therefore conducive to a rigorous film studies.[11]

"Story" and "plot" have often been distinguished in narrative analysis.[12] *Story* represents the causal, temporal, and spatial relationships between narrative events (what happens in time and space). The *plot* refers to what information is presented to the audience in what way (*how* the story is told). *Pulp Fiction* has several linear storylines; in each, one event is causally linked to another. The plot of *Pulp Fiction*, however, is *nonlinear*, where sequences of different stories are mixed together and presented in nonchronological order. Halfway through the film we see Vincent (John Travolta) get killed by Butch (Bruce Willis), even though Vincent appears in the final sequence, the shootout in the diner that bookends the action. It would be possible to change the plotting of the film to make it more chronological while preserving the same stories. The story is "imaginary"[13] ("mental" or "cognitive") in the sense that it emerges internally as the result of how the viewer processes the plot. Thus, we can say that the plot belongs to the film, while the story belongs to the viewer. Drawing on cognitive science, Bordwell believes that in order to bridge the gap between plot and story, viewers must use a variety of *schemas* (mental structures for organizing knowledge).[14]

People tend to use cognitive schemas to establish the consistent identity of things previously encountered. Humans are particularly sophisticated when it comes to differentiating the different people in our lives (friends, family, coworkers, waiters), but we are also able to distinguish significant objects (cars, wallets, clothing). There are individual differences between the quantity of discrete identifications we can make (some people have a better memory for faces or names), but the ability to recognize familiar objects is crucial in daily life, as well as for understanding what's going on in a film. Several types of schemas particularly apply to comprehending film. These are exemplified using *Titanic*.[15]

In *Titanic* we identify the heroes, Jack (Leonardo DiCaprio) and Rose (Kate Winslet), from the villain, Cal (Billy Zane). While this may seem simple enough, we are presented with characters from numerous camera angles, wearing different hairstyles and costumes. Viewers are able to keep track of them because the schema for each character remains constant yet allows for minor variations.

People also rely on schemas to make causal sense of the world. We assume events follow each other and that one event may cause another. As we piece together the events in our lives (some of which we may have witnessed and others we have been told about), we are constantly making adjustments to our schemas to render them plausible. While many Hollywood movies are plotted in sequential order, there are exceptions (including more mainstream films than *Pulp Fiction*). *Titanic's* plot shifts between the modern day exploration of the ocean liner's sunken hull and its actual sailing and sinking in 1912. In order to make these time jumps easier for the audience, the film uses certain associative cues. When we first see *Titanic* sailing, the photography uses sepia tones recalling photography from the early twentieth century, allowing us to keep past and present separate while remaining aware of a relationship between time periods.

Other schemas are used to maintain an awareness of the physical relationship between spaces. We must be familiar with the organization of a room to locate objects in it (a pencil, the TV remote, or a chair). We need to have a schema for the path from our living room to the kitchen so we can get from one to the other when we get hungry. There are also places outside of our awareness that we know can be accessed using other schemas (e.g., the ability to read a map).

All of these spatial relationships apply to watching a movie, with one exception: we are spatially limited by the camera, not by the movement of our bodies. Therefore, our spatial knowledge is generally not as precise when it comes to movies as it is in real life. In order to make clear sense, *Titanic* provides specific information about spatial relations. Early in the film we see that the working class passengers are located in the steerage (lower decks) while the affluent passengers are on the upper decks. This relationship is more than just a socioeconomic metaphor but is a feature of the plot when the ship starts to sink. Jack and Rose are trapped among the passengers in steerage; they must keep moving upwards (literally toward the top of the screen) to escape death. Even so, while the audience knows that Jack and Rose are moving toward the upper decks, the rapid editing and the general chaos of the situation are too disorienting to allow for a accurate precise mental map of the ship.

## The Emotional Comprehension of Movies

There is a tendency to think of feelings and thoughts as separate—the heart is hot and impulsive, while the head is cold and rational. Historically, psychology treated cognition and emotion as distinct areas of study, but most modern theories of emotion argue that the two cannot be easily separated.

Cognitive processes occur virtually simultaneously with emotional processes, and emotional reactions have physiological connections to thought patterns.[16] Consequently, recent contributions to narrative comprehension in film emphasize the emotional dimension, making puns about the "moving" component of moving pictures[17] and referring to film as an "emotion machine."[18]

### Emotional Arousal

When they watch a movie, people experience a range of emotions. The next time you are in a movie theater, watch the people around you. Laughter, tears, expressions of terror, and jolts of surprise can all be witnessed in the audience's physical reactions. Psychological researchers have studied virtually every emotion; in many cases, these studies use movies to evoke emotion. Films are so effective at doing this that they have become a crucial element in emotion research. Typically a movie (or a clip) is shown to participants who are then measured for a particular emotion and compared to other psychological variables such as gender, memory or risk-taking.

Researchers are often clever in devising a range of behavioral, subjective and physiological methods for detecting and measuring emotion.[19] Behavioral techniques include videotaping people while they watch a film, then coding their expressions based on the musculature of the face.[20] Subjective methods include straightforward questionnaires as well as a more sophisticated technique in which participants control a dial indicating degree of emotion over the course of a movie.[21] Physiological methods include measuring skin moisture (galvanic skin response: GSR); brain waves (electroencephalogram: EEG);[22] cortisol levels in saliva;[23] and genital blood flow[24] while subjects watch a film.

Based on such measures, researchers have developed a recommended list of film clips for evoking specified emotions: amusement, anger, disgust, fear, sadness, and surprise.[25] The scene from *Silence of the Lambs* where FBI agent Clarice Starling (Jodie Foster) is trying to find the serial killer hiding in a dark basement is used to evoke fear, while a clip from *The Champ* where a young boy (Ricky Schroeder) cries over his father's lifeless body is used to evoke sadness. Such clips do not *guarantee* all audience members will respond the way the researchers expect them to,[26] but they have been shown to produce high levels of arousal for specific emotions in many participants under controlled conditions. (See Appendix C for a full list of films and target emotions.)

Emotional arousal is not just a random byproduct of the film experience but is closely related to the stylistic qualities of movies. One of the first experiments on the emotional power of film editing was conducted by the Russian filmmakers/theorists Pudovkin and Kuleshov, who discovered what has been called the Kuleshov effect. They took a close-up shot of an actor looking offscreen with a neutral facial expression and then edited in different objects including a bowl of soup; a woman lying dead in a coffin; and a little girl playing with a stuffed bear. Audiences shown the short films were all impressed by the actor's ability, yet the emotion they attributed to him differed from film to film. When audiences saw him "staring" at the soup, they thought the actor looked pensive. In the coffin version, he was thought to be sorrowful. In the little girl version, he seemed cheerful. Of course, in each case, the shot of the actor was the same.[27]

This experiment demonstrates several things about cognitive processes generally, and film editing specifically. In each condition of the experiment, the audience assumed the actor was looking at the object in the second shot, even though it had been superimposed via the editing. Audience members automatically join different parts of an edited film in order to form an intelligible whole.[28] The experiment also demonstrated a tendency to organize ambiguous stimuli via context. Thus, depending on the object with which it was paired, the same neutral expression could be interpreted as pensive, sorrowful, or cheerful.

Camera angle is another stylistic aspect that has an impact on not only the emotional reactions of viewers but how they appraise the emotions of a character. In another study, short movies were created about ordinary activities between two characters such as a fender bender. Several versions were shot in which the camera angles varied. In one version, Character A was shot from a low angle while Character B was shot from a high angle, and vice versa. Even though every other aspect of the movies were identical, characters shot from a low angle (towering above the camera) were perceived as stronger, bolder, more aggressive, and less afraid. The opposite was true of the character filmed from a high angle (being looked down on).[29] The results correspond to a well-known rule about the function of camera angles—low angles convey superiority while high angles convey a character's inferiority.[30] *Citizen Kane* famously employs low camera angles when Kane (Orson Welles) is confidently launching his newspaper empire, while later in the film, after his life has collapsed, the camera looks down on Kane from on high. Such angles echo patterns from outside film. When we physically *look down* on someone (an adult to a child), we typically have a position of superiority and vice versa.

*Emotional Themes*

Ever since Aristotle characterized tragedy as dramas evoking fear and pity, there has been a close connection between emotion and story.[31] Since a narrative film is more than a random series of provocative images, its emotional power is not based just on visual perception but on the fundamental qualities of stories, particularly theme and character.

Try the following experiment: Imagine the fear-inducing basement scene from *Silence of the Lambs*. Take any frame from that scene and turn it into a still photograph. Would that photograph be scary? My guess is that a well-chosen frame might evoke some anxiety, but wouldn't arouse as much fear and anxiety as the scene itself. (I also suspect the photo would arouse more fear in people who have seen the film, due to pre-existing associations between the image and the story.)

Stories provoke feelings, an observation that intertwines emotional theory with narrative theory. The cognitive schemas (mental structures) people use to comprehend their actions and those of others, are called "scripts."[32] We have scripts for all of the actions we perform or witness, from trips to the store to weddings. Since scripted events are important for helping us get through the day, achieve success, and ultimately survive, they have an emotional resonance that lets us make intuitive decisions about what is valuable and what is dangerous.

Scripts not only apply to understanding people and events but to comprehending fictional events in the movies; within a literary or cinematic context, these scripts are called themes. As we watch a movie and witness variations of events we have seen before, certain scripts are triggered, bringing an automatic emotional response. Some scripts (going to a grocery store) provoke mild reactions while others (someone getting married) tend to evoke stronger emotions. Sometimes the stories in movies line up with established scripts (weddings at the end of many romantic comedies); and others contrast starkly (the wedding-turned-massacre in *Kill Bill*). Typically conventional stories allow us to feel comfortable and content (even when they bore us) while unconventional stories make us feel disoriented or alienated.

Experiments have demonstrated that our core scripts or themes affect the intensity of our emotional reactions (as well as subsequent memory of events). In one study, participants were shown excerpts from two films (fiction and nonfiction) that each corresponded to one of three themes: weddings, AIDS, and the life of Gandhi. Emotional reactions were more intense to the AIDS and wedding films than the Gandhi films. In addition, participants remembered the material in these films better than they did the

Gandhi films, a finding that connects emotions with the cognitive process of memory. Unlike the Gandhi films, the wedding and AIDS films corresponded to two powerful scripts—love and death. In contrast, the Gandhi films were about complicated sociopolitical and historical factors that, while not entirely unemotional, could not compete with the immediacy of love and death.[33]

The emotional comprehension of themes can be seen through textual analysis of films. The study of film genres is a robust tradition in film studies. It highlights the role of themes since genres involve a repetition of core themes and stylistic motifs.[34] These motifs trigger particular scripts and accompanying emotions. A successful genre film combines multiple sequences that evoke affective memories on the part of the audience and lead to a response related to one dominant emotion.

Some genres—melodrama, suspense and horror—wear their emotions on their sleeves. Melodramas are more than movies that express oversized emotions but feature plots in which bad things happen to good people, thereby evoking the emotion of pity. Melodramas tend to be less emotionally complicated than tragedies since tragic characters have flaws that make them responsible for the outcome, evoking judgment and diluting audience pity. In melodramas however, the protagonists' flaws are not emphasized—they are in a sense innocents. *Gone with the Wind* is often described as melodramatic, but it is not a *prototypical* melodrama because Scarlet's (Vivien Leigh) vanity contributes to her downfall. *An Affair to Remember* is a clearer example where Terry (Deborah Kerr) is prevented from rendezvousing with Nicky (Cary Grant) through no fault of her own (she's crippled in a car accident). Her character evokes a high degree of pity from as audiences access their melodramatic scripts.

The dominant emotions produced by the horror genre are fear and disgust. We fear for the protagonists because they are explicitly threatened, tapping into personal scripts that involve threat and potential harm. Other genres (thrillers) have elements of threat and harm, but horror distinguishes itself by combining our fear with disgust. We are not just afraid of the monster, we are disgusted by its deformity, lack of humanity, or corruption. The monsters in horror films—vampires, zombies, werewolves possess typically non-human qualities. Even the modern psychopath, while nominally human, is usually masked or made to look grotesque, and demonstrates few identifiable human characteristics. The fear and disgust responses intensify in combination with each other.

Suspense occurs during many movies, and like horror, involves fear. For a film to be categorized in the suspense genre, it must sustain a pervasive sense of anxiety about what is to come; suspense always has a *future* orientation. Suspense films place the future in serious doubt and require the audience to experience dread and anticipation for an extended period of time. Hitchcock films are commonly cited in this category, but other films also qualify. An action film like *Speed* in which a bus must maintain a high speed to keep from exploding also establishes an uncertain future that the audience must contemplate throughout.[35]

### Emotions, Character Motivation and Empathy

The use of provocative themes is not the only way in which films connect comprehension with feelings. Another is figuring out why characters do what they do. Without a sense of character motivation, it would be impossible to follow a string of causally related events. Each character's behavior would be as likely as any other, and any temporal sequence would be arbitrary. To maintain cognitive and emotional involvement, we have to "get inside" the characters.

We do not approach each character as someone entirely new, however. Another variation of schema theory proposes that we also have schemas for people. These are sometimes called stereotypes or, less pejoratively, prototypes.[36] As viewers are introduced to characters in a film, they attempt to fit them into previously held categories.[37] Little information is necessary to begin the associative process: a black hat, a smile, an awkward hesitation—these cues may be all a viewer needs to evoke a familiar prototype.

As the character onscreen is developed, further characteristics are introduced that lead viewers to better understand his or her motivations. While iconoclastic characters are sometimes sufficiently complicated to challenge the range of types viewers have available to them, most characters correspond to available prototypes and are therefore easy to understand. One reason why the audience tolerates the complicated narrative in *Eternal Sunshine of the Spotless Mind* is that the characters are so familiar—the "wacky, imaginative girl" and the "lovable sad sack."

When viewers recognize the motivational structure, they identify with that character. This identification need not be intense or lasting, but it has to occur long enough for the character's actions to make sense and serve the development of the story.[38] Often viewer identification with a particular character is not neutral; we *feel* certain things as we identify with different characters. We empathize with them and experience a range of emotions.

Our empathetic experience affects how we relate to the story. Experimental research has demonstrated the impact of viewer empathy on responses to scary films. Participants who were empathetic to characters found it necessary to deliberately inject "unreality" into their viewing experience, such as focusing on the visual effects. Some viewers were so bonded to characters, they experienced personal distress during scary scenes and withdrew from the narrative world by imagining they were somewhere else.[39] Clearly there is a relationship between characters, viewers' emotional experience, and the story.

Much of what has been said about identification, character motivation, and empathy could be applied to any narrative form, yet there are differences. Readers assert that they bond with literary characters by using their imagination to provide the unwritten details. In contrast, viewers are quite easily drawn into visual narratives as in the common experience of turning on the TV "for just a second," catching a glimpse of a film, and then being "sucked into the story," unable to walk away.

One explanation why films achieve such rapid emotional response has to do with their ability to show facial expressions. Extensive cross-cultural research has demonstrated that a set of basic expressions (sorrow, anger, disgust, happiness) are accurately interpreted by people from all cultures. Humans also have powerful emotional reactions to these expressions. Through close-ups, movies vividly portray facial expressions, thus conveying information about emotions instantaneously. The audience is able to grasp a character's motivations, increasing our empathy. The death scene of the android (Rutger Hauer) in *Blade Runner* is justly famous due to the power of facial expression. The camera focuses on Hauer's upper body and face for an extended period. As he recounts the joys and sorrows of his life, his face continually and unequivocally reflects his inner experience—and ours.[40]

## Brain Functioning and the Movies

While brain research had been progressing at remarkable pace over the past several decades, current understanding is still limited, and applications to complex real world experiences tend to be crude. The application of brain science to film viewing is in its infancy, but the early findings are intriguing. A recent study of narrative comprehension looked at fMRI (functional magnetic resonance imagery) technology, the most sophisticated form of noninvasive neuro-imaging ("picturing" the brain) currently available; it allows researchers to obtain a relatively precise image of brain activity over a period of time.

This particular study focused on cortical activity. The cortex is the large, deeply indented, outer part of the brain responsible for sophisticated abilities (motor functioning, visual processing, language processing, abstract reasoning, etc.). Researchers showed participants short (silent) scenes like the one in *My Girl* in which two children disturb a wasp nest, or montages of clips, randomly edited from different movies. For the narrative sequence, a predictable network of brain parts was activated. For the scrambled sequence, no network was noticeable (i.e., brain activity was more random). The researchers concluded, "The comprehension of edited visual action sequences . . . appears to be based on the coordinated activities of multiple brain areas that are bound together functionally in a high-level cognitive network."[41] Such statements are still a long way from explaining the total viewing experience of *Eternal Sunshine of the Spotless Mind*, but they strongly suggest a mind-brain-film connection.

While direct laboratory research is sparse, we can reasonably speculate that the viewer's emotional experience while watching cinematic stories is related to brain functioning. The autonomic nervous system (the system regulating automatic bodily functions such as the breathing and heart beat) and the subcortical areas of the brain seem particularly involved. Subcortical refers to the diverse areas of the brain that lies just beneath the cortex. These areas deal with the primitive functions necessary for immediate survival—hunger, wakening, breathing, and so on. Strong emotional reactions, particularly negative reactions, are partially located in this primitive zone.

One small subcortical part, the amygdala, is especially responsible for processing responses to aversive stimuli. Recent models of subcortical functioning have suggested that while messages reach the amygdala either directly or indirectly after cortical processing, the direct input happens much faster. Interestingly, only certain stimuli directly stimulate the amygdala including noises such as growling, large, imposing objects, and wriggling movements such as those made by snakes. Such potentially dangerous environmental inputs are processed quickly, allowing us to respond before other parts of the brain can rationally process the threat and figure out what to do.

Even though filmed objects are not "real," our perceptual and cognitive systems often treat them as though they were real, thereby enhancing our emotional reactions. This is particularly true in comparison to books, which though capable of evoking great emotion in readers, are perceptually just inked symbols on paper, requiring greater higher-order (i.e., cortical) processing. In a movie, the image of a beast, the sound of a loud growl, or a quick edit of a snake about to strike momentarily bypass our rational cortex and goes straight for the spontaneity-loving subcortex, in some cases causing us to jump in our seats, even though we rationally know it is "only a movie."[42]

## Closing Shots: An Unlikely Partnership

The pairing of cognitive science and film studies has been fruitful, but there are tensions. Bordwell has argued that the focus on comprehension sets cognitive-based film studies apart from the previously dominant tradition which had been almost exclusively concerned with interpretation (explicating what a film *says* about human nature, politics, cultural values, and so on [43]). Since comprehension is more amenable to concepts grounded in cognitive science, it stands in contrast to a relativistic film studies based on countless alternative readings of a film.[44] However, even at the level of story comprehension, movies are not unequivocal. It is possible to argue about what exactly *happened* in *Eternal Sunshine of the Spotless Mind* just as it is possible to argue about what it *means*. Differences in psychological characteristics such as age, gender, personality, education, and so on can all impact how one understands the story (which, as Bordwell points out, is in the "imagination" of the viewer).

Film studies' movement toward cognitive science is also made difficult by differences in methodology. Cognitive science favors experiments and computer modeling while film studies favors textual analysis. Film scholars have welcomed cognitive concepts, and they have shown a willingness to utilize any tool at their disposal to better understand the object of their passion (movies). From the other direction, cognitively oriented psychologists have frequently utilized movies, but they have tended to see them as methodological instruments (e.g., emotional arousal research), not as art forms. Similarly, scientists often treat different cognitive processes as discreet[45], making it difficult to see the movie viewing experience in a holistic, systemic way. Yet it is crucial that cognitive science address art and narrative forms like film for what they are. Patrick Colm Hogan notes that literary and artistic studies have rich academic traditions that are thousands of years old, and he asserts that "...if you have a theory of the human mind that does not explain the arts, then you have a very poor theory... If cognitive science fails to address this crucial part of our everyday lives, then cognitive science will be left on the dustheap of history."[46]

# Further Reading

Anderson, J.D. (1996) *The Reality of Illusion: An Ecological Approach to Cognitive Film Theory*. Southern Illinois University Press, Carbondale, IL.

Bordwell, D. (1985) *Narration in the Fiction Film*. University of Wisconsin Press, Madison, WI.

Grodal, T. (1997) *Moving Pictures: A New Theory of Film Genres, Feelings, and Cognition*. Oxford University Press, New York, NY.

Hogan, P.C. (2003) *Cognitive Science, Literature, and the Arts: A Guide for Humanists*. Taylor & Francis Books, New York, NY.

Rottenberg, J.; Ray, R.D., and Gross, J.J. (2007) Emotion elicitation using films, in *Handbook of Emotion Elicitation and Assessment* (eds J.A. Coan and J.B. Allen),. Oxford University Press, New York, NY, pp. 9–28.

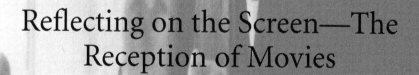

# Reflecting on the Screen—The Reception of Movies

**Illustration 7.1**  Linda Blair & Max von Sydow as Regan & Father Merrin in *The Exorcist* (1973) © Moviestore Collection Ltd/Alamy.

# Chapter 7

# Reflecting on the Screen—The Reception of Movies

William Friedkin's *The Exorcist* was released in 1973, a few years after publication of the novel by William Peter Blatty. If the novel caused cultural ripples, the movie set off shockwaves of controversy, acclaim, and fear.

At the time of its release, *The Exorcist* became the highest grossing film of all time. Adjusted for inflation, it is still ranks #9 on the list of box office earnings (see Appendix B; there are no other horror films in the Top 50). It was nominated for 10 Academy Awards and won two.

*The Exorcist* contains a host of indelible images that, almost 40 years later, have become part of the cultural landscape: the possessed Regan (Linda Blair) with her spinning head, copious amounts of pea green projectile vomit, and blasphemous language; and the exorcist, Father Merrin (Max Von Sydow) approaching the Georgetown brownstone in the dead of night. The film ignited many discussions about the historical and modern practice of exorcism. Some viewers entertained the possibility of real-life demonic possession. Among nonbelievers, it was taken as a serious horror film that made a statement about science and faith in the modern world.

Critics were divided in their evaluation of the movie. Roger Ebert gave the film four stars and claimed that Friedkin uses "the most fearsome resources of the cinema" to create "one of the most powerful [escapist movies] ever made." Yet he also fretfully speculated, "Are people so numb they need movies of this intensity to feel anything at all?"[1] Pauline Kael

*Psychology at the Movies*, First Edition. Skip Dine Young
© 2012 John Wiley & Sons, Ltd. Published 2012 by John Wiley & Sons, Ltd.

of *The New Yorker* was all-out condemning. She criticized Blatty's book as "shallowness that asks to be taken seriously"; she castigated the director for being so "mentally unprotected" that he felt a need to "make everybody sick"; and she argued that "the movie industry is such that men of no taste and no imagination can have an incalculable influence." She ended her review by questioning the state of mind of the 500 parents who had unsuccessfully auditioned their daughter for the lead role: '[As they watch Linda Blair act like a little demon] do they feel, "That might have been my little Susie—famous forever"?'[2]

To kids like me growing up in the 1970s, *The Exorcist* was legendary. Like *Saturday Night Fever*, it was an R-rated film that was a frequent topic of conversation. I was not allowed to watch it,[3] but some kids claimed to have seen it and vividly described the movie's green puke and twisting heads. Not to be outdone, other kids claimed that a distant cousin or family friend had been possessed. There was particular interest in the subliminal insertion of a demonic face into the film which we'd been told was the photograph of an actual demon taken on a spirit-hunting expedition.

I finally saw *The Exorcist* in my late teens in the early 1980s and thought it was a great movie. In the era of *Friday the 13th*, it was at once old-fashioned in its slowly building terror yet up-to-date in its graphic special effects. I was particularly disturbed by the intrusive medical interventions, and I was perplexed how the crucifix scene didn't merit the film an X rating. I appreciated the unrelenting, ominous tone. I definitely took the film seriously.[4] When I read Pauline Kael's review, it disturbed me almost as much as the movie. Her criticism seemed a personal attack on not only my intelligence but my moral sensibility.

When I teach film courses, I sometimes use *The Exorcist* as an example of a film that has had a significant cultural impact. As with all films with graphic violent or sexual content, I give some spoilers and excuse anyone who is likely to be disturbed. Most of the time my students dismiss my warning, but in the case of *The Exorcist*, a few always take me up on it. There is something about the film that still hits a nerve, even among jaded college students. Some report that seeing the movie was terrifying or even traumatic. Others find it unnerving based on their religious beliefs (even non-Catholics). Occasionally students claim they find the film scary because "that can really happen."[5]

When we watch movies, we follow the storyline and become emotionally involved with the characters. Generally, after the credits roll, we never think about them again. Sometimes, however, a movie stays with us, and we reflect on it—for an hour, a week, a year or a lifetime. The story and images run

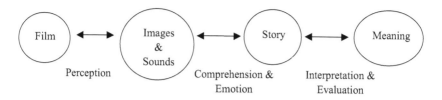

**Figure 7.1** Symbolic activity in film viewing: Interpretation and evaluation.

through our minds. We relive our emotions. We evaluate the quality of the movie and our experience with it. We make connections between the film and the rest of the world around us (maybe to our job or something we read in the paper). Our understanding of the film's story and characters becomes a grid that we map onto the rest of our lives.

Reflecting on a movie is another level of symbolic processing. Evaluation (determining enjoyment of a movie) and interpretation (determining the meaning of a movie) are reflective processes that can be added to perception and comprehension, as we see in Figure 7.1.

Whether we keep these reflections to ourselves, or share them with other people, it is during this phase that movies invade other aspects of our lives.

## Viewer Enjoyment of Movies

The old saying "everybody's a critic"[6] is certainly true of moviegoers. Everyone evaluates their filmgoing experiences. Those who are more articulate, louder and/or verbose become academics or start blogs, but even the most unexpressive viewers base the movies they choose on previous cinematic experiences.[7] For most people, this evaluation has a self-conscious, reflective component. We ask ourselves, was it enjoyable? Was it gratifying? Or was it a waste of time and money? Enjoyment and gratification are the primary issues when considering film as a form of entertainment.[8] When people choose their forms of entertainment, we assume they are making decisions that they consider worthwhile.

The enjoyment of film is closely tied to emotional experience.[9] Presumably, people want their entertainment to make them *feel* good. Yet the relationship between the emotions experienced during a film and the labeling of a film experience as enjoyable is by no means transparent. Even with movies that provoke such positive emotions as wonder, we can question why some people find one movie wondrous and not another? Particularly puzzling are movies that arouse negative emotions such as sadness and fear. Tearjerkers, horror movies, and thrillers have been popular throughout the entire history of filmmaking. Why do people seek out the experience of negative emotions?

*Funny Movies*

Laughter feels good. Comedies make people laugh. Therefore, comedy is perhaps the most robust film genre: To paraphrase the hippie mantra, "If it feels good, watch it." This observation is consistent with a hedonistic theory of film appeal—we enjoy movies because they bring us pleasure.

As with everything that involves the human mind, there are deeper puzzles just below the surface. We may ask what makes something funny. Freud had an explanation that can serve as a starting point.[10] He believed that jokes and humor were socially acceptable expressions of unconscious aggression. Some things in life are frustrating, but social and moral inhibitions prevent people from directly acting on their feelings. We thus use humor to express our longings and frustrations without doing any physical harm. Dirty jokes, sarcasm, and slapstick clearly exemplify this theory. Are people sadists for thinking the abuse dished out to the burglars in *Home Alone* is funny? Freud would answer yes.

Freud's ideas have been modified by modern experimental psychologists to form the superiority or disparagement theory of humor. The joker gains superiority over the object of the humor (an enemy, authority, or ambivalent loved one) by disparaging them. One experiment involved the degree to which a joke about a politician contracting an STD was perceived as funny.[11] Participants who felt animosity toward Bill Clinton found the joke funnier than those who liked Clinton. The same pattern applied when Newt Gingrich was the subject. This finding is an explanation for the famous sight gag from *The Naked Gun* (from the height of the first Gulf War) that involved Saddam Hussein having a bomb dropped in his lap while lounging by his pool.

Not all humor is aggressive. The line, "I'll have what she's having," in response to Sally's (Meg Ryan) faked orgasm in a diner in *When Harry Met Sally* is a cinematic example of a *friendly* joke. The woman who uttered it probably didn't have any aggression toward Sally, the lunch menu, or orgasms. While there is a sexual element to the joke, the attitude is not repressed and therefore doesn't fit Freud's theory.

The enjoyment of friendly humor has been explained by incongruity theory—the listener or viewer starts thinking of an utterance or event in an ordinary way, but the joke takes things to a surprising resolution.[12] "I'll have what she's having" is usually a banal, shorthand method of ordering food. But uttered by a woman after hearing someone experience great pleasure, it implies Sally's food must have special qualities and be highly desirable. Humans find the mental jolts of verbal and visual twists to be cognitively refreshing and energizing.

## Violent Movies

Why do people enjoy watching events filled with violence, destruction and human suffering? According to Freud, in civilized societies people's inborn destructive tendencies are punished when overtly expressed, so they are relegated to the unconscious. Because they don't go away, we experience internal tension. One solution is to displace (or sublimate) our aggressive urges from activities that would get us into trouble (starting a bar fight) to activities that are more socially acceptable (watching a bar fight in a movie).

Evolutionary psychology makes a similar argument using different language. Throughout human evolution, violence has proven to be advantageous to our survival against predators and enemies. Therefore violence as a problem-solving impulse is deeply imbedded in our genetic code. Yet, in the modern world, violence is not an effective way to resolve daily situations. So our violent urges finds expression in symbolic media, and violent movies are experienced as satisfying and enjoyable.

These broad formulations don't explain the enormous variation in violent circumstances depicted in movies. A film of random scenes of explosions and gunfire would not attract a very large audience.[13] Instead, enjoyment of violence likely depends on plot and character. Dolf Zillmann's dispositional theory of media entertainment specifies how certain kinds of media violence are particularly enjoyable. For most viewers, enjoyment comes from the moral dispositions that they feel toward the characters. If a character (usually the hero or the protagonist) is seen as positive, viewers empathize with him or her. They enjoy the film if good things happen to the character but do not when bad things occur (particularly at the end). On the other hand, if a character is viewed as negative, viewers experience gratification when bad things happen to him or her, since these events are felt to be justified by the character's evilness.[14]

This theory applies to all age groups, but is particularly pronounced in younger audience members. In one experimental study, children reported enjoying a film when a likable character received a new bike at the end.[15] In another variation, they appreciated when an obnoxious character fell off his bike. The children didn't enjoy the film when the likable character fell off his bike or when the unlikable character emerged unharmed with a new bike. A quick survey of box office hits (Appendix B) supports this theory: almost all of these films are resolved by the hero getting rewarded and the villain being punished.

*Horror Movies*

Horror films have received a great deal of attention from psychologists studying entertainment.[16] Fans of horror films may detect a patronizing subtext to this research (what kind of person enjoys this stuff?), but the horror genre is defined by a compelling paradox. Horror films are frightening; fear arises when people are threatened by bodily or social harm. Normally people will go to enormous lengths and expense to avoid fear-producing situations. How then does the existence of the horror genre make sense?

Dispositional theory has relevance to horror films. While a horror film may contain fear- and terror-arousing moments, traditional horror films generally end with the monster/villain being vanquished and some of the good characters surviving. When the moral order is restored through the survival of the hero and the destruction of the villain, the anxiety experienced during the film is relieved, adding emphasis to the final payoff.[17] Since horror films combine fear with disgust for a nonhuman monster, the killing of the monster doesn't arouse the residual human sympathies that might be present in suspense movies. This pattern is common and can be vividly seen in *Alien* and *Aliens*[18] which feature extended showdowns between Ripley (Sigourney Weaver) and the oozing alien. While the monster is intelligent, it is also loathsome and unsympathetic. Encounters between Ripley and her nemesis range from slow-building suspense to horrific violence, yet each film ends with the dramatic destruction of the monster. The viewer is rewarded with both relief and moral satisfaction.

The pleasure of perceived justice is also noticeable in the "virgin survivor effect" in slasher movies.[19] The "pure" characters, with whom the audience presumably empathizes, are spared in the end while the "impurity" of sexually active characters is a justification for their gruesome deaths. They find the fate of morally deficient victims gratifying for the same reasons as the death of a villain. Research has found that teenage boys who hold disapproving beliefs about female sexuality along with punitive attitudes ("I like to see the victims get what they deserve") reported enjoying the murders of female characters who are sexually active more than the murders of male characters (regardless of sexual activity) or non-sexually active female characters.[20]

## Sad Movies

The enjoyment of sad movies raises a paradox similar to horror movies. Since most people consider sadness a negative emotion and generally avoid the feeling, then why are so-called "weepers" or tearjerkers so popular? On the surface, this seems to be run up against the idea that people don't do things that don't feel good. In many movies sad events are not much of a problem if the movie is viewed holistically. Depressing events at the beginning or middle of the story establish challenges for the characters which are overcome in the course of the film, thus increasing the pleasure of a happy ending. An epic like *Lord of the Rings* can compile many tragic events over a long narrative, so that the characters can repeatedly triumph in the end.

Movies with unhappy endings are more puzzling since there is no obvious payoff. Why do people subject themselves to *The Notebook* or *Old Yeller*, stories where sympathetic characters (an elderly couple and a Labrador retriever, respectively) die tragically due to no fault of their own or as the result of heroic behavior? One possibility is that viewers are motivated by something other than experiencing a particular emotion. Research has found that participants in a "tender affective state" (warmth, sympathy and understanding) showed a greater preference for sad films than participants in happy or sad affective states.[21] The people in the tender state were also more interested in other movies that explored intimate human relationships, sad or not. When participants adopted a sympathetic attitude, their motivating interest was to watch movies with meaningful insights, not to experience a particular emotion.

*Old Yeller*'s beloved standing among viewers demonstrates a willingness to tolerate heartbreaking emotion if the experience is attached to meaningful events. *Old Yeller* offers themes like courage, friendship and loyalty, and the ending encourages reflections on growing up and responsibility. The emotions associated with watching the movie are important, but they are secondary to the insights that come from viewing the film. This observation expands the notion of what it means to enjoy or to be gratified by films.[22]

## Viewer Interpretations of Movies

Based on what we have seen, viewing movies in order to feel good is a useful starting point, but it is not the whole story. Viewers experience both positive and negative emotions while watching movies. Whether they positively evaluate their overall viewing experience is based in their understanding of the story, their empathy with the characters, and their discovery of the story's meaning or significance. Viewer evaluations and interpretations occur simultaneously, as complementary forms of cinematic reflection.[23]

Interpretation is generally regarded as something that critics do to movies in order to discover the meanings contained within them.[24] In this chapter, however, I treat interpretation as a psychological process that takes place within ordinary viewers (see Figure 7.1).

### Historical Studies

The interpretive approach of film studies is to pick a movie and then analyze it; historical approaches select the film and then look at how other people have analyzed or reacted to it.[25] Researchers use many sources including movie reviews, news stories, opinion pieces, commentaries from filmmakers, industry data, and advertising campaigns. Every source is understood as reflecting the diverse qualities of the film in question and is not evaluated for absolute truth. The sources are not considered to cancel each other out; rather, they suggest that different people can have different perspectives. These artifacts are then pieced together to create a picture of the film's cultural significance and to identify patterns of audience response. The lenses used to evaluate a film's reception often relate to some controversial issue, such as race, gender, or sexuality. Because it involves close analysis, historical reception is a humanities-friendly middle path between textual analysis and the data collection used by social scientists.

*Field of Dreams* received a mixed response when it was released in 1989 and has maintained this contested status today; it is considered a classic by some and an object of ridicule by others. The story focuses on Ray (Kevin Costner) and his mission to build a baseball diamond in his cornfield in hopes of giving the ghosts of the 1919 disgraced White Sox team an opportunity to redeem themselves from accusations that they threw the World Series. Critics who liked the film took Ray's quest to be a celebration of redemption through ritualistic reenactment. This take, however, glossed over the fact that at the time of the scandal, major league baseball was racially segregated. Since *Field of Dreams* was made in the 1980s by a liberal leaning star, this situation was awkward. The solution of casting James Earl Jones as Terence Mann, a political activist from the 1960s, only inflamed the controversy; this was a significant change from the book where Mann was a fictionalized version of J.D. Salinger. Jones was aware of the contrast between Mann and Salinger, but did not address the racial implications in interviews. Critics maligned the character's willingness to collude with Ray's quest to mythologize an all-white team. The conflicted reception of *Field of Dreams* shows how a film can both "evoke and deny race simultaneously."[26]

Reactions to movies are often divided along political fault lines. In response to Mel Gibson's *The Passion of the Christ*, Christian conservatives focused on Christ's faith-affirming sacrifice while liberals pointed to the negative portrayal of Jews and Gibson's obsession with sadomasochistic violence. Sometimes a film's reception does not fall along such clear divisions. *Silence of the Lambs* was hailed as being empowering to women, particularly its portrayal of FBI agent Clarice Starling (Jodie Foster). As she pursues a serial killer who is targeting young women, she is strong, determined, and able to succeed in a male-dominated environment.

Others criticized the film as reinforcing stereotypes of sexual orientation and gender identity by showing the killer as effeminate and demented (using victims' skin to fashion a female body suit). Gay activists were so bothered by Jodie Foster's decision to hide her sexual identity that she was "outed," a situation that was greeted acrimoniously by feminists: "Like their straight brothers, the gay men who condemn Jodie Foster and *Lambs* are out to destroy a woman who doesn't put male interests first and doesn't conform to their ideas of what a woman should be."[27] While both the praise and criticism of the film may be justified from its contents, it's clear that different members of the audience are more likely to key in on certain aspects of the film than others.

The debate over *Thelma & Louise* was primarily related to gender.[28] It is a rare that a Hollywood film includes two female leads (Gina Davis and Susan Sarandon). The script, by Callie Khouri, offers dialogue that highlights the gender roles of both male and female characters. Reviews and opinion pieces were roughly divided into three categories. Those who loved the film viewed Thelma and Louise as interesting, sympathetic characters whose adventures were by turns funny, disturbing, and exhilarating. Not everyone saw them as standard bearers of feminism, but supporters of the film tended to voice their appreciation for the characters' culturally determined predicament.

Another group despised the film based on the perception that the male characters were all "pigs" or "cretins."[29] Seen from this perspective, not only were Thelma and Louise violent criminals, but the movie was viewed as justifying their behavior by holding up a lens of man-hating feminism. Though some assumed this reaction broke down along gender lines (men hated the film, women loved it), this was not the case. Many male reviewers liked the film; not every female critic did. The most vociferous critics, however, tended to be male, such as the newspaper columnist who claimed that "male-bashing has flushed like toxic waste into the mainstream."[30]

The third reaction was also negative, but these reviewers saw *Thelma & Louise* as an example of *false* feminism. They saw the film as a typical buddy film with a revenge theme, which attempts to be subversive by inserting women into roles traditionally played by men (e.g., Newman and Redford in *Butch Cassidy and the Sundance Kid*). For these viewers, the film didn't ring true because Thelma and Louise often relied on macho solutions (guns and fast cars) instead of dialogue and self-revelation (presumably women's problem-solving tools of choice). As the reception of Thelma & Louise is explored further and further, it's clear that any "he said/she said" characterization of the debate is far too simplistic.

## Cultural Studies

In the essay *Encoding/Decoding*, Stuart Hall (1980) argues that complementary processes are involved in understanding any cultural product (television, movies, advertising, etc.). *Encoding* is the process by which creators imbue, either intentionally or unintentionally, a product with signifying codes (meaning). *Decoding* is the process by which the receivers of the product (in this instance, movie viewers) interpret that code and extract meaning from it. Decoding is not simply the mirror image of encoding, because decoders do not always share the same social views as encoders. It is not that the decoders are wrong; they simply have different backgrounds and sets of motivations. Decoders will adjust their interpretations to make them consistent with their worldviews. Since decoders come from different social circumstances, there will invariably be many different interpretations.

Hall's essay had a huge impact on cultural studies because it added a twist to ideological criticism.[31] Interpreting cultural products as reifications of a culture's ideology becomes problematic if we acknowledge that cultural products can be decoded in multiple ways. With Hall's argument in mind, some scholars turned their gaze toward the audience and started asking about their reactions to popular media in personal interviews and focus groups (a group of 8-10 participants gathered to discuss specific research questions).[32]

A seminal audience study done in the late 1970s showed two episodes of a British news program to 29 focus groups representing different socioeconomic classifications in the United Kingdom (university students, technical apprentices, management trainees, and shop stewards).[33] The researchers found that each group responded to the show in different ways. The variations were based on the attitude participants had about the program's messages. Bank management trainees and technical apprentices expressed a "dominant" attitude; they didn't agree with everything, but accepted basic assumptions that the program was accurate. The student teachers and trade union officials expressed a "negotiated" attitude: cynical about the tone of the program, without rejecting it. Black university students and shop stewards took an "oppositional" stance toward the program by rejecting it as intentionally misleading or by being apathetic.

Daytime dramas (or "soap operas") have received a lot of attention from cultural scholars, thanks to the exaggerated picture of dominant cultural patterns they present. In the 1980s *Dallas* was a particularly fruitful object of study because of its popularity around the world.[34] One might speculate there was something universally appealing about the nighttime soap opera, but cross-cultural focus groups failed to identify any silver bullet that provided universal entertainment.

Instead, the insights that emerged revealed an array of culturally dependent interpretations that suggested different notions of selfhood. Arabs and Moroccan Jews tended to focus more on story events. These were evaluated through a moral filter regarding the family roles played by the various characters. In contrast, Americans and Israelis were focused on individuals and displayed a heightened concern for their psychological motivations and their own emotional reactions. Finally, Russian respondents enjoyed the program, but took a distanced, critical stance to the characters' behavior and the production itself. They questioned the intentions of the producers and distributors of the show and were concerned about the potential for certain messages manipulating the audience toward consumerism.

## Other Interpretive Studies

Reader response criticism highlights the importance of the reader in understanding the meaning of literature.[35] In some ways, this approach parallels the spectatorship approaches in film studies: such critics approach the reader's experience indirectly through close analysis of written texts. Some reader response critics however have looked directly at the experience of readers. Norman Holland's accurately titled *Five Readers Reading* (1975) offers an in-depth look at five of his student's readings of short stories by Faulkner, Fitzgerald and Hemingway, while Janice Radway's *Reading the Romance* is an influential audience response study that, like cultural studies, focuses on a form of popular culture, romance novels.

Radway identified a group of women who were avid romance novel readers and used questionnaires and interviews to gain a deeper understanding of the meaning that romance novels had for these women. She documented the functions the books had in their lives (relaxation, escape, education, mood management, self-care) and made the surprising observation that the act of reading was often experienced as an act of defiance, given the various pressures in the women's lives that made taking time for themselves difficult.

Radway also interpreted the women's interpretations. They preferred romances with strong-willed, determined heroines and seemingly brutish heroes. The ultimate purpose of these relationships was to bring about change in the man, provoking the emergence of dormant capacities for tenderness and sensitivity. Radway viewed this as a quasi-feminist attempt to undermine the destructive aspects of masculinity and replace them with virtues associated with femininity (the capacity for intimacy). At the same time, the women's need to find intimacy in romance novels suggested it was not being met in their day-to-day lives.

While Radway offers a global reading of the participants in her study, other approaches emphasize the idiosyncratic psychological position of readers. Since every reader is different in personality and background, every reading is different. Focusing on film, Holland takes an individualized approach in a study that features three viewers viewing a controversial erotic movie from the 1970s, *The Story of O*[36] where O, the heroine, sequestered in an isolated castle, submits to painful and degrading acts in order to win the commitment of her lover.

One study participant, Agnes, related O's oppression to her experiences at a strict Catholic girls school, but ultimately found O too emotionally cold to connect to. A second participant, Norm, did not identify with any of the characters but instead, treated the castle as an exotic realm which operated by alternative rules that were his job to figure out. A third, Ted, brought his moral code to the film, making judgments about O's willingness to submit or dominate. Holland concluded that these different readings were related to variations in the participants' personalities and motivations—Agnes sought connection, Norm sought intellectual mastery, and Ted sought to maintain interpersonal control.

My investigations into audience responses to *Thelma & Louise* complement the historical approach. A year following its 1991 theatrical release, I interviewed people about their reactions after watching it on video. The film aroused strong opinions, but they did not fall along clear gender lines. Women enjoyed the film slightly more frequently, but a fair number of the men mildly enjoyed the film. Some men thought the film did portray men negatively yet still found reasons to value the beautiful scenery or exciting action sequences.[37] I have continued to show the film in my courses through the years and give students an open-ended questionnaire afterwards. By the end of the 2000s, there was no noticeable difference between the genders in terms of the frequency of liking the film. Today's male students don't find the film particularly threatening toward men, perhaps a reflection of the Angelina Jolie era in which women action figures are an accepted part of film-going.

A few subtle differences in gender reception of *Thelma & Louise* remain, at least among college students. Women report loving the film more often than men; female students identify strongly with Thelma and/or Louise. Men report they most strongly identify with one of the male characters (Detective Slocum: Harvey Keitel or Louise's boyfriend Jimmy: Michael Madsen), and their level of identification with the female leads is minimal. While young men are not threatened by the idea of Thelma or Louise as gunslingers, they are still reticent to consciously identify with a female character.

For women who identify strongly with Thelma and Louise, two scenes are cited as powerful instigators: the sexual assault in the parking lot early on in the movie, and the ending in which Thelma and Louise drive off a cliff to escape capture. While some viewers see the latter scene as a consequence of the former, female students report feeling anger and helplessness during the assault, but exhilaration and freedom when they watch the leap into the canyon. Most participants see the act as an affirmation of friendship and a refusal to surrender, not suicide. The students' interpretation of the final scene appears closely entwined with their emotional engagement with the narrative.

Audience studies focused on viewer interpretations provide a means of extending other forms of research. Movies that fall into the category of the "new brutalism"[38] (*Reservoir Dogs, Pulp Fiction, Casino, Natural Born Killers*) challenge Zillmann's dispositional theory in which the enjoyment of violence is based on justice and bad characters being punished.[39] Such movies feature a combination of gruesome violence mixed with witty dialogue and

imaginative cinematic techniques. Characters and actions are morally ambiguous compared with typical mainstream films. In *Pulp Fiction*, when
Butch (Bruce Willis) kills the sadistic neo-Nazis, it could be seen as justified
revenge and self-defense, yet his collusion with Marcellus (Ving Rhames), a
brutal drug dealer who had been trying to kill Butch, is morally convoluted.
Is he being merciful by aiding his enemy? Is he being self-serving in trying
to procure a favor from Marcellus? Is he being irresponsible for releasing a
man who is arguably more dangerous than the neo-Nazis? Such questions
make the straightforward application of disposition theory difficult.

Asking what meaning viewers derived from films like *Pulp Fiction* can
provide alternative reasons for valuing them. Some viewers are willing to
justify or applaud the use of violence because, as one interviewee put it,
"The whole point [is] getting a glimpse of the other side of life that you
don't see very often." Viewers can also judge whether a film's use of violence
is warranted in terms of a particular theme. A fan of Baz Luhrman's *Romeo
+ Juliet* remake commented, "I thought the violence was valid because it
showed the senseless results of groundless family bickering and it shows the
tragedy of young men killing each other for no reason except their father's
argument."[40] Experiences like these are not just a matter of enjoyment but
are acts of meaning making.

## Closing Shots: The Challenges of Audience Response

The study of film reception aims at a place somewhere between traditional
humanities and social science approaches.[41] A tension remains when it
comes to integrating audience response studies.

Most social science research into reflective processes has been limited
to movies as entertainment. Researchers ask people "Did you enjoy this
movie?" and reliably evoke such answers as yes, no, a little, or a lot, that
are manageable using statistical procedures. Meaning-making, on the other
hand, is more elusive to measure. If one asks, "Did you find this movie
meaningful?" an affirmative answer then begs the question, "In what ways
did you as an individual find this particular movie meaningful?" Given
the infinite number of answers, a controlled experiment would be difficult
to conduct. Nonetheless, recent research into the importance of meaning-
making as a form of gratification suggests possible overlap between social
scientists and film scholars, for whom interpretation is a key issue.[42]

It is not that film scholars are not interested in viewers. While attention
to close textual analysis generally prevents them from directly encountering

audiences, the study of spectatorship has been prominent in film studies.[43] Core concepts like identification, voyeurism, and suturing refer to viewers' mental activity. Ambiguous films like *Psycho* or *Blow Up* are frequently analyzed for their contradictory messages and how they frustrate the audience in its search for meaning. However, such insights are generated by looking at the movie and then extrapolating to viewers without ever confronting the experience of a particular viewer. Meaning (including ambiguity) is derived from the film, not the viewer.

Compare the following statements:

> Because readers are superior in wisdom to the heroine at the same time they emotionally identify with her, the reading process itself must lead to feelings of hypocrisy . . . We consider the heroine's emotions important only insofar as they subvert themselves. Reading Harlequin Romances, one has a continual sensation of being in bad faith.

> I am 25, a wife and mother. Sometimes, like so many other people, I get low in spirits . . . I can pick up one of [Essie Summer's] books and see the goodness staring out at me. The heroine makes me feel it's a lovely world, people are good, one can face anything and we are lucky to be alive.

The first quote is from a film and literature scholar. The second is a letter to the editor written by a fan of Harlequin romances. One might wonder if they are reading the same books. Radway's study of romance readers carves out a position somewhere between these poles.[44] While Radway doesn't take her subjects' perspectives at face value, neither does she imply that the emotionally distanced opinions of the world of academics is the definitive word on the matter.

Some scholars worry that film critics do too much interpreting.[45] Studies that solicit the interpretations of audience members multiply this potential. One could see this as a reason to prioritize the study of comprehension and not return to the chaos of interpretive processes. Yet the fact is that all of us, not just film critics, interpret the movies we see. Film interpretation may be confusing and difficult to study, yet it is an essential symbolic process that resonates with the instability of everyday life.

# Further Reading

Bryant, J. and Vorderer, P. (eds) (2006) *Psychology of Entertainment.* Lawrence Erlbaum, New York, NY.

Fournier, G. (2007) *Thelma & Louise* and Women in Hollywood. McFarland, Jefferson, NC.

Liebes, T. and Katz, E. (1990) *The Export of Meaning: Cross-Cultural Readings of Dallas.* Oxford University Press, New York, NY.

Nabi, R.L. and Oliver, M.B. (eds) (2009) *Media Processes and Effects.* Sage, Thousand Oaks, CA.

Radway, J. (1991) *Reading the Romance: Women, Patriarchy and Popular Literature,* 2nd edn. University of North Carolina Press, Chapel Hill, NC.

Staiger, J. (1992) *Interpreting Films: Studies in the Historical Reception of American Cinema.* Princeton University Press, Princeton, NJ.

Stokes, M. and Maltby, R. (eds) (1999) *Identifying Hollywood's Audiences: Cultural Identity and the Movies.* British Film Institute, London.

# The Movies Made Me Do It—The Effects of Film

**Illustration 8.1** Juliette Lewis & Woody Harrelson as Mallory & Mickey in *Natural Born Killers* (1994) © AF archive/Alamy.

# Chapter 8

# The Movies Made Me Do It—The Effects of Film

On April 20, 1999, Eric Harris and Dylan Klebold went on a shooting rampage at Columbine High School in Littleton, Colorado. Using semiautomatic rifles, they killed 13 people and wounded 21 more before killing themselves.

When they entered the school, they wore the black trench coats similar to the ones worn by characters of *The Matrix*, a movie which turned shooting sprees into mesmerizing, balletlike spectacles. Is it possible that Harris and Klebold wanted to emulate the transcendent coolness of Neo (Keanu Reeves), perceiving their victims to be little more than virtual icons, part of a tragic passion play they created for themselves?

A trench coat was also featured in *The Basketball Diaries*, in which an addict named Jim (Leonardo Dicaprio) imagines entering his high school and shooting students and teachers. This massacre eerily resembles the events of Columbine. Could the shooters have used Jim's fantasy sequence as a model?

*Natural Born Killers* is another movie in which a lot of people get killed—not in a school, but nearly everyplace else. While Mickey (Woody Harrelson) and Mallory (Juliette Lewis) cause plenty of devastation, the film also documents the abuse and hardship they experience, providing a hint of justification for their crimes. Harris and Klebold used the acronym

*Psychology at the Movies*, First Edition. Skip Dine Young
© 2012 John Wiley & Sons, Ltd. Published 2012 by John Wiley & Sons, Ltd.

**Illustration 8.2** A still from a security video shows Dylan Klebold & Eric Harris on the day they killed twelve students and one teacher at Columbine High School, Colorado. April 20, 1999. © Reuters/Corbis.

NBK for the diaries and videotapes where they secretly recorded plans for their own devastation.[1] Did they believe they were "natural born killers" waiting to get payback against those who they felt deserved it?

Did these movies cause the teens to go on a deadly rampage? Or are violent movies a reflection of cultural conditions that were already present? Or does the answer lie somewhere in between?

The broader issue is what kind of impact movies have on the real world. Clearly, they arouse emotion and consume our time and money, but do they really affect the way people behave and think after they leave the theater? Beyond being fun to watch and talk about, *do movies really matter?*

Ultimately I believe that the answer is yes. Or at least, some movies matter to some people some of the time. The psychological processes we have considered—perception, comprehension, and interpretation—are the mental means by which viewing films impacts people's lives. Figure 8.1 illustrates this relationship.

**Figure 8.1**  Symbolic activity in film viewing: Function and effect.

Occasionally the meanings viewers form about a film will be so powerful and relevant that they will have an influence on people's lives. This chapter considers research on the behavioral and cognitive effects of media which occur largely outside of viewers' awareness.[2] (Sometimes viewers are able to identify the influence a film has on them.[3] The conscious functions of film are discussed in the next chapter.)

In the late 1920s, investigations into the psychological impact of film led to a series of books with names like *Movies and Conduct*[4] (concerning college students) and *Movies, Delinquency and Crime* (about teens in a juvenile detention center).[5] Although they were not a blanket indictment, they did raise concerns about the potential hazards of movies. The focus on dangers has continued as we will see below, but a minority of studies has considered the possibility of prosocial effects.[6]

Effects research entered another fertile period in the 1960s, with no signs of letting up. It has become a vast field, numbering thousands of articles and books. Over time, the primary target has shifted from film to television and, in recent years, videogames and computer use. Because of this broadening scope, such research is known as "media effects."[7] While I provide a broad overview of the scope and significance of effects research, I will refer to movie examples whenever possible.

## Effects on Behavior

"Subliminal seduction" (subconscious media messages that influence our behavior) was a term popularized in the 1970s.[8] Frequently referenced examples included "Buy popcorn" messages secretly flashed on the screen to prompt concession sales, innocuous sounds (waves on a beach) containing undetectable spoken messages meant to inspire success in business, and satanic voices on Led Zeppelin's song "Stairway to Heaven" that could only be understood when played backwards. Subliminal effects are sensory stimuli undetectable to conscious awareness which are nevertheless dutifully processed by the brain and subsequently influence behavior. While the claims regarding such stimuli are dramatic, laboratory research has been unable to confirm any significant impact on behavior or thought (at least at the level of buying more popcorn or becoming a success in business) as a result of seeing or hearing subliminal message in popular culture.[9]

Most effects on behavior are outside our awareness, but it is not that viewers are being affected by things they can't see or hear. Instead, it is simply that they do not know that one thing (a violent movie) is causing another thing (their own aggression). When asked, most audience members will deny that media has anything to do with their behavior, yet there is considerable evidence that it does.[10] And while effects researchers almost never use the term "subliminal," they assume that many effects and the underlying cognitive processes are indeed "nonconscious."

Since most human behavior can be captured by media, it is theoretically possible that media can influence any given human behavior. Advertising has pushed this possibility as people are induced to buy soap, cars, beer, iPods, Chia pets, and so on. While commercial theatrical films are intent on selling themselves, they have clearly impacted consumer behavior at times (such as the boom in Reese's Pieces after being featured in *E.T.*). Despite all the possible behaviors that a researcher might study, a disproportionate amount of attention has been given to three domains—violence, sex, and substance use.[11] Each domain is an area of social concern related to important public issues—crime, war, family planning, moral values, health problems, unemployment, and so on. The social mirror theory suggests that media merely reflect social behaviors, but there is considerable evidence to suggest that media can influence behaviors.

### The Copycat Phenomenon

Sometimes it is clear that a movie has an impact on behavior based on parallels between film and real life so precise they could not be mere coincidence. Most of the time, the copycat phenomenon is relatively innocuous. Take the sale of undershirts which supposedly plummeted after Clark Gable appeared without one in *It Happened One Night*.[12] "The Rachel" hairstyle became ubiquitous after Jennifer Aniston modeled it on *Friends* in the early 1990s. Catch-phrases like "Go ahead, make my day" have been uttered by millions of people based on Dirty Harry's cinematic inspiration.

Other behaviors can be more dramatic and compelling. Some movies have inspired gross negligence. Several people were injured or killed after emulating a scene in the football drama, *The Program*, in which players lie on the median of a busy road.[13] *The Deer Hunter* provoked as many as 30 imitations of the Russian roulette scene in the film, resulting in numerous deaths.[14] A teenager set his friend on fire copying a stunt in *Jackass*. Numerous crimes have also been associated with movies. Beyond John Hinckley's attempted assassination of Reagan and the Columbine shootings, other infamous examples include: women setting their abusive partners on fire after seeing the TV movie *The Burning Bed*; and a cross-country killing spree by an Oklahoma couple who had repeatedly watched *Natural Born Killers*.[15] Incidents like these get a lot of attention in the news,[16] but the frequency of copycat crime may be even greater than it appears. One study reported that one-fourth of the incarcerated adolescents they interviewed had attempted at least one copycat crime.[17]

Copycats are aware of the impact of a movie on them to the extent that they can point to the film as their inspiration. At the same, there is a striking lack of critical reflection and reality testing. The influence of the film appears to start with a strong identification with the characters. Although such identification is a part of the normal viewing process, these incidents extend beyond the immediate viewing experience. The copycat's personality and external environment also have to support their actions, often in ways they are unaware of. [18] Fortunately, since most environments do not support destructive acting out, most people do not end up following through on their cinematic identifications.

The significance of copycat incidents are sometimes downplayed, either because the behavior is trivial (adopting a popular hairstyle) or because the perpetrators of such atrocities/acts of stupidity display pre-existing mental, moral, or developmental limitations. In the case of Harris and Klebold, school bullying, psychiatric problems, negligent parenting, and other factors were implicated and debated as causes of the Columbine rampage. Yet even if Harris and Klebold were destined to commit murder anyway, the events at Columbine would probably not have been *exactly* as they were (no trench coats) if it were not for media. The movies likely affected how Harris and Klebold saw their world and colored their behavior, even if the seeds of that behavior were much deeper.[19] Percolating movie images attached to destructive behavioral tendencies should not be dismissed out of hand especially since other effects have been identified that are subtler but perhaps more pervasive.

*Effects on Aggressive Behaviors*

More research has been conducted on the effects of violence in movies than any other area.[20] This preeminence certainly relates to the frequency of media violence[21] and concerns about violence in the real world. The typical American sees violence in the media on a daily basis, yet for most people, acts of actual physical violence are relatively rare. Media violence thereby calls attention to itself. When it comes to possible behavioral effects of violence (particularly those causing aggressive behavior), research has disproportionately focused on the effects on children, echoing public sentiment that minors are vulnerable and therefore more susceptible to media effects than adults.[22]

The classic Bobo doll experiment performed by Albert Bandura and his colleagues has been one of the most influential studies with regard to the effect of media aggression.[23] In a laboratory setting, children were led into a room one at a time, given some craft materials and told to wait. After a short period of time, the researchers came and escorted the child to another room that contained a variety of toys including an inflatable punching bag (a Bobo doll), toy guns, hammers, and dolls. Researchers observed the children's play and recorded any action they defined as aggressive—hitting the Bobo doll, shooting the gun, throwing objects, and so on.

In another condition, an adult was in the room while the child waited. The adult pretended to get angry and began pummeling a Bobo doll with a toy hammer, saying things like "Sock him in the nose." Afterwards, the children were taken to the playroom to be observed. In another condition, the researcher turned on a film camera that showed a scene of the adult hitting the Bobo doll.[24]

While virtually all of the children in the experiment engaged in some form of aggression, those who witnessed aggressive modeling by an adult (either live or filmed) engaged in a significantly greater number of aggressive acts than children who were not exposed to an aggressive model. Some of the exposed children closely imitated the adult's behavior, right down to repeating the same phrases while beating the hapless plastic clown.

Bandura interpreted the findings as evidence that children model behavior on what they see around them, especially when such behaviors are not punished. This effect occurs at the level of direct imitation (hitting the Bobo doll) and more general instigations of aggression (shooting a gun). There appears to be nothing magical about film's influence on the children, since live modeling had the same result. Consistent with social learning theory, Bandura claims that film is one of many forms of observational learning

There were limitations to this study: only young children were observed, and even those who weren't exposed to modeling showed some degree of aggression. The definition of aggression the researchers used was broad and could not be characterized as violent since there were no other people in the room. The aggressive behavior occurred soon after exposure to the model and therefore might have been short-lived. Finally, the laboratory situation, as well as the film, bore little resemblance to the real world.

These are all good qualifications, many of which Bandura addresses in the study's conclusion. Watching violent movies alone cannot make people violent, yet it would be a mistake to dismiss the study simply because of its limitations. No one experiment can look at all variables at once, just as no single film can capture all the important dimensions of cinema. Building on this study, other researchers designed further studies with additional variables of interest. As studies have accumulated, several patterns have been noted.

Many people may not consider aggression toward Bobo dolls to be worrisome, but other researchers have inquired about whether a relationship between media exposure and real-life violent behavior exists. One study observed that boys who watched the most violent television programs were most aggressive at school.[25] A large-scale longitudinal study followed children over 20 years and found that eight year-olds with the most exposure to violent TV were more likely to be involved in serious crimes (including murder, rape, assault, and robbery) by age 30.[26]

Studies that only look at a relationship/correlation between two variables have a methodological limitation that constrains interpretation. Just knowing that the variables are related does not tell us which came first or caused the other.[27] Thus, it's possible that watching a large amount of television caused violent tendencies, manifesting in crime. However, it's also possible that the children with violent tendencies were already drawn to violent media. Or it could be that other factors influenced both behaviors; for example, lack of parental guidance leading to both inappropriate viewing choices and lack of respect for the law. In real life, many factors affect any given behavior, leading some researchers to make a distinction between the media *contributing* to certain behaviors (along with other many factors) versus media single-handedly causing behaviors.[28]

One of the ways that researchers explain how media can contribute to behavior but not directly cause specific behaviors is priming theory.[29] Parallel to the way a well must be pumped a number of times before it actually starts producing water, psychologists believe that exposure to media provides a range of images and behavioral examples that remain dormant until a relevant situation emerges that matches the priming. Therefore, repeated exposure to bar fights do not necessarily lead men to go to bars looking for fights. However, if men happen to be in a bar and they are threatened, they have already been primed for how to respond in such a situation. They may then act aggressively, even if they are unaware of the source of the influence on them.

### *Effects on Sexual Behaviors*

As a topic of great research interest, the impact of sexualized images on viewers is second only to violence.[30] Both address social concerns, but depictions of sexuality seem to cause even more worry than violence. Why would an MPAA rating system that routinely gives R ratings to brutal depictions of torture (like the *Saw* films) saddle a critically lauded film such as *Blue Valentine* with an NC-17 rating for the depiction of marital sex? This situation strikes many as misguided, but its rationale is based on American parenting anxieties. Most parents of teenagers are more worried that their children will commit acts of sexuality than violent crimes. The fear is that sexual depictions in movies that condone sexual activity will "give the kids ideas."

Does viewing sex in the media actually inspire teenagers to "do it," as parents fear? While the results are far from definitive, some evidence suggests that it is a contributing factor. One study of nearly 2000 respondents indicated that the teens who watched a lot of sex on TV initiated sexual activity (including intercourse, heavy petting, and oral sex) at a significantly greater rate than those who did not.[31] As a correlation-based study, the causal relationship between variables remains unclear (teens with greater interest in sex may seek it on TV).[32] Other factors (parental disapproval, a two-parent household, a high degree of parental monitoring) also predicted the teens who would postpone sex. This finding exemplifies that while media may have a modest effect in the short term, it usually combines with other cultural and personal variables to have an overall influence on behavior.

Demographic data has led to speculation that there might be a connection between media and deviant acts such as rape and other acts of sexual aggression. From the 1960s to the 1990s, the frequency of reported sexual assaults increased as sexually explicit material became more available. However, changes in attitudes toward sexuality during the same time may have led women to report assaults without fear of humiliation or public reprisal. Cross-cultural data leads to even more questions: much sexually explicit material comes from Japan, which historically has a relatively low rape rate.[33] Some studies narrow the focus by comparing the consumption of sexually explicit material by men convicted of sex crimes with non-offenders. While it is difficult to find reliable findings on the typical man's pornography usage, these studies have found that sexually aggressive men are exposed to more violent pornography than non-sex offenders.[34]

## Effects on Substance Use

Completing the sex, drugs, and violence triumvirate, significant research has looked at the influence of media on substance use, particularly tobacco and alcohol. Drinking and smoking have a long Hollywood tradition, often used to suggest rebellion and dangerous behaviors. The concern is that such adult behaviors might have an impact on children and teens.

A recent study looked at the relationship between smoking in movies and smoking by children aged 9–12 (the age when nearly 20% of all children try cigarettes for the first time). The children most exposed to smoking in G, PG and PG-13 movies were more likely to try smoking than those with minimal movie exposure. This result was found one and two years after the study was initiated.[35] This finding is somewhat surprising, given that in recent years, it was the "negative characters" who were most likely to be smoking.[36] Some children may be influenced to try smoking precisely because of cigarettes' negative images.

A recent study considering the relationship between R-rated movie viewing and alcohol initiation found differences based on personality type. Though no relationship between R-rated movies and alcohol use was found among individuals classified as high sensation seekers (those who seek exciting/dangerous behavior), a significant relationship was established for people who measured low on the sensation-seeking scale. These individuals had less overall exposure to risky-decision making so movies appeared to leave a greater impression. For high sensation seekers, movies had a minimal influence compared with other variables regarding alcohol use, such as choice of peers.[37]

# Effects on Thoughts and Emotions

Focusing on outward behaviors like hitting a blow-up doll or committing a crime is tempting since these behaviors are so vivid. However, cognitive psychology is just as interested in the thinking and emotion that underlie behaviors. Over the years effects research has shifted toward investigating the impact that visual media have on the ways viewers think about themselves and the world around them.

Movies often provoke powerful emotional reactions, but occasionally people will respond to a movie so strongly that they develop symptoms of trauma, depression, or psychosis. The psychiatric literature is sprinkled with case studies of these acute clinical reactions. After seeing *Invasion of the Body Snatchers*, a 12 year-old boy came to believe that a foreign entity had entered him and that if anyone touched him, their hands would go through him.[38] Subclinical reactions to *Jaws* are common (such as refusing to swim in the ocean), but one 17 year-old girl experienced episodes of seizure in which she screamed "Sharks, sharks!" and briefly lost consciousness.[39]

*The Exorcist* not only provoked strong opinions, it was the reported catalyst for seven different cases of psychiatric disturbance.[40] One 22 year-old woman developed severe anxiety symptoms, including sleeplessness, abdominal cramps, and panic attacks. A teenage boy had intrusive memories of the movie, heard noises at night, and went on a drug binge in an attempt to eradicate memories of the film.[41]

Reactions requiring psychiatric hospitalization are rare, but they are at one end of the emotional continuum that is part of the film experience. While movies do not have the power to make secure individuals into nervous wrecks, these examples exemplify the interaction between symbolic images presented in cinema and the psychological makeup of a particular individual. All the people cited above had experienced interpersonal stressors before watching the film in question, and some had histories of psychiatric treatment. Thus, the combination of symbols in the film ignited their existing personal issues. The theme of possession was particularly disturbing for an unmarried pregnant woman struggling with Catholic guilt when she viewed *The Exorcist*. Her borderline personality structure split off a part of herself that she considered evil. Demonic possession in the film symbolized this "evil part" as well as her anxiety about her unborn child.[42]

*Effects on Fear and Imagination*

Fear and anxiety are common emotions when viewing films, and they are central to the enjoyment of horror films and thrillers.[43] However, sometimes fear is an aftereffect that lives on when the movie is over. The psychiatric disturbances already discussed are extreme, but in a milder form this phenomenon is common. Whenever I ask my students if they have seen a movie that severely scared them, most report at least one, citing horror movies like

*Saw, Final Destination,* and *The Exorcist,* or reality-based war films like *Hotel Rwanda* or *Saving Private Ryan.* This finding is confirmed in formal surveys.[44] Typical reactions include difficulty sleeping or intrusive memories of disturbing scenes. Some of these emotional reactions were of short duration, but many people have reported such fright reactions lasting over a year.[45] Most reactions were not treated, but retrospective surveys suggest that the symptoms reported by a fourth of the participants appeared to be clinically significant stress reactions.[46]

Strong fright reactions in children have been frequently documented.[47] The most common is sleep disturbance, but other studies suggest that children avoid activities that they associate with a scary scene from a movie. For example, children who witnessed a house fire on *Little House on the Prairie* were less interested in learning how to build a fire in a fireplace than children who had not witnessed the scene.[48]

The reason why children have greater fear reactions relates to their level of cognitive ability and developing sense of self. Children sometimes react fearfully to stimuli that adults would not find scary. Younger children are particularly influenced by vivid perceptual factors that override the subtleties of context and narrative. In one study, children were very frightened by television show *The Incredible Hulk,* despite the fact that the Hulk typically acted in beneficial ways. Older children did not find the character scary, but younger children reacted to the Hulk's bright green skin, oversized musculature, and angry facial expression to such a degree that nothing else mattered.[49] Perceptual concreteness can also explain why children do not fear other subjects, such as the made-for-TV movie, *The Day After,* about a nuclear attack on America. While the film was disturbing to adolescents who comprehended the significance of nuclear devastation, younger children lacked any concrete images to associate with fear.[50]

One reason why children are so vulnerable to strong emotional effects is that their imaginations are active and malleable. Visual images from the media leave a strong impression and take on lives of their own. This process, which can be both good and bad, has received considerable research attention.[51] On one hand, children often integrate the characters and storylines they have been exposed to in movies such as *Toy Story* and use them in their imaginative play, telling additional stories and deepening characterizations. At the same time, children who are exposed to high levels of visual images on television and in the movies, often are less imaginative and display a diminished capacity to role play. They appear to become reliant on external media as sources of stimulation and are less able to access their own imagination.[52]

## *Effects on Attitudes, Beliefs and Stereotypes*

Adults may not be as impressionable as children, but research has demonstrated that media affects how viewers categorize, understand, and evaluate their world. These critical cognitive processes touch nearly every aspect of life. Gender socialization, the process by which people learn what a society expects from boys and girls, is a central concern of social psychology, and many scholars believe media plays a fundamental role. If media depictions of male and female characters are skewed in a particular direction, viewers' self-concepts and vision of the future will be similarly affected. A young girl may have difficulty imagining herself a lawyer unless she sees female lawyers on television and in movies.

Survey and experimental research have identified a relationship between media consumption and sex-role stereotyping in how visual narratives get mixed up with the real world. At the same time, most studies have found that the relationship was relatively weak.[53] This is not surprising if we consider that other factors (biological, environmental) factors may also play a role. Thus, movies appear to be part of a cultural web of influences which reveal themselves not so much as solid patterns but rather as the shadow of such patterns.

The documentary *Killing Us Softly* and its sequels highlight media depictions of women's bodies in a psychologically and physically unhealthy way. While the majority of examples were from advertising, images of excessively thin film actresses (Keira Knightly, Gwyneth Paltrow, Angelina Jolie) are readily available. The documentary contends that women and men are constantly bombarded by images of women whose body shapes are unhealthy, not to mention unattainable by the majority of the female population. Such unrealistic images can damage the psyches of women and men alike, but adolescent girls are thought to be a particularly vulnerable population. Survey and experimental research into the influence of media on negative behaviors and attitudes (increased personal body dissatisfaction, a distorted image of beauty ideals and unhealthy eating habits) supports the contention of *Killing Us Softly*. Since most of these studies looked at the impact of media exposure in general, the problem appears to be broader than watching too much *Project Runway*.[54]

Concerns about racial stereotyping based on fictional characters predates effect research. Mark Twain's *The Adventures of Huckleberry Finn* has always been a source of controversy. When readers praise the book for its progressive view on race relations, they focus on the escaped slave Jim's courageousness and wisdom. Whenever the book is criticized as racist, the focus is often on Jim's childishness and buffoonery. This debate is grounded in the belief that reading the book will strengthen pejorative stereotypes of African-Americans.

This debate continues today. There was considerable controversy about the contemptible hyenas (voiced by Whoopi Goldberg) in the animated movie *The Lion King* which exhibited urban black dialects. Other movies are praised when they run counter to stereotype (a homeless man played by Will Smith becomes a successful stockbroker in *The Pursuit of Happyness*). Studies support the possibility that media contributes to stereotyping both positively and negatively. When white college students watched a lot of TV news disproportionately presenting African-Americans as criminals, they tended to underestimate the education level and socioeconomic status of African-Americans and attribute these conditions to a lack of motivation. However, when students watched more sitcoms, a genre in which African-Americans are represented relatively positively and proportionally,[55] they gave higher estimates of the educational achievement of African-Americans.[56] (Studies with younger children have also demonstrated that exposure to visual media have an impact on racial stereotyping.)[57]

A variation on the concern that media causes particular thoughts and emotions is that media also has the power to diminish emotional response. For example, if people are exposed to excessive violence, they may become numb and stop feeling distress. This effect has been demonstrated on men who were exposed to a series of slasher films that paired sex and violence. When these men were subsequently asked to witness a videotape of a rape trial, they not only expressed feeling less upset than men who had not seen the slasher films, they were also less empathetic with the victim in the trial.[58] Findings such as these raise concerns that people are becoming desensitized to violence and will therefore be less likely to try to prevent it in the real world.

## Propaganda and Effects on Culture

Propaganda is designed to cause large numbers of people to think in a particular way. There have been many overlaps between propaganda and narrative film history. *Battleship Potemkin* is considered one of the greatest movies ever made, particularly in its use of montage (editing). It is also a propaganda film intended to celebrate the mutiny aboard the *Potemkin* as a critical event in the Russian Revolution. An infamous example of film propaganda is the technically brilliant *Triumph of the Will*. Directed by Leni

Riefenstahl, the documentary commemorates the 1934 Nuremberg rally coalescing Nazi power, and is a stunning glorification of Nazi ideals of order, authority, and power. Hollywood filmmakers also engaged in propaganda efforts during World War II.[59] Frank Capra made the influential series *Why We Fight* (1942–45). John Ford became head of the photography unit for the Navy. Even Hitchcock was commissioned by the British Ministry of Information to make short films in support of the French Resistance.

Because propaganda is intended to have a diffuse impact, its effects are hard to measure. These films are usually created under dire circumstances, in which the emphasis is on action, not analysis. Whether *Triumph of the Will* had its desired effect cannot be known, but it certainly generated admiration and discussion and is forever connected with Nazism. Even movies not considered propaganda can become connected to particular ideas. Was *Casablanca* propaganda for American involvement in World War II? Is *Avatar* an argument in favor of the environmental movement? Perhaps all films are propaganda in that they are having a broad and cumulative effect on the way people think about the world? This process has been called the cultivation effect of media.[60]

Many of the discrete effects we have considered can be imagined for the entire culture, creating a variety of nightmare scenarios: desensitization becomes zombification by technology—mindless viewers plugged into visual media that keep them passively entertained, falsely informed, and disconnected from real human intimacy (essentially the plot of *The Matrix*). Variations include concerns that the media makes people stupid, self-indulgent, narcissistic, flabby, and/or weak—a society of couch potatoes.

The assumption behind such fears is that the media affect not only our thoughts and behaviors but an entire way of understanding the world. This brand of cultural critique can be traced to Marshall MacLuhan and his famous phrase, "The medium is the message"[61]—essentially, that the forms of media upon which a culture relies are more important than its content. Our thinking adjusts to new forms of technology as they are introduced. When we watch movies, we are more affected by the fact that it *is* a movie than by its genre (whether it is a comedy or a drama) or its overall quality (whether it is a good movie or a bad movie). The more movies we see, the more we begin to see the world like a movie.

In his book *Amusing Ourselves to Death,* Neil Postman observed that in the modern age, public discourse (the way information is communicated) must look and sound good on camera.[62] Politicians, newscasters, preachers, healers, teachers, and so on must filter everything they say through the lens of what it will look and sound like. Along the way, the message can be altered, beautified, or even fabricated in order to give it the right visual appearance.

The medium is determining what the message will be. The standards of entertainment, including those refined by Hollywood over many decades, are now applied to news or political rhetoric. Postman worried that the ultimate impact of this "dumbing-down" of information could spell the death of Western culture.[63]

## Closing Shots: The Great Debate over Media Effects

Media effects research is not an example of a value-neutral pursuit of understanding. The media are often perceived as a public health threat, particularly to children, and are grouped with such medical and social dangers as cancer, crime, and racism.[64] A noticeable aura of anxiety hangs over the field. Even though the Bobo doll study was central to the development of social learning theory and therefore more concerned with psychological theory than most studies in this area, Bandura chose to introduce it with the report of a teenage boy injured while emulating the knife fight in *Rebel Without a Cause*.[65] Recognizing the real-world implications of his theory, Bandura used the incident as a provocative rhetorical device to capture the reader's attention.

Many researchers believe that social scientific study of the effects of media can help mitigate its potential damage, and they take the role of concerned activists as they comment and advise on policy issues such as film ratings, the television V-chip, and government policy.[66] Social scientists rarely advocate for censorship, but there is an emphasis on promoting "media literacy" (learning how to critically evaluate media) and on educating and supporting parents in their quest to protect their children. For example, Joanne Cantor's *Mommy I'm Scared: How TV and Movies Frighten Children and What We Can Do To Protect Them* (1998) applies the research on the effect of frightening images on children to develop a guidebook for parents.

Effects researchers feel confident in their advice because they believe the evidence is overwhelming that the media does indeed affect individuals and society:

> This [overview] is based on the assumption that the mass media *do* [italics in original] have effects ... it is clear that mass communication is an agent or catalyst to a variety of shifts and changes in people and institutions.[67]

> The research results reveal a dominant and consistent pattern in favor of the notion that exposure to violent media imagine *does* [italics in original] increase the risk of aggressive behavior.[68]

> The results from [this] research ... *should* [italics added] lead objective sci-
> entists to conclude that exposure to media violence increases a child's risk for
> behaving aggressively in both the short run and the long run.[69]

But, despite an appeal to consensus, other scholars don't accept this basic
premise:

> Many people are convinced that media violence is harmful ... There is a
> considerable amount of research on the topic, and contrary to these claims,
> the results of the research generally do not demonstrate that exposure to
> media violence causes aggression.[70]
>
> While certain groups of researchers (primarily in the social sciences) con-
> tinue to assert that violence in media is bad, firm conclusions about why it is
> bad have failed to materialize.[71]

The debate among scholars is characterized by opposite conclusions,
and the rhetoric sometimes gets nasty. One article by a prominent effects
researcher characterized critics as "glib," asserted that they argued with an
attitude of "careful inattention and misrepresentation," and accused them
of being in "denial."[72] Critics of effects researchers responded with rancor
of their own, representing the entire movement as overly zealous, and
characterizing one researcher "as the enforcer on the violence/aggression
causality hockey team."[73] Clearly, the media effects debate is not for the
faint of heart.

Why is this debate so heated? Partly because the media plays such a
significant role in the lives of most people. If media cause negative impacts,
these should be addressed. Some effects researchers take it as a responsibility
to help address social concerns. Critics, however, are wary about limits
placed on information, images, and ideas in a free society. To the extent
that there is a tension between the desire to improve social conditions
and the caution against premature, ineffective solutions with unintended
consequences, it is a healthy debate.

The debate is complicated by disciplinary differences however. Effects
researchers are generally psychologists and social scientists with strong
methodological preferences for carefully constructed surveys and experimental methods. They are concerned about the intellectual pitfalls of broad
cultural analysis, or over-interpreting unique events. While a football coach
might believe that showing his players *The Fast and The Furious* was a good
way to let off steam after a practice, a social scientist would have important
questions: How does the coach know that the players were calmer after the

movie? Couldn't the players have calmed down if they just sat around for a couple of hours? Is it possible the players only seemed calm but were ready to go and race cars afterward?

Insights about the impact of cinema from outside the social sciences are sometimes dismissed as anecdotal. Even rigorous textual and qualitative studies are not integrated into research conclusions or policy recommendations. On the other side, the critics of effects research, often from the humanities, are skeptical of the scientific study of people, particularly artistic experience. They value techniques like textual analyses and case studies because of attention to details, complexities, variations and contexts. In contrast, laboratory experiments are seen as an unnatural attempt to force broad generalizations about media reception when the experience is complicated by personal, cultural and aesthetic factors. Critics sometimes move too quickly from qualifying the interpretation of a particular study to dismissing the study entirely.[74]

Communication (including mass communication) is an interdisciplinary field that manifests this tension. While it shares a social science dimension with psychology and a rhetorical dimension with literary studies, these alternative perspectives often seem to be in opposition rather than complementing each other.[75] Because effects researchers and their critics do not hear each other well, they get stuck in a never-ending cycle of overstatement and misinterpretation. For example, effects researchers have set themselves up for a backlash with some unjustifiable rhetorical flourishes. One researcher claimed that if TV had never been invented, there would be 10 000 fewer murders every year.[76] By arguing that the television industry instigates mass murder, the standard of proof for judging social scientific research shifts. In light of incendiary claims, studies which would otherwise be simply seen as incomplete pieces of a larger puzzle are now judged as woefully inadequate.

On the other side, there is overstatement as well. For example, the title of the book *The Myth of Media Violence* by art scholar David Trend might lead to the conclusion that he believes that concerns about the impact of media violence are a myth (a falsehood). However, Trend states the following: "My research over the past decade has convinced me that violent media do plenty of harm."[77] Instead of denying the effect of media violence, he claims to bring balance and context to the debate. Unfortunately, the subtleties of his argument may be undermined by the book's polarizing title. The heightened rhetoric provokes both sides to come out with their guns blazing and minds closed. The resulting disconnect is unfortunate for students and the public.

There is, however, a middle ground. Effects research provides a focused snapshot of discrete elements to a complex problem. I believe that there is strong evidence that media do sometimes have an effect on audiences. Movies are not inert; they play a contributing role in some of the behavior and thoughts of many people. However, several qualifications of this claim can be highlighted:

*Media effects are not overwhelmingly large.* When research results are statistically aggregated across individual studies, the measured effect (whatever it may be) is quite small. There is no evidence that large numbers of people are radically transformed by exposure to media, especially in the short term. This lack of dramatic effect is typical of the social sciences. When the degree of media effect is compared to such interventions as reading instruction, psychotherapy, and psychotropic medications, media effects are found to be comparable. [78] Therefore, while effect sizes are not dramatic, such research should not be dismissed.

*Media do not affect everyone the same way.* There are always individual differences; that is why statistics are necessary in the social sciences. The results of an experiment in which everyone responded the same way would be convincing (as they are in physics), but they never happen in the social sciences because people are the most oppositional of scientific subjects. The fact that effects studies always report general trends is relevant but not definitive.

*Media exposure never causes anything by itself.* All behaviors are over-determined (caused by more than one factor). A well-designed experiment may succeed in temporarily isolating an important influence, but additional factors are always present that could be revealed by other well-designed experiments.

I also believe that the critics of effects research have an excellent point. Movies are artistic creations. They vary along many different aesthetic criteria, and these criteria matter in how people receive them. As complicated symbolic objects, movies are open to an enormous variety of meanings by the billions of people who watch them. Scientific research will never be able to conclusively define and weigh all of the possible influences on all possible people.

One of the biggest limitations of effects research is that, as a rule, it tends to downplay essential aesthetic and narrative variations. All movies are treated as essentially the same, or are differentiated along gross criteria: Does it contain violence? Does it contain sex? Does it contain sex and violence?

When I was an undergraduate, I remembering reading a study where one of the experimental conditions was referred to as "R-rated sex comedies" and included *Fast Times at Ridgemont High*, *H.O.T.S.*, and other films from the early 1980s.[79] As a teenager when these movies were released, I had seen several of them, including *H.O.T.S.* (at a drive-in theater I infiltrated by hiding in the trunk of a car—the movie still wasn't worth the price of admission).[80] The idea that *H.O.T.S.* was placed in the same category as *Fast Times*, a well-constructed cultural satire made by respectable filmmakers,[81] struck me as ridiculous. Its similarity was superficial, based on featuring horny teenagers. It made me wonder if researchers ever really watched the movies they were using.

Effects researchers sometimes lose aesthetic subtlety in statistical analysis and experimental design. Driven by social concern more than an appreciation of movies, they are better at imagining possible negative influences than positive ones. While one could stand in the checkout line at the grocery store and curse the invention of the printing press, we can step back and note the cultural advantages to the printed word that balance out whatever harm is being done by *The National Enquirer*. Technological innovation is always introduced with great hope and excitement, and while disillusionment is inevitable, most technologies retain the potential for good, including the movies.

## Further Reading

Bandura, A.; Ross, D., and Ross, S.A. (1963) Imitation of film-mediated aggressive models. *Journal of Abnormal and Social Psychology*, **66** (1), 3–11.

Bryant, J. and Oliver, M.B. (eds) (2009) *Media Effects: Advances in Theory and Research*, 3rd edn. Routledge, Taylor & Francis, New York, NY.

Grimes, T.; Anderson, J.A., and Bergen, L. (2008) *Media Violence and Aggression: Science and Ideology*. Sage, Thousand Oaks, CA.

Gunter, B. (2002) *Media Sex: What are the Issues?* Lawrence Erlbaum, Mahwah, NJ.

Postman, N. (1985) *Amusing Ourselves to Death: Public Discourse in the Age of Show Business*. Penguin Books, New York, NY.

Singer, D.G. and Singer, J.L. (2001) *Handbook of Children and the Media*. Sage, Thousand Oaks, CA.

Sparks, G.G. (2006) *Media Effects Research: A Basic Overview*, 3rd edn. Wadworth, Cengage Learning, Boston, MA.

# Movies as Equipment for Living—The Functions of Film

Illustration 9.1 Al Pacino as Sonny in *Dog Day Afternoon* (1975) © Photos 12/Alamy.

# Chapter 9

# Movies as Equipment for Living—The Functions of Film

*Dog Day Afternoon*, directed by Sidney Lumet and starring Al Pacino, was released in 1975, with supporting roles played by John Cazale, Charles Durning, and Chris Sarandon. Frank Pierson won the Oscar for Best Adapted Screenplay, and the film was nominated for five other Academy Awards including Best Picture. It was a critical and popular success and is now seen as a 1970s classic. It was also a watershed film in featuring a gay character played by a major star. Much of the dialogue was improvised, including Pacino's famous chant, "Attica! Attica!" The story, based on real events about a couple of robbers, Sonny (Pacino) and Sal (Cazale), who hold up New York City bank on a hot summer day only to find the money gone. When the building is surrounded by police, Sonny and Sal take hostages and tense negotiations ensue. It emerges that Sonny attempted the robbery to pay for his lover's sex change operation. When Sonny requests a getaway car to take them to the airport, Sal is shot and killed by a police officer, and Sonny is arrested.

For writer Patrick Horrigan, the movie was more than an interesting plot, a critically acclaimed Oscar winner, or a biting cultural commentary.[1] Patrick was 15 when he saw the film in 1979. He was from a large Catholic family in suburban Pennsylvania, and at the time he watched it on TV, he

*Psychology at the Movies*, First Edition. Skip Dine Young
© 2012 John Wiley & Sons, Ltd. Published 2012 by John Wiley & Sons, Ltd.

was struggling with his own sexual orientation. He was particularly struck by the film's portrayal of New York City, a place he found gritty yet inviting and pulsing with life.

Horrigan was attracted by the Pacino character at the same time he identified with his dilemma. He found the authorities well-meaning, but paternalistic and ineffectual in finding a resolution to the dire circumstances in which Sonny was trapped. Patrick interpreted the scenes in which Sonny is coaxed to *come out* of the bank building as a metaphor for the complexities of coming out as a homosexual. Even his mother's pleas for Sonny to leave the building could have had deadly consequences. Since Patrick was aware of the dangers associated with coming out as a gay teenager, such scenes evoked a great deal of turmoil. Patrick was particularly moved by the intimate phone conversation between Sonny and Leon. While that scene has been subsequently criticized because the use of the phone prevented the filmmakers from visually depicting any physical contact, the opportunity for Patrick to witness emotional intimacy between two men was more important than physical intimacy.

*Dog Day Afternoon* became part of Patrick's inner life. Prior to the film, he had engaged in a series of elaborate daydreams in which he was a famous actor and director. He integrated these fantasies into the movies he saw. He imagined writing a quasi-sequel to *Dog Day Afternoon* in which he played the part of Sonny's younger partner. His experience of the film and his elaborations ended up having a profound effect on him: "The real possibility of a gay identity and a loving relationship with another man, glimpsed in the film's portrayal of the hero's relationship to his boyfriend, first entered and altered my mind."[2]

Sometimes people know that a movie is having an impact on them. They feel the film enter them, and are aware of the role it plays in their thinking and their actions. This is one of the powers of a symbolic form like film. In these situations, symbols are not just stand-ins for abstract concepts like love and oppression. Sometimes symbols really matter to how people live their lives.[3]

This chapter picks up where the previous chapter on media effects leaves off. Both deal with how watching movies filters into our lives, but with one a major difference: "effects" (impacts, influences) happen *to* people. When we say that a movie had an impact on us, we are treating the film as the active agent. Sometimes however, we self-consciously use a film for our own purposes. We apply the film to our lives, and it serves a particular function. In this scenario, we are the agents and movies are the tools.

## Professional Functions of Movies

If we wish to influence people, film is one way to accomplish that goal. Used properly as communication tools, films can educate people on a wide range of subjects—oral hygiene, history, politics, coping with grief, and so on. The latent power of visual images can be harnessed and molded with any educational, therapeutic or moral goal in mind.

### The Use of Movies in Education

The melodramatic and/or fantastic content of mainstream films do not match the standard picture of disciplined learning. Movies may appear much too fun to impart anything of value. The apparent ease with which people process visual images could discourage careful analysis promoted by reading and traditional teaching methods. Despite these concerns, many educators are energized by the accessible qualities of motion pictures. While higher education favors the written word, movies have become widely accepted as auxiliary teaching methods on a remarkable variety of topics.

Visual images for film, television, and computers are created explicitly for the educational market and there is substantial literature on the effectiveness of these methods.[4] Even theatrical films are found to have educational value, particularly their potential for teaching values, virtues, and morals to children and adolescents. My childhood education provides a good case study. I was part of the first generation of viewers for PBS's *Sesame Street*. I can't say I definitively learned my ABCs from a television show, but I am quite sure that the depiction of communal harmony left a strong impression on me. In elementary school, we were occasionally shown short films with prosocial messages. One film in particular, *Paddle-to-the-Sea*, in which a carved wooden boat with an Indian is released into a small stream and eventually to the sea, resonated in my memory. I believe the film helped me identify with the interconnected natural systems and appreciate the importance of endurance and chance in the journeys of life.[5]

Educators have sought to catalog films that, with the help of a skilled teacher, can be used to teach certain values.[6] *Bridge to Terabithia*, a live action Disney movie, features themes of friendship, death and bullying. A teacher might ask students about scenes in which the main character is taunted because of his poverty: How do you think it made Jess feel when the other kids laughed at him about his shoes? Why does it seem wrong to make fun of the fact that Jess is poor? How would you have reacted to the teasing if you were in Jess' position? This cinematic technique has an advantage over simply teaching moral propositions ("It's wrong to tease people") because the film heightens the emotional and empathetic experience.

For years, film's dubious intellectual standing made professors wary of using it as a teaching aid, but the progressive swing in the 1960s opened up a greater range of pedagogical methods. Professors started using movies to teach the classic liberal arts.[7] In the new millennium, entire textbooks devoted to narrative films exemplify important concepts for many disciplines including sociology,[8] political science[9] and environmental science.[10]

There is still concern that using movies for higher education is a cheap tactic, pandering to unengaged students to increase enrollment. My own Psychology of Film course is always overenrolled, to the envy of colleagues teaching Kant or Spanish Imperialism. I am quick to acknowledge its popularity derives largely from the word "film" in the title. Clearly students perceive that watching movies will only minimally interfere with the campus wiffle ball tournament and the other spring pursuits of young people. While I make sure to include rigorous reading and writing assignments to offset my colleagues' suspicions, I am not above exploiting the visceral appeal of film to draw students to the material, deepening the learning experience.

Movies can also be used as educational tools in applied arts like medicine. "Cinemeducation" describes the use of commercial films in medical education by demonstrating situations and raising questions about a variety of medical concerns.[11] While few movies would be helpful in studying the anatomy of the circulatory system, health treatment is more than anatomy, medicines and physical procedures. The practice of medicine involves psychological, interpersonal, and social dimensions that films depict well (or poorly, which can also be instructive):

> *The impact of chronic illness on a family*: Steel Magnolias shows the impact a young woman's terminal illness has on her mother and extended family.
>
> *Giving bad news*: The indelible scene in *Terms of Endearment* in which a physician is uncomfortable conveying a patient's poor prognosis contrasts with ideal doctor-patient communication.
>
> *Pediatric illness*: Lorenzo's Oil features a husband and wife struggling to combat their son's chronic illness. The impact on the spousal relationship is highlighted as well as the mother's attempts to explore all possible treatments.

Despite distortions in depicting counseling and mental illness on film, some films have been embraced by psychotherapists as a means of teaching psychology. Several books use movies to instruct students about personality theory[12] and psychopathology,[13] and workshops are available for helping therapists refine their skills using movies.[14] Film is utilized for its vividness, but it is also encourages identification, decreasing the stigma of mental illness among medical students[15] and increasing empathy for patients.[16]

## *The Use of Movies in Psychotherapy*

Cinematherapy is the use of movies as tools in psychotherapy.[17] Since movies allow viewers to make metaphorical connections between the content of the film and the real world, a skilled therapist can help clients make these connections to solve problems and facilitate therapeutic progress.[18] Cinematherapy should be thought of a *technique* for therapy, not a unique type of therapy. While any therapist who uses film must assume the symbolic potential of film, there are many possible directions in which to proceed. One therapist may use movies as a means of helping clients understand troubling thought patterns (cognitive-behavioral therapy). Another might use movies to facilitate their clients' understanding of their values and aspirations (humanistic therapy). Yet another therapist could use film to assist clients in understanding their inner conflicts (psychodynamic therapy).

*Nightmare on Elm Street* was used by a therapist in his work with a hospitalized adolescent boy, "C."[19] C. was initially hospitalized for substance abuse, oppositionality, poor school performance, and an incident in which he destroyed his guardian's home. Abandoned by his mother at the age of nine, he had a difficult relationship with his strict uncle. The boy was a fan of slasher films, which were banned as his problems escalated. After a period of isolation in the hospital, his therapist made a connection with him by talking about his favorite horror movies, something he was emotionally invested in.

The therapist made an agreement with C. to watch segments of *Nightmare on Elm Street IV: The Dream Master* during their sessions and then discuss them. This coviewing improved the therapeutic relationship between therapist and patient, increasing C's trust, and allowed the therapist to carefully observe C's reactions. C. revealed that while he admired the power of Freddy Krueger, he also identified with his helpless teenage victims. He associated Freddy with authoritarian adults, particularly his uncle. The therapist helped C. identify his fear of abuse and abandonment as the source of his anger. Family therapy applied this insight, helping C. communicate his pain (not just his anger) to his guardians. This facilitated C.'s discharge and successful reintegration into family life.

In another variation, therapists match an appropriate film with the client's situation (problem type, age, gender, culture, etc.). After the client watches it, the film is discussed. Sometimes therapists rely on clients making their own connections, but in other situations, clients are oriented to the purpose of the video and may even reflect on particular questions.[20] *Searching for Bobby Fischer* is used for working on parent-child issues. The young chess prodigy (Max Pomeranc) is pushed by his father (Joe Mantegna) and coach (Ben Kingsley) to abandon his kindheartedness in order to develop an aggressive attitude about winning. Eventually the father realizes he is hurting his child. The film can help parents realize how they project their own aspirations onto their children and warns of the danger of this kind of vicarious gratification. This insight can help parents nurture their children's talents while at the same time balancing the other needs of childhood. (A list of psychological issues connected to particular films is offered in Appendix IV.)

The use of movies in psychotherapy has the advantage of having a therapist present. Recent research suggests that the most important predictor of progress in psychotherapy is the strength of the interpersonal relationship between client and therapist.[21] Still, movies offer important therapeutic qualities: they are both emotionally engaging and highly metaphorical. Because of this, psychologists and other writers assume value in movie-inspired self-reflection even when it is not led or shared with a therapist; their self-help books assert that reflecting on movies can lead to richer, healthier or more virtuous lives.

Jones' *Killing Monsters: Why Children Need Fantasy, Super-Heroes, and Make-Believe Violence* makes the case for why fantastical and violent images can help stimulate the imagination and facilitate a healthy sense of self through identification with powerful figures.[22] Other books argue that movies can facilitate communication between parents and children on all topics including divorce, drugs, death, and even paranormal activity.[23] Solomon's *Reel Therapy: How Movies Inspire You to Overcome Life's Problems* (2001) reviews several hundred films for their capacity to address a host of different life situations. Grace's *Reel Fulfillment* takes a similar path, except that the author arranges her movie suggestions within the context of a step-by-step plan for life improvement.[24]

The movie book most grounded in established psychological perspectives is Niemiec and Wedding's *Positive Psychology at the Movies: Using Film to Build Virtues and Character Strengths*.[25] Positive psychology claims that throughout its history, psychology has focused on what is wrong with people—psychopathology, social atrocities, cognitive errors—rather than offering a vision of optimal human functioning.[26] In contrast, twenty-four character strengths are associated with six core virtues. Systematic analyses are used to argue that that these strengths have been associated with human excellence throughout human history.[27]

*Positive Psychology at the Movies* identifies the presence of these characteristics in various films and creates a compendium. For example, creativity is associated with *Life is Beautiful* where Guido (Roberto Benigni) creates an imaginative world for his son confined in a concentration camp, the most soul-deadening of situations. Vitality is exemplified in *Cool Hand Luke* in the form of Luke (Paul Newman), who cannot repress his individuality even if it means death. *It's a Wonderful Life* captures the importance of gratitude when George (Jimmy Stewart) learns the true importance of his life after contemplating suicide. These and other films are presented as works of art that have the potential for improving human life.

## General Functions of Movies in Everyday Life

Research on uses and gratifications is a social science approach to studying how the media fulfills the needs and desires of its audience.[28] Gratification was reflected in the film preferences and enjoyment of film discussed in Chapters 5 and 7. But beyond enjoyment, do movies serve any other functions in people's lives? How do people "use" the movies they watch?

Uses and gratifications complement effects research; both fields seek to identify the practical consequences of media, with several important differences. Fundamentally, the guiding question of the uses and gratifications approach has been what people do with the media (as opposed to what the media do to people). Such researchers believe that viewers have a basic system of motivations, emotions, and cognitions, and that media provide an avenue to meeting these motivations. They also believe people are sufficiently self-aware to access their motivations and their media experience. And, in contrast to the social activism of effects research, this approach resists judgments about whether these uses of media are good or bad.[29]

The uses and gratifications approach identifies different types of function that films and other media fulfill. While distinguishable, they overlap considerably. A film may be useful for one person, and not another; one film might have many uses for different people. One viewer might get more than one need met by the same film, while another uses a particular film one way and a different film another.

One of the functions of film is *entertainment*, although this category is often used as a kind of black hole when other functions cannot be articulated. To refer to a movie as "just entertainment" implies that it does nothing else. Similarly vague descriptions of film functions include "leisure" or "killing time." Questions about why something is entertaining or a preferred form of leisure hang in the background. While entertainment is closely related to pleasure, media enjoyment is a complex phenomena that requires deeper exploration.[30]

Another use of film is *adjusting emotions*. People frequently use films to relax/alleviate anxiety, and comedies are a favorite genre. It is evident that people often use action adventure movies for an emotional kick when they are bored and seeking excitement. These functions are complementary processes referred to as "mood management": using media to achieve an optimal level of arousal (either to get higher or to come down),[31] a use of media that parallels how drugs and alcohol are used.

Movies and other media can be used for *social purposes*. Going to the movies is a social activity that can be relatively unrelated to the cinematic content. Some people look at a Cineplex marquee with *The Hangover, Part II*, Terrence Malick's *The Tree of Life*, or Woody Allen's *Midnight in Paris* and declare they don't care which movie they go to see. Content is not so much a motivator as an excuse for getting out: meeting a friend or date, driving to the theater, sitting next to each other, talking about the movie afterwards, and so on.

Movies also serve a social purpose even when people are alone, providing a feeling of human contact that can *mitigate loneliness*. Since films are created by people, they are in themselves a form of communication.[32] This communication may be indirect and one-sided, but is still a way to symbolically connect with other people through engagement in a universal story and identification with characters. While TV is most commonly used in this manner, home video and movie theater attendance can play a similar role.[33]

Mass media also allow people to *share information*. Primarily these are the functions of news and telephone communication, but it can also apply to forms of entertainment. Janice Radway's study revealed that a common reason for reading romance novels was "to learn about faraway places and times"[34] even though education is not what most people typically associate with these books. Education is not the primary reason that people go to a Cineplex either, yet, since film vividly depicts places and activities to which most people aren't otherwise exposed, instruction serves a secondary function. People can learn about African genocide from *Hotel Rwanda,* British history from *The King's Speech,* or schizophrenia from *A Beautiful Mind.* Experts in particular areas may be concerned about the inaccuracies of cinematic portrayals[35] but the realistic appearance of movie images creates strong impressions for people who would not know about them any other way.

Movies are commonly used as a means of *escape.* This function is so pervasive that it is sometimes manipulated in advertising and reviews—"Movie X is a great way to set your troubles aside." This is a robust function because there are so many way of escaping.[36] Seeking to escape one's current emotional state is another way of talking about mood management. Other times, viewers might seek to escape routine and do something different (one reasons why movie theaters still hold a special appeal for many viewers). Finally, some viewers use movies to escape from themselves.[37] Rather than being bored or anxious, for such viewers movies provide an alternate reality superior to own current lifestyle. This alternative form of escape is exaggerated in films such as *Spider-Man, Lord of the Rings,* and *Sex in the City.*

Another function of movies is *self-development.* Although it may appear to be the opposite of escapism, the two are related. Though self-escape allows people to avoid the reality of their daily lives, sometimes the experience of escape can offer a glimpse of other ways of being, serving as a catalyst for reflection on their own lives. Making meaning through movies is not only a form of pleasure, [38] it can make self-improvement possible.

Like effects researchers, uses and gratifications researchers prefer experimental and survey methodologies that provide a broad picture of film functions across the population. These methods are not designed to confront the symbolism of particular movies and the interpretive processes of particular individuals. A function like self-development, which is different for everybody, opens up subtler dimensions when individualized methods of data gathering are employed.

## Personal Functions of Movies in Everyday Life

In his influential essay "Literature as Equipment for Living," Kenneth Burke points out that the metaphorical use of words can affect human action, as in the proverbs "A rolling stone gathers no moss" or "The higher the ape goes, the more he shows his tale." They serve as instructions on how to react to a particular life event. For Burke, the proverb is the most concise form of literature. Shakespeare's plays also influence our behavior, although in a more complicated and open-ended manner. For Burke, it is the critic's job to tease out the various categories through which literature can be used:

> They [the categories] would consider the works of art, I think, as strategies for selecting enemies and allies, for socializing losses, for warding off the evil eye, for purification, propitiation, and desanctification, consolation and vengeance, admonition and exhortation, implicit commands or instructions of one sort or another. Art forms like "tragedy" or "comedy" or "satire" would be treated as *equipments for living*.[39]

Burke contrasts this approach to literature with the attitude that literature exists in a pure aesthetic realm untouched by the outside world. From his perspective, literature is alive in how it intermixes with the lives of readers. Literature is not the only art that has this living quality. Any symbolic medium has the power to affect life.[40] To borrow Burke's phrase, movies as equipment for living describes what happens when viewers self-consciously apply the meanings they find in movies to their own lived experience.[41]

Narrative films use symbols to tell stories about events that are linked in time and space, and audiences must understand and interpret these symbols.[42] Making sense of the world through the stories we tell is a major component of the way the mind works.[43] Dan McAdams argues that not only do we use narratives forms to understand fiction, we use narratives to understand ourselves.[44] The reason people are always telling stories to each other (in the form of conversations, novels, plays, and movies) is because we are always telling stories to ourselves. Our "selves" are nothing but a collection of stories. The insights we glean from the books of neurologist Oliver Sacks (*The Man Who Mistook His Wife for a Hat* and *The Mind's Eye*) don't come from a technical analysis of neuroanatomy, but from his ability to capture his patients' stories. In these stories, he captures subjective experience and readers are able to empathize.

When we talk about using literature or movies as equipment for living, we are using a narrative art form to understand our own narratives. Fictional stories become part of our life stories. Fiction is a symbolic *simulation* of experience. Anything that can be experienced in life can be expressed by artists in a compressed form as fictional narratives. Stories are laboratories that provide lifelike situations in which audiences can test possible reactions.[45] By engaging with these stories, we learn a great deal about many aspects of the social world, including extraordinary circumstances that we would never directly experience. These narrative simulations symbolically prepare us for future challenges, as well as help us understand situations from the past. Because engaging with stories often has an emotional component and involves identification and empathy, it can increase our capacity to empathize with real-life "characters": other people.

Every fictional medium has advantages and disadvantages in the way it can be used as our equipment of living. Written stories require intellectual energy because there is a perceptual difference between the medium (ink marks) and the world of the story. In contrast, movies are pictures allowing for a relatively easy entree into the fictional world.[46] This ease sometimes encourages viewers to escape, and discourages them from doing the difficult reflective work of comparing the fictional world to the real one. When viewers are able to achieve reflective distance from a film, however, the fact that the cinematic simulations are so vivid and lifelike can make the experience particularly fruitful, since the viewer *feels* like he or she has "been there and done that."

Equipments for living can be identified through textual analysis, just like other approaches of spectatorship. For example, haunted house films (*The Shining*, *The Amityville Horror* and more recently, *Paranormal Activity*) can be analyzed for how they establish apocalyptic scenarios that mirror modern anxieties yet offer viewers examples of means of copying.[47] However, looking directly at first person viewer accounts allows for the exploration of individual differences and can provide more vital examples.[48] Many personally meaningful film experiences have been published (such as Horrigan's response to *Dog Day Afternoon*), and I will refer to some of these as examples. In addition, I will utilize unpublished interviews (each 45–90 minutes long) in which I asked 50 participants, "Thinking back on your life, has there been a movie that was personally significant to you? What was the movie, and why was it important?" I gave participants at least a day to reflect on these questions. The resulting interviews produced rich and moving stories about the power of movies to touch lives.

### *"The Movie I Will Never Forget": Autobiographical Functions*

Memory has received a great deal of attention in psychology. While much of this has been concerned with recalling numbers, word lists, and factual information, an offshoot has focused on autobiographical memory (the recollection of personal experience).[49] Results have consistently demonstrated that our memory of life events is subject to many inaccuracies, but some scholars have argued that autobiographical memories are not just an issue of accuracy—rather, memories of past experience may be incorrect with regard to the objective details, yet still capture the emotional and interpersonal essence of the events experienced. These kinds of memory often take a narrative form.[50]

In this way, movies can become a vivid part of one's personal memory system. This is not the case for all films, of course. Some movies leave no memory trace. A few years or even months after viewing them, people cannot recall details of the plot or characters (and sometimes forget having seen the movie at all). Still, scattered among the forgotten movies, a few stand out. Some of these vivid memories may even be traumatic,[51] but other may be transcendent.

The people I interviewed about meaningful movies conjured up powerful memories of movies, particularly early ones. One respondent recalled that his earliest memory was seeing *The Wizard of Oz* on television. Another remembered movies like *The Golden Voyage of Sinbad*, and that the film merged with his memories of playacting the characters in the film, to the point that he couldn't remember which was which. Movie memories mixed with other memories can also be seen in the recollections of the participant who associated *White Christmas* with holiday events such as wrapping presents and decorating the tree.

Not all memories were wholesome. Another respondent remembered sneaking into movie theaters with his hoodlum friends to see movies condemned by the Catholic Church (*Town Without Pity*). Since movies are often viewed with other people, some recollections are shared. One interviewee talked about reconnecting with a former girlfriend and renting *Tromeo & Juliet*, a violent, satiric punk version of *Romeo & Juliet* they had watched as teenagers. Seeing the film again led the couple to other reminiscences and helped them view their relationship more positively.

Like all autobiographical memories, cinematic memories can be inaccurate. A psychoanalyst vividly remembered *Three Came Home*, a 1950 film about a Japanese prison camp he had seen when he was young. When he watched the film again 40 years later, he was surprised by important elements he had forgotten, most notably, the fact that the film featured a young boy around the age he'd been when he first saw the film. In fact, numerous scenes seemed to echo his own life (the boy's fondness for monkeys and his mother being pregnant). As a psychoanalyst, he concluded that forgetting about the boy character was a defense against the anxiety of the storyline, but might also have been a result of oedipal guilt at enjoying scenes in which male prisoners, including the boy's father, were segregated by the Japanese guards, leaving the women and children alone.[52]

## "The Movie That Defines Me": Identity Functions

Autobiographical memories are the stories that make up our identity, our personal sense of who we are. For developmental psychologists like Dan McAdams, the study of narrative is essentially the study of identity. It is almost impossible to think of ourselves or describe ourselves without using stories. If a person describes herself as courageous, such a claim may be followed up by the question, "In what ways?" To answer that, she relates the time she stood up to bullies or saved her family from a house fire (like the Meryl Streep character does in Albert Brooks's poignant *Defending Your Life*).

Stories—and identities—take many forms. Some people see themselves as helpers, and their stories are about the times they helped people. Other stories are about people seeing themselves as fighters or lovers. McAdams believes that all these types are variations of the fundamental dimensions of self-concept—the agentic dimension (how we conceive ourselves as individuals with the power to leave our mark on the world) and the communal dimension (the way we see ourselves connected to the people around us).[53] All of our stories express our uniqueness or our relationships to other people (or sometimes both).

When we watch a movie, we temporarily identify with many or even all of the characters. We may identify with the tone or style of the film. Most experiences, like memories, are fleeting. Every once in a while, we come upon a film where our identification is so strong that we become aware of it, and will continue to identify with an aspect of the film (or at least our memories of the film) long after it is over. At this point, movie memories will become a part of our personal identity. It's what people mean when they say a movie truly defines who they are or some period of their lives.

As we have seen in Chapter 2, one can apply many psychological interpretations to a movie like *The Wizard of Oz*. But, although the interpretations imply something about the viewer, they are abstractions. On a more personal level, novelist Terry McMillan asserts that the film was important to her during her childhood. While she was aware of the contrast between her own life as an African-American growing up in an industrial town in Michigan compared with a white girl on a farm in Kansas, these differences weren't as important as the things to which she *could* relate: Aunt Em's bossiness, which reminded her of her mother; Dorothy's feelings that nobody really cared about her; the trip to Oz, reflecting McMillan's fantasies about escaping her drab circumstances for a world that was colorful and exciting.

Ultimately, the part of McMillan that craved adventure and delighted in the imagination would inspire her to become a novelist as an adult.[54]

One of my interviewees related how a film can define a whole era in a person's life.[55] In his mid-thirties Ethan[56] described the impact that *Animal House* had on him. He and his college fraternity emulated the wild partying, anti-authority antics of Bluto (John Belushi) and the rest of the animals. They frequently got in trouble with the administration, and evoked disparaging parallels between Dean Wormer (John Vernon) and the actual dean of students at their college. While Ethan and his friends were aware of the connections they were making, they probably didn't reflect deeply on it at the time. However, as Ethan matured, he came to regard his former self in a highly critical manner. Now, whenever he watches the film, he remembers his previous identification with the film, even as he is offended by it.

Another participant, Judy, a married mother of two in her early forties, spoke of how *To Kill a Mockingbird,* particularly Atticus Finch (Gregory Peck), defined her complex relationship with her father. The movie first became significant when she was eight, and watched it with her dad. The bond was solidified when her father began to call her Scout after the daughter in the movie. When Judy was a teenager, her father died in a fishing accident. She began to see the similarities between Atticus and her father, a respected doctor who frequently treated the poor without payment. In contrast with Atticus, however, Judy realized her father had "a major flaw": he was "not willing to sacrifice his drinking for the safety and love of his children." At the time of his death, their close relationship was already becoming distant due to his alcoholism. Judy experienced a difficult adolescence after her father died, followed by "a string of really bad trying-to-save-my-father boyfriends" in her early adulthood. While *To Kill a Mockingbird* had always been important because of the role it played in her early relationship with her father, she didn't become aware of the complex feelings she had about Atticus (or her father) until after she married and entered therapy.

Identity formation is particularly visible in the phenomenon known as "fandom."[57] Fans form an intense attachment with some aspect of popular culture, such as a movie (*Gone with the Wind*), genre (horror or sci-fi films) or director (Quentin Tarantino). Fans typically share their interests through clubs, conferences, chat rooms, and so on. This communal spirit can have a major impact on identity. The arena of action moves away from private reflection to interpersonal dialogue and elaborate social exchanges.

The cult popularity of *The Rocky Horror Picture Show* in the 1970s and 1980s exemplifies this social side of identity development. It is difficult to imagine anyone who unwittingly stumbled on this rather disjointed movie finding it profoundly meaningful. However, in a midnight show, surrounded by fellow fans wearing elaborate costumes and engaging in animated rituals, the film becomes a spectacular exercise in community building.[58] The entirety of this social experience affects aspects of identity related to peer bonding, self-expression, struggles with sexual identity and the exploration of non-mainstream values.

### "The Movie That Changed My Life": Transformative Functions

Stories have always been used by parents, clergy, and dramatists as informal forms of therapy, but therapists have develop forms of narrative therapy in which counselors help clients to revise the stories they tell about their lives.[59] Narrative film facilitates this revisioning process through not only cinematherapy, but the personal insights we gain from everyday viewing. More than just healing (which implies a wound that needs to be mended), the notion of transformation suggests that movies can be used to facilitate our ongoing development as human beings.[60]

Judy's affinity for *To Kill a Mockingbird* is an example of the transformative use of film. She not only used the film to understand her past, but she now sees it as echoing her present life with her children. In particular, she sees Atticus as a model for parenting:

> I certainly am parenting very differently than my parents parented me, with the idea to teach tolerance and to teach respect and self respect and all the things that I feel like are in that character, and to stand up for what you think is right in the world. To be fair.

While rarely conscious of the movie in day-to-day life, she becomes aware of those connections in moments of reflection. The movie underscores realities of her life, but also offers possibilities for what her life and her children's can become.

Sometimes transformation occurs over a period of many years and viewing multiple films. This complicated process can be seen in Norman Holland's memoir *Meeting Movies*, in which he reflects on movies that have been important to him (2006). One theme that runs throughout is his love of literature and stories. This passion became a source of conflict, when Holland struggled over whether to become a writer or a critic. His ambivalence manifested itself with John Huston's biopic *Freud*. When Holland approaches the film as a scholar, he found he could flex his analytical muscle, and his psychoanalytic training gave him a deep understanding of the film's subject. Yet, when Holland tried to come to terms with the creator of the film, he felt threatened by Huston's larger-than-life persona and ability to create masterpieces like *The Maltese Falcon*. Comparing Huston's seemingly boundless energy to his own sense of repression and stalled efforts to become a writer forced Holland to realize that no matter what strengths or flaws he might find in *Freud*, his own work as a scholar was overshadowed by Huston's brilliance as a director.

Holland's take on *Children of Paradise* emphasizes this theme. He sees Baptiste's (Jean Louis Barrault) early infatuation with Garance (Arletty) as an example of how the romantic ambitions of youth are dimmed by the realities of adulthood. While he successfully rebelled against his father's wish that he become a lawyer, he never became the great artist that he imagined he would be. In contrast, his reaction of *Shakespeare in Love* reflects his coming to terms with this conflict. While he always loved Shakespeare's work, Holland confessed that he had been envious of Shakespeare's apparently limitless talent. By the time *Shakespeare in Love* was released, Holland was late in his career. He found the film to be a delightful fantasy that celebrated young Will's artistic and sexual triumphs and found he could enjoy the film without guilt or longing. This experience helped him finally accept his place in the world.

## Closing Shots: Seeing Movies from a Different Angle

Movies as equipment for living grew out of many of the approaches discussed in this book, yet it involves looking at movies from a different position. The process of interpretation in numerous guises is not an end in itself but a crucial symbolic mechanism by which movies may become functional. Before someone can consciously act on a message, they have to understand the message. As viewers reflect further, they can begin to consider how the meaning of a film is related to the meaning of their lives.

The richer one's interpretive capacity, the wider the range of significance that film and other art forms can have. In a study I conducted, some participants were asked to interpret a film they had just seen, others were asked to describe the film's plot, and still others were asked to reflect on an event from their day unrelated to the film.[61] Following this reflection, all of the participants were asked to imagine what applications the film might have in the future. The most personal ideas came from those who had been encouraged to interpret the film's meaning.

Using movies as equipment for living assumes the ability to put a psychological distance between oneself and the film. Therefore, this process is not the same as "merging" with a film, in which viewers believe they are living in a movie (or that the movie is living in them). While such blending may often occur in the immediate experience of watching a movie, it typically dissipates once people leave the theater. People who continue to confuse the real and the cinematic suffer from cognitive immaturity or even psychosis (perhaps resulting in some of the copycat behaviors discussed in the previous chapter). Instead, movies as equipment for living implies that viewers know who they are and what is happening on the screen, and have the wisdom to tell the difference.

Self-reflection is required in order to use movies as equipment for living. It is therefore difficult to observe in a strictly controlled laboratory setting. Narrative, qualitative, and journalistic methods such as case studies, interviews, personal testimonials, and even textual analysis can be provide avenues for studying the phenomenon, but it can be difficult to prove that a movie changed someone's life. This approach places a premium on human experience: how people perceive, feel, and understand the events that happen to them. While mercurial, these processes are the materials of self-awareness. Scholars, teachers and therapists who are exploring the possibility of self-consciously using film in professional and daily life tend to be excited about movies and are hopeful that films may be beneficial to the never-ending goal of human beings to understand ourselves.

# Further Reading

Burke, K. (1973) *The Philosophy of Literary Form: Studies in Symbolic Action.* University of California Press, Berkeley, CA.

Dine Young, S. (2000) Movies as equipment for living: A developmental analysis of the importance of film in everyday life. *Critical Studies in Media Communication,* **17** (4), 447–468.

Hesley, J.W. and Hesley, J.G. (2001) *Rent Two Films and Let's Talk About It in the Morning: Using Popular Movies in Psychotherapy,* 2nd edn.. John Wiley & Sons, Inc., Sommerset, NJ.

Mar, R.A. and Oatley, K. (2008) The function of fiction is the abstraction and simulation of social experience. *Perspectives on Psychological Science,* **3** (3), 173–192.

McAdams, D.P. (1993) *The Stories We Live By: Personal Myths and the Making of the Self.* Guilford Press, New York, NY.

Niemiec, R.M. and Wedding, D. (2008) *Positive Psychology at the Movies: Using Films to Build Virtues and Character Strengths.* Hogrefe & Huber, Cambridge, MA.

Rubin, A.M. (2009) Uses-and-gratifications perspective on media effects, in *Media Effects: Advances in Theory and Research*, 3rd edn. (eds J. Bryant and M.B. Oliver), Routledge, Taylor & Francis, New York, NY, pp. 165–184.

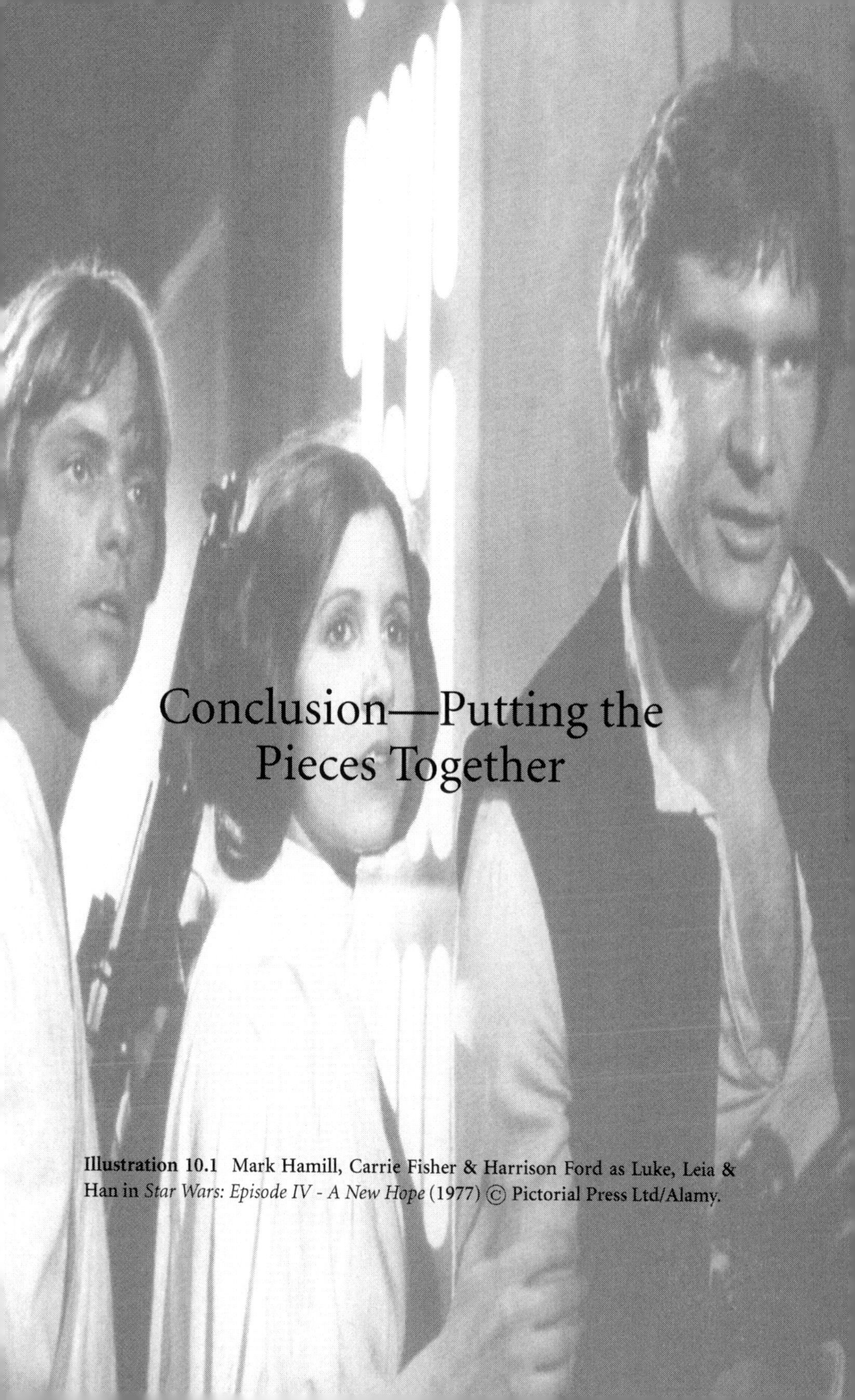

# Conclusion—Putting the Pieces Together

Illustration 10.1  Mark Hamill, Carrie Fisher & Harrison Ford as Luke, Leia & Han in *Star Wars: Episode IV - A New Hope* (1977) © Pictorial Press Ltd/Alamy.

# Chapter 10

# Conclusion—Putting the Pieces Together

The summer of 1977 was a time of transition. I was 10 years old, sandwiched between childhood and adolescence, that period captured in *Stand By Me*. Since the age of five, I had lived in Stuttgart, Germany on a small American military post, but my dad, an Army major, was being transferred back to the US.

Although I had few conscious memories of America, for me and my friends it was a promised land. Anything touched by America's glow took on irrational value; a bag of Pixie Sticks candy sent by grandparents could be sold for 50 cents apiece or bartered for all manner of contraband.

Now I was going back to this mythical place, and despite my excitement, the impending move was scary. The army post had been an idyllic place to grow up. Kids were free to roam in packs throughout the post on one side of the gates and endless woods on the other. I felt sad and scared to leave.

A few weeks before we were to move, I was watching the only English-language television station available and saw a story about a movie that was causing a sensation in the States. There were genuine Americans, in a real American city, lining up for blocks to buy a ticket. I watched a film clip where an oddly shaped spaceship narrowly escaped some exotic planet. There were laser guns, bad guys wearing white body armor, a giant hairy ape, and a man in a black vest who was clearly the coolest human being who

*Psychology at the Movies*, First Edition. Skip Dine Young
© 2012 John Wiley & Sons, Ltd. Published 2012 by John Wiley & Sons, Ltd.

**Illustration 10.2**   Alec Guinness & George Lucas on the set of *Star Wars: Episode IV - A New Hope* (1977) © AF Archive/Alamy.

**Illustration 10.3**   Skip Young, *Star Wars* fan, age 10.

had ever lived in any galaxy. I was mesmerized. The thought that I would be able to see this movie in a few weeks, instead of having to wait a year before it got to the always behind the times post theater was exhilarating.

As I said goodbye to my friends and the only home I knew, my excitement about seeing *Star Wars* soothed my anxiety and focused my attention. Once the move to Colorado Springs was over and the boxes unpacked, one of the first things my family did was take a trip to a sparkling new mall that had a movie theater right inside. Though *Star Wars* had been out for months, we still waited in line for an hour as my anticipation built.

Finally it was time. As the opening titles scrolled up the screen, John Williams's score awoke something in my soul. The space battles were strikingly realistic. The characters were compelling, new yet familiar. Exotic creatures popped up faster than I could process. Glimpses of Darth Vader, masked and towering, were terrifying yet thrilling. Occasionally, at just the right moment, tension was followed by comic relief, and the audience would explode with laughter (Han Solo after shooting Greedo: "Sorry about the mess"). In the end, the characters did what they should, with Luke believing in the Force and Han finding redemption. *Star Wars* captured my imagination like nothing else I had ever seen.

The movie became my transition object, helping me connect to my new home. Many of my activities were filtered through it. Before its first theatrical run was over, I'd nagged my mom into taking me four more times (an unimaginable indulgence). I bought the magazines, the bubblegum cards, and the action figures. These objects formed a shared playing field for making new friends.

Looking back, it seems like no accident that *Star Wars* consumed those of us on the cusp of adolescence, as dawning self-consciousness was turning internal lives of loosely related episodes into something interconnected and epic. It was the first time I remember contemplating good and evil, vowing to do what's right. In Sunday school, as the teacher was talking about the Holy Spirit, I had what felt like a profound theological revelation: it dawned on me that he was in fact talking about The Force. Films I would later see, like *The Hustler*, *The Grand Illusion*, and *The Last Temptation of Christ*, would offer more complicated takes on morality and spirituality, but it was *Star Wars* that first called my attention to such matters.

Many of the characters were important to me, but I remember being particularly challenged by Princess Leia. She was attractive in an odd way (those buns!), yet so different from the other action movie babes (like the Bond girls) who had been fueling my preadolescent hormones. Leia did not act the way she was supposed to. I found myself identifying with her to a certain extent—it made sense she would rather pick up a blaster and do something with her life instead of waiting around for male characters to act. I have to believe that when I was first exposed to the basic tenets of feminism, they made a lot more sense because of Leia.

The unconscious impact may even have been greater. In a class I co-taught, I was lecturing about Princess Leia as a "quasi-feminist icon." My colleague smiled and added, "Well, of course you think Leia is an interesting character—you married her." Though I was momentarily stunned, when I quickly did the comparison between Leia and my wife, it was clear that he was right.

Not all my memories of *Star Wars* are positive. At the height of my fanaticism, I got the flu and had a high fever. I had a dream in which I was at the bottom of a reverse gravity tube. I knew if I jumped up into the tube I would "fall" upward and crash into the ceiling that had the *Star Wars* logo on it. A friend was trying to stop me, but I insisted on jumping anyway. I woke up sweating, screaming and disoriented. Apparently the images of the film had entered my psyche in ways that were not entirely uplifting.

George Lucas became an important figure for me. I don't think I'd ever really thought about the "author" of anything prior to that. Movies, books and music presented themselves in their pure form, and I either liked them or didn't. But after reading some articles, I realized that this Lucas guy was responsible for creating a world I loved. He soon became something of a mythical figure. Like Obi-Wan, he had chosen to share his wisdom with ordinary mortals. It made me giddy to think that *Star Wars* was one small part of a nine-story series he would slowly reveal.[1] This promise meant a continuing flow of wonder that would sustain me for the rest of my life. As time went on, of course, Lucas became less superhuman, but he has remained an interesting figure as an artist, entrepreneur and corporate leader attempting to balance family values, personal disappointments, a media empire and the *Star Wars* legacy.

In part my passion for *Star Wars* has been sustained because I am not alone in my appreciation. My story is almost a cliché for members of Generation X. When I interviewed people about movies that had a significant impact on them, *Star Wars* came up more often than any other film (for both men and women). In part this shared experience can be explained by the well-established themes Lucas used in the film. It did not emerge from a narrative and cinematic vacuum. The filmmakers were drawing upon techniques used in westerns, serialized cliff-hangers, and other action-adventure movies. What was innovative about the movie (its state-of-the-art special effects, funny robots, "space opera," etc.) wasn't as crucial as the themes that had been working in Hollywood and on the human imagination since well before my time.

Yet *Star Wars* was also very much of its time. When it was released in the late 1970s, it sent a ripple through the culture, soothing an American spirit troubled by the post-Vietnam era. *Star Wars* signaled (caused?) a trend in which mainstream American entertainment became increasingly escapist and divorced from reality. It also set the standard for movie merchandise. Action figures, trading cards and emblems slapped on T-shirts were ways that my friends and I tried to invoke the film's mythic qualities in our everyday lives. The success of that endeavor obviously inspired the partnership between film and merchandizing that is so pervasive today.

Through the years, my *Star Wars* obsession cooled to an enduring appreciation. Images continue to resonate—Luke looking out at twin setting suns; the fateful light-saber confrontation between Darth Vader and Obi-Wan; Leia in a white dress wielding a blaster; and so on. As I enter middle age, it is clear that ideas about goodness, divine intervention, men and women, and many other things have become intertwined with my own personality, values, and background. In a real sense, *Star Wars* is part of who I am.

## An Appeal for Interdisciplinarity

I have chosen to include this personal reflection on *Star Wars* because it contains elements of all the chapters of *Psychology at the Movies*. There are examples of the interpretations presented in Chapters 2—*Star Wars* as the triumph of good over evil or a salve for the cultural wounds of Vietnam. And while there are no mental health professionals in the faraway galaxy, how far is Obi-Wan's guidance of Luke from the caring counselors discussed in Chapter 3? Lucas's personal values speaks to the overlap between artists and their art (Chapter 4), while the success of *Star Wars*, both in terms of box-office and public acclaim, is an intriguing phenomenon related to audience preferences (Chapter 5). Chapter 6 explores the narrative and emotional aspect of movies, something I experienced acutely when I first saw the film in the theater. I have continued to reevaluate and reflect on *Star Wars* over the years (Chapter 7), which has ultimately had a significant impact on my life and played a role in my personal development (Chapters 8 and 9).

Figure 10.1[2] captures all these important symbolic dimensions.

All of these dimensions are important, and they all interconnect. While the methods of particular disciplines tend to focus on one element at a

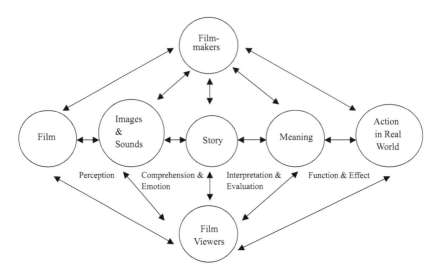

**Figure 10.1** Symbolic activity in film (expanded).

time, I hope that the interdisciplinary approach I have used in this book demonstrates the ways these pieces weave together.[3]

> *Viewers interact with films.* Even though I think *Star Wars* is a great movie, I am aware that there are people who don't relate to it at all. Some movies speak to us at different points in life while others do not. I saw *The Goodbye Girl* not long after I saw *Star Wars*, but I don't remember anything about the film.[4] It just didn't have what it takes to inspire a 10 year-old boy.
>
> *Filmmakers interact with their films.* They write dialogue, they act, and they point the camera; it all adds up to a movie. Not just any filmmaker could have made *Star Wars*. It required George Lucas and his personal preoccupations (not to mention Harrison Ford's surliness to embody Han; James Earl Jones's authority to give voice to Vader; and the special effects team's obsessiveness to make a model of the Death Star seem the size of a moon).
>
> *Viewers interact with filmmakers.* The screening of a film is the place where the filmmakers and the audience meet—not face-to-face, but symbolically. This indirect relationship is nevertheless a powerful one. I idolized Lucas, a man I had never met. Some fans would later express rage at him when he made changes to the movie franchise they loved. Lucas himself seems to have become ambivalent toward his audience:

appreciative of the adoration, yet defensive toward those who would tell him what to do.

The different levels of psychological processing in the center of Figure 10.1 interact with each other. *Star Wars'* theme of the superiority of intuition over rationality has been and encouragement for me to trust my gut. I see this theme manifested in the scene where Luke destroys the Death Star. Before I can make this interpretation though, I have to comprehend what is going on technically in the scene (certain camera shots are meant to simulate Luke's subjective viewpoint, and the voice about "trusting the force" does not from someone sitting behind Luke but is an internalization of Obi-Wan's voice). And of course I have to be able to see what's on the screen.[5]

All the pieces and processes fit together. The more this overlap is recognized (e.g., the more experimentalists pay attention to aesthetics, and the more critics consider the actual experience of audience members), the richer any study of psychology and film will be.

## Movies as Art

Along with the advantage of looking at the psychology of movies from multiple perspectives, my other take home message is that movies are powerful. They should be treated carefully, but their positive potential should be embraced. I want to create a frame for a psychological approach to film that helps readers not only understand films but embrace them.

We have seen that academic psychology has often focused on how to respond to the dangers of visual media.[6] Encouraging media literacy (teaching skills on how to critically interpret and filter messages) is one of the most common reactions to these dangers and it is a compelling idea. However, sometimes it is used in a way that assumes movies are inherently toxic and that the only reason to properly read a film is to dilute its negative potency.

At other times, the motivation for media literacy goes beyond mitigating negative effects. The argument for written literacy focuses on the benefits to citizens of a democratic society (reading traffic signs, understanding laws, participating in elections, and so on). The same argument is applied to visual media that blend words, sounds and images. Media literacy advocates believe that a medium like film is a tool that modern society uses to communicate and organize itself, and that to function efficiently and productively, people should know how to accurately interpret media.

There is still something missing in this outlook. By considering the intertwined symbolic qualities of movies, filmmakers, and viewers, we can conceive of movies as more than hazards and more than cultural documents we need to be able to understand. After all, the written word allows people to do more than copy recipes and read owner's manuals; it gives us the ability to create epics, novels, and poetry. Films educate and entertain, but they are also forms of visual, narrative poetry. They can be disturbing and beautiful, and they have the capacity to enlighten and inspire. Like all art, movies can be dangerous, but they are also a gift—a dangerous gift that is potentially destructive and potentially elevating.

# Appendix A

# Mental Health Professionals in Top Box Office Grossing Movies, 1990–1999

| Title | Character |
|---|---|
| *Ace Ventura: Pet Detective* | Dr Handley |
| *Analyze This* | Dr Ben Sobel, Jr. |
| *Analyze This* | Dr Sobel, Sr. |
| *Armageddon* | Psychologist |
| *As Good As It Gets* | Dr Green |
| *Awakenings* | Dr Malcolm Sayer |
| *Awakenings* | Dr Copeland |
| *Awakenings* | Nurse Costello |
| *Awakenings* | Dr Peter Ingham |
| *Awakenings* | Anthony |
| *Awakenings* | Hospital Director |
| *Basic Instinct* | Dr Elizabeth Garner |
| *Basic Instinct* | Dr Lamott |
| *Basic Instinct* | Dr Myron |
| *Basic Instinct* | Dr McElwain |
| *Batman Forever* | Dr Chase Meridian |
| *Batman Forever* | Dr Burton |
| *Casper* | Dr James Harvey |
| *Conspiracy Theory* | Dr Jonas |
| *Die Hard with a Vengeance* | Dr Fred Shiller |
| *Dr. Doolittle* | Dr Blayne |
| *First Wives Club* | Dr Leslie Rosen |

*(Continued)*

*Psychology at the Movies*, First Edition. Skip Dine Young
© 2012 John Wiley & Sons, Ltd. Published 2012 by John Wiley & Sons, Ltd.

| Title | Character |
| --- | --- |
| *Fried Green Tomatoes* | Group Therapist |
| *Fried Green Tomatoes* | Assertiveness Trainer |
| *The General's Daughter* | Elisabeth Campbell |
| *The General's Daughter* | Sarah Sunhill |
| *The General's Daughter* | Dr Slezinger |
| *The General's Daughter* | Dr Robert Moore |
| *Goldeneye* | Psychologist |
| *Good Will Hunting* | Dr Sean Maguire |
| *Good Will Hunting* | Hypnotist |
| *Good Will Hunting* | Dr Henry |
| *Groundhog Day* | Psychologist |
| *Hot Shots* | Dr Ramada Thompson |
| *Lethal Weapon 3* | Dr Stephanie Wood |
| *Lethal Weapon 4* | Dr Stephanie Wood |
| *Mrs. Doubtfire* | Ms Selner |
| *Nine Months* | Samuel Faulkner |
| *Phenomenon* | Dr Nierdorf |
| *The Santa Clause* | Dr Neil Miller |
| *The Silence of the Lambs* | Dr Hannibal Lecter |
| *The Silence of the Lambs* | Dr Frederick Chilton |
| *The Silence of the Lambs* | Clarice Starling |
| *The Silence of the Lambs* | Jack Crawford |
| *The Sixth Sense* | Dr Malcolm Crowe |
| *The Sixth Sense* | Dr Hill |
| *Sleepless in Seattle* | Dr Marsha Fieldstone |
| *Space Jam* | Doc |
| *Star Trek: Generations* | Deanna Troi |
| *Terminator 2* | Dr Silverman |
| *Terminator 2* | Douglas |
| *A Time to Kill* | Dr Willard Bass |
| *A Time to Kill* | Dr Rodeheaver |
| *There's Something About Mary* | Therapist |
| *Twister* | Dr Melissa Reeves |
| *What About Bob?* | Dr Leo Marvin |
| *What About Bob?* | Dr Carswill |
| *What About Bob?* | Dr Tomsky |

Note: These films were each among the top 20 box office grossing films for the year of its theatrical release.

* *The Prince of Tides* (1991) was a highly successful film with a mental health professional, Dr Susan Lowenstein, as a main character. It was not included in this list because it was one of those rare movies that made a significant portion of its box-office gross in two different years and subsequently did not appear in the Top 20 in either year. It therefore fell through the cracks of the sampling method, even though it is clearly related to the other films on the list.

Adapted from Dine Young, S., Boester, A., Whitt, M.T., and Stevens, M. (2008). Character motivation in the representations of mental health professionals in popular film. *Mass Communication and Society*, 11(1), 82–99.

# Appendix B

# Three Top 50 Lists
# of Acclaimed Movies

| Top Box Office Films*<br>(Adjusted for Inflation) | AFI's Greatest American<br>Films** | IMBD.com Users Top Rated<br>Films*** |
|---|---|---|
| 1. Gone With the Wind (1939) | 1. Citizen Kane (1941) | 1. The Shawshank Redemption (1994) |
| 2. Star Wars: Episode IV-A New Hope (1977) | 2. The Godfather (1972) | 2. The Godfather (1972) |
| 3. The Sound of Music (1965) | 3. Casablanca (1942) | 3. The Godfather: Part II (1974) |
| 4. E.T. The Extra-Terrestrial (1982) | 4. Raging Bull (1980) | 4. The Good, the Bad and the Ugly (1966) |
| 5. The Ten Commandments (1956) | 5. Singin' in the Rain (1952) | 5. Pulp Fiction (1994) |
| 6. Titanic (1997) | 6. Gone with the Wind (1939) | 6. Schindler's List (1993) |
| 7. Jaws (1975) | 7. Lawrence of Arabia (1962) | 7. 12 Angry Men (1957) |
| 8. Doctor Zhivago (1965) | 8. Schindler's List (1993) | 8. Inception (2010) |
| 9. The Exorcist (1973) | 9. Vertigo (1958) | 9. One Flew Over the Cuckoo's Nest (1975) |
| 10. Snow White and the Seven Dwarfs (1937) | 10. The Wizard of Oz (1939) | 10. The Dark Knight (2008) |
| 11. 101 Dalmatians (1961) | 11. City Lights (1931) | 11. Star Wars: Episode V-The Empire Strikes Back (1980) |

*(Continued)*

*Psychology at the Movies*, First Edition. Skip Dine Young
© 2012 John Wiley & Sons, Ltd. Published 2012 by John Wiley & Sons, Ltd.

| Top Box Office Films*<br>(Adjusted for Inflation) | AFI's Greatest American Films** | IMBD.com Users Top Rated Films*** |
|---|---|---|
| 12. Star Wars: Episode V – The Empire Strikes Back (1980) | 12. The Searchers (1956)<br>13. Star Wars (1977) | 12. The Lord of the Rings: The Return of the King (2003) |
| 13. Ben-Hur (1959) | 14. Psycho (1960) | 13. Seven Samurai (1954) |
| 14. Avatar (2009) | 15. 2001: A Space Odyssey (1968) | 14. Fight Club (1999) |
| 15. Star Wars: Episode VI-Return of the Jedi (1983) | 16. Sunset Blvd. (1950) | 15. Goodfellas (1990) |
| | 17. The Graduate (1967) | 16. Star Wars: Episode IV-A New Hope (1977) |
| 16. The Sting (1973) | 18. The General (1927) | 17. Casablanca (1942) |
| 17. Raiders of the Lost Ark (1981) | 19. On the Waterfront (1954) | 18. City of God (2002) |
| 18. Jurassic Park (1993) | 20. It's a Wonderful Life (1946) | 19. The Lord of the Rings: The Fellowship of the Ring (2001) |
| 19. The Graduate (1967) | 21. Chinatown (1974) | |
| 20. Star Wars: Episode I-The Phantom Menace (1999) | 22. Some Like It Hot (1959) | 20. Once Upon a Time in the West (1969) |
| | 23. The Grapes of Wrath (1940) | 21. Rear Window (1954) |
| 21. Fantasia (1940) | 24. E.T. The Extra-Terrestrial (1982) | 22. Raiders of the Lost Ark (1981) |
| 22. The Godfather (1972) | | 23. The Matrix (1999) |
| 23. Forrest Gump (1994) | 25. To Kill a Mockingbird (1962) | 24. Psycho (1960) |
| 24. Mary Poppins (1964) | | 25. The Usual Suspects (1995) |
| 25. The Lion King (1994) | 26. Mr. Smith Goes to Washington (1939) | |
| 26. Grease (1978) | 27. High Noon (1952) | 26. The Silence of the Lambs (1991) |
| 27. Thunderball (1965) | 28. All About Eve (1950) | 27. Se7en (1995) |
| 28. The Dark Knight (2008) | 29. Double Indemnity (1944) | 28. It's a Wonderful Life (1946) |
| 29. The Jungle Book (1967) | 30. Apocalypse (1979) | 29. Memento (2000) |
| 30. Sleeping Beauty (1959) | 31. The Maltese Falcon (1941) | 30. The Lord of the Rings: The Two Towers (2002) |
| 31. Shrek 2 (2004) | 32. The Godfather Part II (1974) | |
| 32. Ghostbusters (1984) | | 31. Sunset Blvd. (1950) |
| 33. Butch Cassidy and the Sundance Kid (1969) | 33. One Flew Over the Cuckoo's Nest (1975) | 32. Toy Story 3 (2010) |
| 34. Love Story (1970) | 34. Snow White and the Seven Dwarfs (1937) | 33. Forrest Gump (1994) |
| 35. Spider-Man (2002) | | 34. Leon: The Professional (1994) |
| 36. Independence Day (1996) | 35. Annie Hall (1977) | 35. Dr. Strangelove or: How I Learned to Stop Worrying and Love the Bomb (1964) |
| 37. Home Alone (1990) | 36. The Bridge on the River Kwai (1957) | |
| | 37. The Best Years of Our Lives (1946) | 36. Apocalypse Now (1979) |
| | | 37. Citizen Kane (1941) |

*(Continued)*

| Top Box Office Films* (Adjusted for Inflation) | AFI's Greatest American Films** | IMBD.com Users Top Rated Films*** |
|---|---|---|
| 38. Pinocchio (1940) | 38. The Treasure of the Sierra Madre (1948) | 38. American History X (1998) |
| 39. Cleopatra (1963) | | 39. North by Northwest (1959) |
| 40. Beverly Hills Cop (1984) | 39. Dr. Strangelove (1964) | |
| 41. Goldfinger (1964) | 40. The Sound of Music (1965) | 40. American Beauty (1999) |
| 42. Airport (1970) | | 41. Taxi Driver (1976) |
| 43. American Graffiti (1973) | 41. King Kong (1933) | 42. Terminator 2: Judgment Day (1991) |
| 44. The Robe (1953) | 42. Bonnie and Clyde (1967) | |
| 45. Pirates of the Caribbean: Dead Man's Chest (2006) | 43. Midnight Cowboy (1969) | 43. Saving Private Ryan (1998) |
| | 44. The Philadelphia Story (1940) | 44. Alien (1979) |
| 46. Around the World in 80 Days (1956) | | 45. Vertigo (1958) |
| | 45. Shane (1953) | 46. Amelie (2001) |
| 47. Bambi (1942) | 46. It Happened One Night (1934) | 47. Spirited Away (2001) |
| 48. Blazing Saddles (1974) | | 48. The Shining (1980) |
| 49. Batman (1989) | 47. A Streetcar Named Desire (1951) | 49. WALL-E (2008) |
| 50 The Bells of St. Mary's (1945) | 48. Rear Window (1954) | 50. Paths Glory (1957) |
| | 49. Intolerance (1916) | |
| | 50. The Lord of the Rings: The Fellowship of the Ring (2001) | |

* Retrieved from http://www.filmsite.org/boxoffice.html; April 13, 2011.
** Retrieved from http://www.afi.com/100years/movies10.aspx; April 13, 2011.
*** Retrieved from http://www.imdb.com/chart/top; April 13, 2011.

# Appendix C

# Emotionally Arousing Movie Scenes

| Emotion | Film | Scene |
|---------|------|-------|
| Amusement | *When Harry Met Sally* | Discussion of orgasm in café |
|  | *Robin Williams, Live* | Comedy routine |
|  | *Bill Crosby, Himself* | Comedy routine |
|  | *Whose Line is it Anyway?* | Helping hands comedy routine |
| Anger | *The Bodyguard* | Bully scene |
|  | *Cry Freedom* | Police abuse protesters |
| Disgust | *Pink Flamingos* | Person eats dog feces |
|  | *Amputation* [Non-feature Film] | Amputation of arm |
|  | *Foot Surgery* [Non-feature film] | Surgery on a foot |
| Fear | *The Shining* | Boy playing in a hallway |
|  | *Silence of the Lambs* | Basement chase scene |
| Neutral | *Abstract Shapes* [Non-feature Film] | ScreenPeace screen saver |
|  | *Alaska's Wild Denali* [Non-feature Film] | Summer in Denali |
| Sadness | *The Champ* | Boy with dying father |
|  | *The Lion King* | Cub with dead father |
|  | *Return to Me* | Dog and man after death of wife |
| Surprise | *Capricorn One* | Agents burst through door |
|  | *Sea of Love* | Man is scared by pigeon |

Adaptation of material from chapter "Emotion elicitation using film" by Rotternberg, Ray and Gross (pp. 9–28) in *Handbook of Emotion Elicitation and Assessment* edited by James Coan and John Allen (2007). (Reprinted by permission of Oxford University Press, Inc.)

# Appendix D

# Therapeutic Movies

| Therapeutic Issue | Examples |
| --- | --- |
| Abuse | *This Boy's Life* (1993) |
| Adolescence | *Breaking Away* (1979) |
| Adoption and Custody | *Losing Isaiah* (1995) |
| Aging | *Strangers in Good Company* (1990) |
| Chronic Illness | *Philadelphia* (1994) |
| Commitment | *High Fidelity* (2000) |
| Communication and Conflict Resolution | *The Story of Us* (1999) |
| Death and Dying | *My Life* (1993) |
| Divorce | *Kramer vs. Kramer* (1979) |
| Emotional Disorders | *Dead Poets Society* (1989) |
| Family-of-Origin Issues | *Like Water for Chocolate* (1993) |
| Support Systems | *Steel Magnolias* (1989) |
| Grief and Loss | *Ordinary People* (1980) |
| Inspiration | *The Shawshank Redemption* (1994) |
| Intimate Relationships | *About Last Night* (1986) |
| Marriage | *The Four Seasons* (1981) |

(*Continued*)

*Psychology at the Movies*, First Edition. Skip Dine Young
© 2012 John Wiley & Sons, Ltd. Published 2012 by John Wiley & Sons, Ltd.

| Therapeutic Issue | Examples |
| --- | --- |
| Women's Issues | *How to Make American Quilt* (1995) |
| Parent-Child Relationships | *Searching for Bobby Fischer* (1993) |
| Blended Families | *Fly Away Home* (1996) |
| Substance Abuse | *When a Man Loves a Woman* (1994) |
| Values and Ethics | *Shortcuts* (1993) |

Adapted from Hesley, J.W., & Hesley, J.G. (2001). *Rent Two Films and Let's Talk in the Morning: Using Popular Movies in Psychotherapy* (2nd ed.). New York: John Wiley & Sons. (Reprinted with permission of John Wiley & Sons, Inc.)

# Endnotes

## Chapter 1

1. Keyser (1992).
2. Diamond, Wrye and Sabbadini (2007) point out that when Freud published his first significant work, *Studies in Hysteria* in 1895 (co-authored with Josef Breuer), the Lumiere brothers were screening what is widely considered to be the first nonfiction film, *Workers Leaving the Lumiere Factory*. The scientific-minded American Psychological Association had been founded a few years earlier in 1892 (Wertheimer, 1987).
3. Freud's appearance at Clark left an aura that pervaded even the physical space. Many of us were convinced that the reason the university never remodeled the worn wooden staircase was because Freud had made the stairs sacred by setting foot on them.
4. Werner (1980).
5. Many of the professors at Clark at that time had been mentored by Werner, including Bernard Kaplan, Leonard Cirillo, Roger Bibace, Seymour Wapner, Robert Baker, and the neuropsychologist Edith Kaplan. Other Clark professors who influenced my thinking were socioculturalists James Wertsch and James Gee and narrativists Michael Bamberg and Nancy Budwig.
6. Kristen and Dine Young (2009).

*Psychology at the Movies*, First Edition. Skip Dine Young
© 2012 John Wiley & Sons, Ltd. Published 2012 by John Wiley & Sons, Ltd.

7. Amateur short films are becoming much more available, thanks to digital cameras and YouTube. Even as I write, my children are collaborating with neighborhood kids to make their own movie. Perhaps in another decade someone will write a book on *The Psychology of YouTube*.

8. Wade and Tavris (2005) define psychology as "the discipline concerned with behavior and mental processes and how they are affected by an organism's physical state, mental state and external environment" (p. 3).

9. Method has strong religious connotations, deriving from the Greek root *methodos*, meaning "the way." The derivation calls to mind Jesus' proclamation, "I am the way, the truth and the life" (John 14:6). Psychologists have been known to be *almost* as serious about their methods.

10. Interestingly, the only book on psychology and the movies as free-ranging as Gladwell's approach is Munsterberg's 1916 work which mixes history, technology, experimental psychology, textual interpretation, aesthetic philosophy and imaginative speculation.

11. Sternberg and Grigorenko (2001).

12. Another effective way of making this point is John Saxe's poem *The Blind Men and the Elephant* in which several blind men investigate an isolated body part (tusk, trunk, ear, etc.) of an elephant and come to erroneous conclusions about the nature of an elephant (concluding it is a spear, snake, fan, etc.). This poem is used by Tavris and Wade in their novel textbook, *Psychology in Perspective,* which introduces the field of psychology in a more cohesive manner.

13. The symbolic framework presented here is a simplification of the model presented by Werner and Kaplan (1984) in *Symbol Formation*. They draw their perspective, in part, from the symbolic philosophy of Ernst Cassirer (1955–1957) and the rhetorical method of Kenneth Burke (1973). Symbolization, as understood by Werner and Kaplan, is as amenable to literary interpretation as it is to experimentation.

14. Since most of the examples used in this book refer to how visual and linguistic symbols are embedded in *stories*, narrative theory (i.e., theories about how stories are constructed and how they are received by listeners/viewers) pops up with some regularity. This theme is central in Chapter 9 in which parallels are made between stories in movies and stories in identity construction (McAdams, 1993).

15. The fact that symbols have *more than one level of meaning* is taken by numerous writers, including Carl Jung (1964) and Paul Ricoeur (1970) in his study of Freud, as the defining aspect of symbolization.

16. Even if a small, independent film reaches "only" a few thousand viewers, it is still a significant social event, especially if a passionate "cult" audience becomes strongly attached to it.
17. These symbolic events are *psychological* both because interpretations comment on human nature (e.g., how people displace unacceptable tendencies like aggression on to acceptable actions such as heroism) and because the transformation between a symbolic object and its meaning requires thought (i.e., mental activity or cognitive processing).

## Chapter 2

1. Greenberg (1975).
2. Payne (1989b).
3. Hopcke (1989).
4. Indick (2004).
5. Murphy (1996).
6. The open-ended use of "text" as an underlying narrative runs counter to the everyday definition of text as something written (as in a "textbook"), but going with the convention in literary, film and rhetorical studies, I sometimes refer to films as "texts."
7. Kracauer (1960) and Bazin (1967) are commonly associated with championing film as an exercise in realism; this attitude found expression in Italian neo-realism (*Rome, Open City*) and cinema verité (*Don't Look Back*). Andrew (1976) asserts that realism ran counter to the earliest trends in film criticism that highlighted films for their dreamlike qualities exemplified by German expressionism (*The Cabinet of Dr. Caligari*) and surrealism (*Un Chien Andalou*). Many modern studies of film in both psychology (Packer, 2007) and philosophy (McGinn, 2005) continue to emphasize film as dream.
8. Bordwell (1989a) steps outside particular theoretical frameworks to cogently explicate the general process that all interpreters use to make meaning out of films.
9. The most prominent interpretive approaches in the early history of film are reviewed by Andrew (1976). Casetti (1999) continues the task of reviewing film theory through 1995.
10. There are many possibilities for types of behavior (e.g., farming, flying airplanes) and types of people (e.g., private detectives, butlers) that could receive attention from social scientists but have not. Psychotherapy and mental illness, however, have been the topics of so much special interest, I consider them in detail in Chapter 3.

11. How movies impact the attitudes of audiences is considered in more detail in Chapter 8.
12. Rendleman (2008).
13. See Krippendorff (2003) for an overview of content analysis methods.
14. The interpretations of clever critics are discussed later in this chapter. Such critics are typically unimpressed by content analyses since content analytic categories *have to be* stated in a way that *everybody* can understand. The joke goes that they need to be so obvious, they could be identified by trained monkeys (or graduate students, whichever are available). The virtues of critics—cleverness, subtlety, and originality—may become liabilities when it comes to content analyses.
15. It is not an accident that these topics correspond to the social concerns of recent decades. Despite occasional claims of neutrality, the social sciences do indeed swim in the cultural stream, either as reflections or agents of change. The topics that receive attention in this chapter have also been studied for their *effects* on audience members considered in Chapter 8.
16. Wilson *et al.* (2002).
17. *Mean Girls* is partly based on *Queen Bees and Wannabes*, Rosalind Wiseman's nonfiction self-help book about adolescent female cliques, which itself draws on research on relational aggression by developmental psychologists such as Nicki Crick (2002).
18. Coyne and Whitehead (2008).
19. Greenberg (1994).
20. See Gunter (2002) for review of research on sexual content in media.
21. Cowan *et al.* (1988).
22. An original content analysis by Molitor and Sapolsky (1993) was followed by a critique by Linz and Donnerstein (1994) and then a rebuttal by Molitor and Sapolsky (1994).
23. Welsh (2010).
24. See Sarafino (2008) for summary.
25. Glantz and Kacirk (2004).
26. Hazan, Lipton, and Glantz (1994).
27. Ricoeur (1974: pp. 12–13).
28. Ricoeur (1974: p. 99).
29. Examples of the numerous book-length studies that use traditional psychodynamic theory to analyze film include Greenberg (1975; 1993) and Indick (2004); many other interpretations have appeared in journals like *Psychoanalytic Review* and *The International Journal of Psychoanalysis*.

In addition, semiotic and post-modern variations of Freudian theory are discussed in the "Spectatorship" section of this chapter.

30. There are periodic attempts to declare Freudian theory dead. Literary critic Frederick Crews' (1995) sharp dismissal of the scientific validity of psychoanalysis was at the center of a 1990s debate known as the Freud Wars (see Forrester, 1998 for a defense of Freud). Despite such battles, Freudian theory continues to thrive in the humanities, and modern variations of psychoanalysis remain a powerful force in mental health treatment, with some psychologists and psychiatrists arguing that crucial elements of Freud's approach are validated by both research on effective psychotherapy (Shedler, 2010) and modern neuroscience (Schore, 2003).

31. See Hall's *A Primer of Freudian Psychology* (1999) as a classic summary of Freudian theory.

32. Freud (1960b: p. 58).

33. Psychodynamic is a broad term that covers Freud's original psychoanalysis and the many spin-off theories that came later.

34. Greenberg (1975).

35. Greenberg (1975: p. 14).

36. Cocks (1991).

37. When it comes to Stanley Kubrick, one can never be sure what was intended. One of my professors warned us never to underestimate Kubrick's attention to detail since the only thing more obsessively conceived than one of his films was big-time advertising.

38. Modern cognitive science has a mixed view of the psychoanalytic contention that people unconsciously perceive every aspect of their environment. On one hand, there is evidence that the mind is highly selective about what information it processes and remembers. At the same time, people do process and react to certain environmental stimuli which they cannot consciously identify, although there is no evidence that these "subliminal" stimuli are actually having an effect on behavior (see Chapter 8).

39. Hill (1992) and Iaccino (1998) provide traditional Jungian analyses of a range of movies while Singh (2009) explores "post-Jungian" approaches to film criticism.

40. The best summary of Jungian theory is the succinct overview he wrote just prior to his death, *Man and His Symbols* (1964).

41. Jung's theory has often been accused of being mystical. One of Jung's (1969: pp. 43–44) most compelling responses to this criticism is an analogy he makes to instincts. He points out that the existence of inborn

instincts—simple *patterns of behavior* that are not learned but crucial to survival (e.g., the rooting reflex in which newborns turn their heads and suck when their cheeks are lightly stroked)—are not controversial. He claims that the archetypes are merely *patterns of thought* that give people templates for making sense out of a complicated world.

42. *Star Wars* is a clear example of Jungian theory because George Lucas was explicitly inspired by the prominent mythologist Joseph Campbell (1968), whose approach to mythology is grounded in Jungian theory. Lucas says, "It was very eerie because in reading *The Hero with a Thousand Faces* I began to realize that my first draft of *Star Wars* was following classic motifs . . .so I modified my next draft according to what I'd been learning about classical motifs and made it a little bit more consistent" (Larsen and Larsen, 2002: p. 541).

43. Iaccino (1998).

44. Hill (1992).

45. Ricoeur (1974: p. 99).

46. Ray (1985: p. 14), quoting Althusser (1977).

47. Many of the critical topics related to cultural psychology are reviewed in Cole (1996).

48. The ideological approach of Louis Althusser had a significant impact on the foundation of cultural studies. Storey (2009) provides an introduction to cultural studies while Ryan (2008) has edited a comprehensive anthology of significant contributions to the field.

49. See Fiske (1989) for a prominent example.

50. Haskell (1973: pp. 327–328).

51. Ray (1985: p. 57).

52. See Andrew (1976) and Casetti (1999) for reviews of the history of film theory.

53. Metz integrated his previous work on semiotics, *Film Language* (1974), with psychoanalysis in the highly influential, *The Imaginary Signifier* (1982). Other psychoanalytic interpretations in film studies are compiled by Kaplan (1990). More recent approaches to Lacanian interpretation can be found in McGowan and Kunkle (2004).

54. Greenberg (1993: p. 5), a practicing psychoanalyst, recounts a humbling experience he had at a conference where his traditional psychoanalytic reading of a film got a cool reception from the film scholars in the audience. In contrast, great excitement was created by a hyperclose Lacanian reading of 20 seconds of a Marlene Dietrich movie that "discovered" sexual hostility in an edit between seemingly unrelated scenes. In the first scene, a gun was fired off screen; if one followed the

hypothetical trajectory of the bullet into the next scene (in a completely separate space), it would presumably hit a male character squarely in the crotch.

55. This difficulty may be intentional. Depending on who you ask, the complexity is either a reflection of the unstable nature of knowledge, or it is a neo-elitist tactic designed to aggravate concrete-minded Philistines (e.g., most Americans).

56. Postmodern philosophy and criticism are associated with Jacques Derrida, Michael Foucault, Richard Rorty, and many others.

57. Summarized from Casetti's (1999) analysis of Metz's concepts of identification, voyeurism, and fetishism.

58. Silverman (1986).

59. Mulvey (1986).

60. The phallocentric nature of mainstream film parallels Haskell's argument except that Mulvey (1986) is more concerned with the *mechanisms* of film, not just the *content* of film.

61. Other authors such as Modleski (1988) argue that Hitchcock films intentionally create discomfort in the audience by self-consciously manipulating the power differentials Mulvey discusses. The significance of *Vertigo* to Hitchcock himself is discussed in Chapter 4.

62. The "text only" approach to criticism is associated with the New Criticism. Classic essays have recently been anthologized by Davis (2008).

63. The implied viewer is a spin on the implied reader, a term coined by Iser (1974).

64. The danger of too many possible criticisms has been made within film studies itself. After analyzing the process of film interpretation at its most abstract, Bordwell (1989a) expresses a weariness for the seemingly endless interpretations that litter his field. He demonstrates this point by juxtaposing seven separate critical interpretations of *Psycho*, arguing that while all are reasonable, the benefit of having this many different readings lying around is unclear.

65. The tension between the desire for absolute interpretations of movies and relativistic "eye of the beholder" approaches are in sharp relief on internet discussion boards like those on IMDB.com. Many criticisms are expressed that take the form "This film sucks and anybody who thinks otherwise is an idiot"; these criticisms are then inevitably followed by pleas for tolerance because "everyone is entitled to his or her opinion."

66. Bruner was a major figure in the "cognitive revolution" in the 1960s in which strict behaviorism was supplanted by cognitive approaches that allowed for the exploration of mental concepts like memory and

imagination. Later in his career, Bruner found that cognitive psychology had become narrower and more constricted than he intended, and he wrote two influential books, *Actual Minds, Possible Worlds* (1986) and *Acts of Meaning* (1990), which argue for a merging of methodologies between the humanities and the social sciences.

67. Bruner (1990: p. 2).
68. Bruner (1986: p. 13).

## Chapter 3

1. Camp, *et al.* (2010).
2. Fleming and Manvell (1985), a psychologist and a film historian, offer a thematic analysis of representations of insanity. Zimmerman (2003) takes a literary perspective to demonstrate the relative sensitivity of certain films. Robinson (2003) and Wedding, Boyd, and Niemiec (2010) use formal diagnostic criteria argue that some films are useful in teaching students about mental illness (discussed further in Chapter 9). Some authors have focused on mental illness in films for children, especially Disney films (Wahl, *et al.*, 2003; and Lawson and Fouts, 2004). All contain extensive lists of films depicting mental illness.
3. I use "psychological disorder" as an approximate synonym for "psychiatric disorders," "behavior disorders," "abnormal psychology," "mental illness," and "psychopathology." Terms like "mad," "crazy" or "loony" are more informal, dramatic and pejorative. In one way or another, they all suggest problems in behavior and thinking that prevent people from functioning to their fullest capacity.
4. Camp, *et al.* (2010; p. 148).
5. The image does call to mind serial killer, John Wayne Gacy, but Gacy acted alone and was not the head of a crime syndicate.
6. Fifty years after its release, *Psycho* holds up moderately well as a thriller, but it was when I realized Hitchcock thought of it as a comedy (Truffaut, 1985: pp. 200–202) that I realized its true genius.
7. DID is an official diagnosis in current psychiatric nomenclature (American Psychiatric Association, 2000). However, it is controversial, and some professionals do not believe it exists in the extreme form of people developing distinct "personalities."
8. Believing that an inanimate object is possessed with sentience is a delusion while seeing a dead body talk is a hallucination. Both are common symptoms of schizophrenia, not DID. Students often confuse

DID (which is very rare) with schizophrenia (which is common). *Psycho* is at least partially to blame for this confusion.

9. The film is based on the book *Psycho*, by Robert Bloch (1989). Bloch based his story on the serial killer, Ed Gein, who lived on an isolated farm in Wisconsin in the 1950s where he killed and dismembered at least 10 women. This case is also the inspiration for the horror classics *The Texas Chainsaw Massacre* and *The Silence of the Lambs*.

10. As documented in Rebello's fascinatingly detailed, *Alfred Hitchcock and the Making of* Psycho (1990).

11. Truffaut (1985: p. 269).

12. Hyler, Gabbard, and Schneider (1991). A few recent examples have been added.

13. While still used in everyday language, nymphomania has not been a formal diagnostic category for decades.

14. Some filmmakers have actually hired professional consultants to insure that their depictions are realistic—e.g., the psychological aspects of imprisonment and brutality in *Midnight Express* (Farber and Green, 1993).

15. Additional examples of accurate portrayals are provided in Robinson (2009).

16. The DSM-IV-TR (*Diagnostic and Statistical Manual of Mental Disorders, 4th Edition, Text Revision*, American Psychiatric Association, 2000) is the diagnostic reference used by most mental health providers in the US. It contains 16 major diagnostic classes, but a system of sub-classification can lead to hundreds of distinct diagnoses. The major classifications that are most common in cinematic depictions include psychotic disorders (schizophrenia), mood disorders (depression and bipolar), anxiety disorders (post-traumatic stress disorder), personality disorders (narcissism and paranoia), dissociative disorders (dissociative identity disorder), and substance-related disorders.

17. The primary criticism is that the film suggests that Nash managed his symptoms without medication which is not consistent with the account in the biography, *A Beautiful Mind* (Nasar, 2001).

18. Greenberg (2003) notes that visual hallucinations (Nash's imaginary roommate) are relatively rare when compared to auditory hallucinations (hearing voices), but of course, movies always prefer to *show* things.

19. See also Brandell (2004), Rabkin (1998), and Walker (1993).

20. Rabkin (1998) offers detailed information about thousands of psych related movies.

21. I use psychotherapy and counseling as synonyms, and I use psychologist or mental health professional as shorthand for anybody who works with people to solve interpersonal and emotional problems. There are differences between forms of treatment (psychoanalysis versus psychotherapy) and disciplines (psychology versus psychiatry) although many people are confused by these differences. In part, the inconsistent and inaccurate use of these terms in the movies is responsible for the confusion.

22. There are exceptions. *Psycho* was released at heart of the Golden Age yet its depiction of Dr Richman is a parody of psychiatric mumbo jumbo.

23. In addition to Drs Dippy, Evil and Wonderful described by Schneider (1987), other categories have been advanced by Orchowski, Spickard, and McNamara (2006) and Winick (1978).

24. Orchowski, Spickard, and McNamara (2006).

25. Pirkis, *et al.* (2006).

26. Schultz (2005).

27. Martin (2007).

28. Gabbard (2001) and Schultz (2005).

29. Bischoff and Reiter (1999) and Dine Young, *et al.* (2008).

30. Dr Melfi from the *Sopranos* was another prominent female therapist that struggled with her attraction to her mobster client although she uncharacteristically resisted temptation.

31. Some passages in the section have been taken verbatim from Dine Young, *et al.* (2008).

32. Perlin (1996).

33. Pope and Vasquez (1998).

34. Edelson (1993: p. 311).

35. Lambert and Bergin (1994).

36. Gabbard (2001).

37. McDonald and Walter (2009) document the almost universally negative portrayal of ECT despite the fact that modern techniques have minimal side effects and have been shown to be an effective treatment for some cases of severe depression.

38. Movies and television make it appear that psychological profilers are a substantial professional group when in actuality, there are very few outside of the FBI. I have disillusioned numerous entering college students with this unfortunate fact.

39. The impact of movies on viewers in general is the subject of Chapters 8 and 9.

40. Jorm (2000).

41. Wahl (1995).
42. Kondo (2008: pp. 250–251).
43. Pirkis, *et al.* (2006).
44. Granello, *et al.* (1999).
45. Philo (1996).
46. Domino (1983).
47. Fleming and Manvell (1985: p. 17).
48. Sullivan (1953: p. 32). I always start my class in abnormal psychology with this quote in order to diminish the tendency of students to approach the topic in a "disorder of the week" manner.
49. Gender is a good example of similarity getting lost in diversity. While there are some notable differences between men and women, across many psychological dimensions the genders are very similar (Hyde, 2005). These similarities are often overshadowed in such popular tomes as Gray's mega-selling: *Men are from Mars, Women are from Venus.*
50. Werner (1980). I use the term here in a broad way that simply suggests that two domains of human action are similar in at least one important dimension (although in other ways they may be substantially different).
51. Sleek (1998).
52. Siegel (1999).
53. Gabbard (2001); Eber and O'Brien (1982); Ringel (2004).
54. Jamieson, Romer, and Jamieson (2006).
55. Schill, Harsch, and Ritter (1990).
56. Dine Young, *et al.* (2008).
57. Edelson (1993: p. 307).
58. Brandell (2004).
59. Stein (2003).
60. The use of film to teach psychology and pass along life lessons is further explored in Chapter 9.

## Chapter 4

1. Corliss (1992).
2. Lax (2000: p. 397).
3. Bjorkman (1994).
4. See Schultz (2005) and Elms (1994) for overviews of psychobiography. Both authors point out that as psychology has established itself as an experimental science, the method has been marginalized. Lives are too

big to fit into laboratories (even the ones at large universities). Early psychologists like William James thought that the study of lives could exist side by side with experimental approaches. Gordon Allport (1965) advocated case studies as a way to balance statistical generalization. He observed that it might be useful for a man to have a general understanding of what most women like when shopping for his wife, but that he was better off knowing his wife's personal preferences (p. 159).

5. Erikson (1962).
6. See Schultz (2005) for chapters on these and other artists.
7. Freud (1957).
8. Examples of projective tests include the Thematic Apperception Test (test-takers tell stories in response to a picture) and the Kinetic Family Drawing Test (test-takers draw their families in action).
9. There are a few exceptions such as a biography of Charlie Chaplin written by a psychiatrist (Weissman, 2008).
10. Wollen (1976).
11. While many directors (Scorsese, Tarantino, Polanski, etc.) have adopted the Hitchcockian trick of popping up in their own movies, these appearances don't generate as much excitement.
12. Spoto (1983: p. x).
13. Spoto (1983: p. 9). There is some question whether the event actually happened. Spoto declares that he was unable to find evidence to confirm it or refute it (p. 16).
14. Spoto (1983: p. 36).
15. Spoto (1983: p. 37).
16. Spoto (1983: p. 65).
17. Spoto (1983: p. 343).
18. Spoto (1983: p. 387).
19. LoBrutto (2008: p. 32).
20. Keyser (1992: p. 7).
21. LoBrutto (2008: p. 33).
22. Quoted in Keyser (1992: p. 10).
23. Cohen-Shalev and Raz (2008).
24. Cohen-Shalev and Raz (2008: p. 36).
25. Dyer (1998: p. 43).
26. McGilligan (1994: pp. 42–47).
27. McGilligan (1994: pp. 262–264).
28. McGilligan (1994: p. 263).
29. McGilligan (1994: pp. 51–52).
30. Morton (2010: p. 105).

31. Morton (2010: pp. 108–109) attributes these quotes to Franziska De George and Iris Martin respectively but does not provide a context for how these professional opinions were acquired, opening up the possibility they were interpreted out of context.
32. This saying is associated with Gestalt psychology, a school of psychology that focused on sensation and perception.
33. Bertolucci, Shaw, and Mawson (2003: p. 20).
34. Bertolucci, Shaw, and Mawson (2003: p. 25).
35. Quoted in Bertolucci, Shaw, and Mawson (2003: p. 28).
36. D'Arminio (2011).
37. Recent developments in method acting are summarized in Krasner (2000). Method acting has made the psychobiography of actors easier since such actors self-consciously access aspects of themselves in playing their roles.
38. Indick (2004).
39. Farber and Green (1993: p. 21).
40. Farber and Green (1993: p. 80).
41. Farber and Green (1993: p. 311).
42. For me, Allen's presentation of psychotherapy in his movies seemed at once cautionary and intriguing. Growing up in a rural town, I watched *Annie Hall* and *Manhattan* repeatedly on cable. Woody's New York seemed an alternative universe in which people spent their days browsing bookstores, pursuing romance, and going to therapy. As an undergraduate, I went to New York to interview for graduate school with a genuine psychoanalyst. I waited while he argued with his secretary about whether I actually had an appointment. After an awkward interview during which he glared at me, I made my way downstairs to find that my car had been towed. I wasn't accepted by the school, and my Woody wannabe days were over.
43. Lax (2000: p. 79) and Baxter (1999: p. 73).
44. Farber and Green (1993: p. 192).
45. Cohen (2004) and Philaretou (2006).
46. Schultz (2005).
47. Based on these criteria, none of the biographical sketches presented here should be considered definitive. My examples are meant to capture certain tendencies in psychobiography but are not complete and accurate pictures of the complicated lives of the filmmakers. The full biographies I draw upon for my summaries are more detailed, yet it is an open question as to whether they are accurate, coherent and consistent.
48. Spoto (1983: p. 36).

49. Elms (2005).
50. Schultz (2005: p. 10).
51. Seligman and Csikzentmihalyi (2000).
52. Nettle (2001).
53. Rothenberg (1990: p. 6).
54. Nettle (2001: p. 145).
55. Freud (1959) emphasized the unconscious desires of storytellers, but filmmakers often seem aware of the personal significance of their movies. Consciousness and unconsciousness are not discrete states but exist on a continuum and are therefore a matter of degree.

## Chapter 5

1. Zillmann and Bryant (1985).
2. Fuller (1996).
3. Austin (1989: pp. 35–36). These attendance figures don't necessarily refer to the number of different individuals who attend a movie since some may have attended more than one movie a week.
4. Television Facts and Statistics (n.d.).
5. Austin (1989: p. 36).
6. Austin (1989: p. 40).
7. Austin (1989: pp. 87–92).
8. Taylor (2002).
9. Krugman and Johnson (1991).
10. Yearly Box Office (2011).
11. On an individual level, psychologists occasionally use reading or viewing tastes as a measure of personality. It seems likely that someone who watches only horror movies will be different from someone else who chooses to watch only romantic comedies. This chapter focuses on general trends in movie viewing. A closer look at movie enjoyment is considered in later chapters, particularly Chapter 7.
12. Lists of box office champs as well as other movies lists are available at www.filmsite.org. The list I am using has been adjusted for inflation and is therefore historically balanced. Movie admissions in 1939 when *Gone with the Wind* was released were much cheaper than a 3D showing of *Avatar* in 2009. This explains why *Avatar*, though the highest grossing movie of all time, is ranked below blockbusters from different economic eras such as *Titanic, The Sound of Music,* and *Gone with the Wind.*

13. To the extent that I am a representative movie fan, I have seen 45 of the 50 films and am generally familiar with every movie on the list except *The Robe*.
14. Dean Simonton (2011) has compiled a large database of box office performance, awards, critics' ratings and other publicly available information.
15. Simonton (2011: pp. 53–78).
16. Simonton (2011: p. 82).
17. Simonton (2011: p. 102).
18. McIntosh, *et al.* (2003).
19. Simonton (2011).
20. Roberts and Foehr (2004).
21. Worth *et al.* (2008).
22. The effects of film are discussed in detail in Chapter 8.
23. See Pritzker (2009) for example.
24. Marich (2005).
25. Retrieved from the American Film Institute's website at www.afi.com/100years/movies10.aspx. AFI is an association of filmmakers, producers and critics who, according to their website, are dedicated to film preservation and educational activities.
26. Accessed from the Internet Movie Database at www.imdb.com/chart/top on April 1, 2011.
27. Another difference is the handful of foreign films (e.g., *Seven Samurai*) on the IMDB list; AFI only ranks American movies.
28. Compared to the exclusive selection process for members of the American Film Institute, IMDB allows access to anyone who is online. Still, there is a strong element of self-selection, as individuals must choose not only to use the site but also its rating function.
29. Fischoff, *et al.* (2002–2003).
30. This survey was conducted in the early 2000s before the *Twilight* craze. Therefore, the results aren't confounded by this massively successful book/movie series. However, its findings may have anticipated the neo-vampire craze of the new millennium.
31. Banerjee, *et al.* (2008).
32. Lincoln and Allen (2004).
33. Thinking about movie viewing in terms of "before, during, and after" establishes a cyclical process. If someone goes to a movie and has an experience which they evaluate as positive, they will likely develop a preference for a particular genre or actor and seek to reproduce it in subsequent movie choices.

## Chapter 6

1. This figure is a variation of Figure 1.1 inspired by Werner and Kaplan (1984). The symbol is the film, and the "referent" is divided up into multiple of levels of "images and sound" and "story." It is important that the arrows go both ways. My example starts with perceptual details and move toward the overarching story; this approach has been described as "bottom-up" processing. However, viewers come to films with expectations about how stories work that impact the perceptual elements they pay attention to; this is "top-down" processing. Humans appear to engage in both types of processing simultaneously.

2. Classical Hollywood style is surveyed in Bordwell, Staiger, and Thompson (1985).

3. Cognitive psychology is an important sub-discipline of psychology and is summarized in numerous textbooks such as Sternberg and Sternberg (2011). Cognitive science is an interdisciplinary field that includes psychology, biology, computer science and philosophy. Neuroscience focuses on how the functioning of the brain and the rest of the nervous system impacts thinking and behavior.

4. Bordwell (1985; 1989a; 1989b), heavily influenced by early psychological studies of film by Munsterberg (1970) and Arnheim (1957), has written several seminal texts outlining a cognitive approach to narrative comprehension of film. Turner (1996) has made a similar case in regard to literature. Other early proponents of the cognitive turn in film studies include Noel Carroll (1988) and Edward Branigan (1992).

5. Grodal (1997), Tan (1996) and Plantinga (2009) are example of cognitive-based theories of film comprehension and emotion. Hogan (2003) provides an accessible overview of cognitive approaches in literature, film and art. Bordwell and Carroll (1996), and Plantinga and Smith (1999) compile a variety of essays on film that take cognitivism (as opposed to Lacanian interpretation) as their starting point.

6. See Anderson (1998) and Hochberg (1989) for overviews of film perception.

7. Anderson (1998: pp. 54–61).

8. Anderson (1998: pp. 99–101).

9. Hochberg (1989).

10. While most scholars agree that there is an interaction between cultural influence and innate endowment, the relative contribution of these factors remains controversial in all areas of the social sciences.

11. Bordwell (1985).

12. Chatman (1978) makes a similar distinction between story and discourse, while Bordwell (1985) borrows terms from Russian literary theory: *fabula* (story) and *syuzhet* (plot).
13. Bordwell (1989a: p. 49).
14. The way people are able to take the concept of "dog" and apply it to a variety of objects in the world is an example of a simple linguistic schema. A physicist's understanding of atomic structure is a more complicated schema.
15. Hogan (2003).
16. The state of modern emotion research is surveyed in Lewis, Haviland-Jones, and Barrett's (2008) edited volume.
17. Grodal (1997) and Plantinga (2009).
18. Tan (1996).
19. Mauss, *et al.* (2005) reported that behavioral, self-report, and physiological responses tend to be modestly correlated, supporting a connection between body, consciousness, and behavior.
20. See Mauss, *et al.* (2005) and Hoffner and Cantor (1991) for examples using adults and children respectively.
21. Mauss, *et al.* (2005).
22. Tomarken, Davidson, and Henriques (1990).
23. Hubert and de Jong-Meyer (1991).
24. Laan, *et al.* (1994) and Koukounas and Over (1997). Methods that involve contact between genitalia and laboratory equipment typically provoke giggles from my students, and indeed they are among the most intrusive social science methods. However, for ethical purposes, studies of human sexuality usually involve thorough education of participants before they make an informed decision to participate.
25. Rottenberg, Ray, and Gross (2007).
26. Yes, there are even hardened souls out there who would mock *The Champ* or laugh at *Silence of the Lambs*.
27. Holland (1989). There is some question as to whether the audience exposure part of the Kuleshov experiment was ever actually conducted or whether Pudovkin extrapolated from his own introspective observations. The experiment has been a reference point in film theory and provides a simple example of how an experiment in editing can be accomplished. I predict that Pudovkin and Kuleshov's hypothesis would stand up today.
28. This observation is consistent with Lacanian psychoanalysis' claims that spectators "suture" juxtaposed scenes together.
29. Kraft (1991).

30. This pattern is often summarized in introductory film text books such as Barsam and Monahan (2010).
31. Aristotle (1967).
32. Schank and Abelson (1977).
33. Pouliot and Cowen (2007).
34. Wollen (1976).
35. Summarized from Carroll (1999: pp. 35–46).
36. This idea is closely related to Jung's archetypes discussed in Ch. 2 although the two concepts emerged from different theoretical traditions.
37. Hogan (2003).
38. Identification is a crucial issue in film theory, psychology and psychoanalysis. Similar terms include "involvement," "engagement," and "participation." Grodal (1997) reviews some of the important variations of identification as used in film studies. While most of these subtleties are not relevant here, the nature of identification (in regard to type, intensity, and duration) can impact the effect of film on viewers discussed in Chapters 8 and 9.
39. Hoffner (1995).
40. Summarized from Plantinga's (1999) application of Paul Ekman's (2007) theory of universal facial expressions.
41. Anderson, *et al.* (2006: p. 7).
42. Summarized from Hogan (2003: pp. 174–179).
43. Major theories of psychological interpretation are overviewed in Chapter 2.
44. Bordwell (1989a).
45. The tendency to isolate discrete processes is comparable to the tendency of medicine to divide up the body in various subsystems.
46. Hogan (2003: p. 3).

## Chapter 7

1. Ebert (1986: pp. 173–174).
2. Kael (1976: pp. 247–251).
3. Thank you, Mom and Dad.
4. I didn't take the film *entirely* seriously. At a high school debate camp held in Georgetown, we amused ourselves by holding races up and down the infamous *Exorcist* stairs.
5. Some student reactions hardly reflect the film's reputation: "How could people ever have thought that was scary?," "I laughed during the exorcism scenes," and "That's nothing compared to *Hostel*."

6. Kenneth Burke (1984) has noted that all living things are critics, using a trout's dilemma of whether or not to take the bait as a metaphor for the people, places and things that we either pursue or avoid.

7. Viewer preferences for types are considered in Chapter 5.

8. The psychology of entertainment is surveyed in edited volumes by Bryant and Vorderer (2006) and Zillmann and Vorderer (2000).

9. See discussion of emotions and comprehension in Chapter 6.

10. Freud (1960a).

11. Zillmann (2000).

12. Zillmann (2000).

13. Critics argue that many modern action movies are indeed random expressions of violence. Yet not all movies with explosions and gunfire are successful, leading to the probability that even action films draw something from character and plot.

14. Dispositional theory is reviewed in Zillmann (2011).

15. Zillmann (2006).

16. See Weaver and Tamborini (1996) for overview of research on horror.

17. Tamborini and Stiff (1987).

18. The *Alien* series has a third and fourth installment, but they weren't financially or critically successful. The fact that they do not *end* well is consistent with my point.

19. The tendency of the virgin female characters to survive while sexually active female characters are killed is discussed in Chapter 2.

20. Oliver (1993).

21. Oliver (2008).

22. Oliver and Woolley (2011).

23. It is possible to see evaluation as a subtype of interpretation since judging a movie as enjoyable can be viewed as a form of meaning.

24. See overview of theoretical approaches to interpretation in Chapter 2.

25. Historical approaches have been used to look at the reception of many art and narrative forms. For example, Freedberg (1989) surveys the intense, visceral, and sometimes violent reactions that audiences have had to public displays of artworks (both low and high) over the centuries.

26. Mayne (1993: p. 148).

27. Staiger (2000: p. 162).

28. Gina Fournier (2007) offers an exhaustive historical look at the reception of a single film.

29. Fournier (2007: p. 31).

30. White and Robinson (1991: p. 29).

31. See overview of ideological approaches to film interpretation in Chapter 2.
32. Television has been given more attention than film in cultural studies. This is a reflection of the Marxist roots of the field since television viewing provides a more pervasive immersion in ideological messages than film viewing.
33. Morley (1980).
34. Ang (1985) and Liebes and Katz (1990) cover the reception of *Dallas*. The latter is the focus of my summary.
35. Reader response criticism has been advocated by many literary scholars such as Iser (1974), Bleich (1978) and Holland (1989). Tompkin's (1980) is a compilation of essays by key figures.
36. Holland (1986).
37. Young (1992).
38. Hill (1999).
39. Zillmann (2011).
40. Shaw (2004: p. 140–141).
41. Film scholars Mayne (1993) and Staiger (1992) explore various approaches to film spectatorship and reception, while edited volumes by Bryant and Vorderer (2006), Bryant and Zillmann's (1991) and Zillmann and Vorderer (2000) survey social science approaches to media reception and enjoyment.
42. Oliver and Woolley (2011).
43. Spectatorship approaches are overviewed in Chapter 2.
44. Quotes from the introduction to the first edition of *Reading the Romance* (pp. 3–4). They were removed from the 1991 second edition, because the author felt that the juxtaposition simplified the positions of the other scholars. While this may be true, putting such divergent quotes side by side is a useful rhetorical technique for highlighting the difference between textual interpretation and the lived experience of fans.
45. Bordwell (1989a).

## Chapter 8

1. Block (2007).
2. Effects tradition has been subject to many overviews like Sparks (2010) an undergraduate text. Other texts such as Giles (2003) and Harris (1999) provide concise summaries of a variety of subdomains. Perse (2001) is a more advanced overview. Bryant and Oliver (2003) and

Nabi and Oliver (2009) are edited volumes of contributions by many scholars in the field.

3. Ultimately the line between consciousness and nonconsciousness is not clear-cut. It is not an all-or-nothing phenomenon. Sometimes we are partially aware of things, other times we are aware of things and then forget them. Consciousness varies across time and is best understood as a continuum. The type of impact of a film will vary depending on factors such as when it was viewed, the conditions of viewing and recall, etc.

4. Blumer (1933).

5. Blumer and Hauser (1933).

6. Overviewed in Giles (2003).

7. See Sparks (2010) and Bryant and Zillman (2009) for historical summaries of effects research.

8. Key (1973).

9. Sparks (2010).

10. Perloff (2009).

11. These topics have been the frequent objects of content analysis discussed in Chapter 2.

12. The Snopes website for debunking media myths claims this widely reported incident has never been verified. Certain claims—T-shirt sales dropped 75% after the movie—are improbable based on the fact that even a successful film is only seen by a relatively small proportion of the population.

13. Hinds (1993).

14. Wilson and Hunter (1983).

15. Sparks (2010).

16. This is an example of the nonfiction media pointing a finger at its fictional counterpart.

17. Surette (2002).

18. Wilson and Hunter (1983).

19. Movie imagery even influenced how I see Harris and Klebold. I can't separate the image of them stalking the halls wearing flowing overcoats and holding high powered weapons from those of *The Matrix* and *The Basketball Diaries*.

20. See Kirsh (2006) for an overview, and Gentile (2003) for an edited overview of media and violence with a special focus on children.

21. One can safely conclude there is "a lot" of violence in the media, but for a more subtle look at the amount and type of violence, see Kirsh (2006).

22. Recent overviews of media and children include Singer and Singer (2001) and Strasburger and Wilson (2002).

23. Bandura, Ross, and Ross (1963).
24. In a fourth condition a film is shown that features an adult dressed like a cartoon cat; the aggressive behavior is staged using unrealistic props.
25. Eron (1963).
26. Huesmann and Eron (1986).
27. "Correlation does not imply causation" is a mantra taught in all social science research courses. While it's probably true that the more years of education one has, the more Woody Allen movies one has seen, it may not be the case that watching Woody Allen movies makes one smarter.
28. This distinction between "cause" and "contribution" is used by Grimes, Anderson and Bergen (2008) to distinguish between the "causationists," those researchers who take a strong position that media violence alone causes negative behavioral effects, and the "contributionists," who believe that media violence is one factor that interacts with many others.
29. Roskos-Ewoldsen and Roskos-Ewoldsen (2009).
30. Much of this research is summarized in Harris and Bartlett (2009) and Gunter (2002).
31. Collins *et al.* (2004).
32. However, in regard to college students, another study (Wilson and Liedtke, 1984) took a straightforward copycat approach and surveyed college students about which movies had been a "significant stimulus" for a sex act. 64% of the males and 39% of the females indicated that at least one film had inspired them (including *10, Endless Love, The Blue Lagoon, Saturday Night Fever*, and *An Officer and a Gentlemen*).
33. Harris and Bartlett (2009).
34. Harris and Bartlett (2009).
35. Titus-Ernstoff *et al.* (2008).
36. Hazan, Lipton, and Glantz (1994).
37. Stoolmiller *et al.* (2010).
38. Mathai (1983).
39. Ballon and Leszcz (2007).
40. Ballon and Leszcz (2007); Bozzuto (1975); Hamilton (1978); and Tenyi and Csizyne (1993).
41. Bozzuto (1975).
42. Ballon and Leszcz (2007).
43. See Chapter 7.
44. Hoekstra, Harris, and Helmick (1999).
45. Harrison and Cantor (1999).
46. Johnson (1980).
47. Cantor (2009).

48. Cantor and Omdahl (1999).
49. Sparks and Cantor (1986).
50. Cantor, Wilson, and Hoffner (1986).
51. Singer and Singer (2005).
52. It is primarily for this reason that, despite my personal love of movies, my wife and I have chosen to limit screen exposure with our children while they are young.
53. Smith and Granados (2009).
54. Levine and Harrison (2008).
55. Mastro (2009).
56. Busselle and Crandall (2002).
57. Perse (2001).
58. Linz, Donnerstein, and Penrod (1988).
59. Jowett and O'Donnell (1992).
60. Gerbner *et al.* (2002)
61. McLuhan (1964).
62. Postman wrote his book in the 1980s. Today's prominence of the computer screen adds another dimension to his argument.
63. McLuhan, Postman, and other cultural critics typically don't refer to surveys or experiments, but they do share concerns about the negative impact of media on society. If one extrapolates the results of some effects studies across the culture, similar conclusions may be reached.
64. Strasburger and Wilson (2002).
65. Following Bandura, Ross, and Ross (1963), psychological theory has been overshadowed by a litany of atheoretical findings. This paucity of theory was documented in a content analysis by Potter and Riddle (2007). Recent attempts such as Nabi and Oliver's (2009) edited volume are designed to give the field more conceptual weight.
66. A variety of perspectives on public policy as it relates to media and children are discussed in Singer and Singer (2005).
67. Perse (2001: p. ix).
68. Sparks, Sparks, and Sparks (2009: p. 273).
69. Huesmann and Taylor (2003).
70. Freedman (2002: p. ix).
71. Trend (2007: p. 3).
72. See Huesmann and Taylor (2003: pp. 112, 130, 111) for the three claims, respectively.
73. Grimes, Anderson and Bergen (2008: p. 49).
74. In particular, the criticism seems to imply that a study must be perfectly randomly sampled, that there can be no variation in participant

response, and that the measure for the study must exactly and completely capture the effect (the "construct") of interest. Such studies do not exist in the social sciences.

75. I once attended a media effects presentation at a national communication convention where I asked a question about the experiential dimension of the participants in the study. I intended it as a friendly question to move the discussion into a slightly different direction. One of the researchers, however, took my question as an implied denunciation of the work and suggested I "go down the hall where the rhetoricians are doing that kind of thing."

76. Centerwall (1993).

77. Trend (2007: p. 1).

78. Perse (2001).

79. Linz, Donnerstein, and Penrod (1988).

80. For those unfamiliar with this movie, the tagline on IMDB.com says it all: "Danny Bonaduce and a cast of Playboy playmates get H.O.T."

81. Directed by Amy Heckerling, written by Cameron Crowe, and featuring talented young stars including Sean Penn and Jennifer Jason Leigh.

## Chapter 9

1. In *Widescreen Dreams: Growing Up Gay at the Movies*, Horrigan shares his experience of *Dog Day Afternoon*, as well as films like *Hello Dolly!*, *The Sound of Music*, and *The Poseidon Adventure*, mixing personal reflection with film commentary. In explaining his choices, he says, "I focus on these [films] . . . because they happened to be the movies that meant the most to me as I was growing up and because in writing about them, I'm trying to understand as fully as possible who I am and why I think and feel as I do" (p. xix).

2. Horrigan (1999: p. xix).

3. Using movies self-reflectively is not inherently a good thing. A viewer may make life choices based on a film that she subsequently comes to regret (e.g., "I should never have believed that Prince Charming would rescue me after seeing *Pretty Woman*"). Alternatively, a viewer could be happy with the impact of a film on his life ("*Rambo* convinced me that might makes right"), yet have that impact judged negatively by others.

4. Fisch (2009).

5. This is an example of multimedia synchronicity. While writing this section, I recalled a movie about a wooden Indian in a boat, but couldn't remember the title. I Googled the plot and, to my delight, found it was

called *Paddle-to-the-Sea*. On IMDB.com I learned it was a short film based on the book of the same name by Holling Clancy Holling. The next day I happened to be watching the 1990s TV show, *Northern Exposure* on DVD. In the episode, "The Final Frontier," the erudite disc jockey Chris (John Corbett) is reading *Paddle-to-the-Sea* on air. *Northern Exposure* is a favorite of mine. The episode "Rosebud," which uses *Citizen Kane* to make the point that movies are modern healing myths, was first aired at the same time I was reading Kenneth Burke's essay "Literature as Equipment for Living." These influences shaped my research program and much of this chapter. And taking it back even further, *Northern Exposure* is clearly a version of *Sesame Street* transplanted to Alaska with adults and no Muppets.

6. Wonderly (2009: p. 12).
7. Murray (1979).
8. Sutherland and Feltey (2009).
9. Van Belle and Mash (2009).
10. Murray and Heumann (2009).
11. Alexander, Lenahan, and Pavlov (2005).
12. Paddock, Terranova, and Giles (2001).
13. Wedding, Boyd, and Niemic (2010).
14. Dr Fritz Engstrom leads summer workshops at the Cape Cod Institute where therapists reflect on psychology and film in the morning and enjoy the beach in the afternoon—the good life.
15. Kerby *et al.* (2008).
16. Gladstein and Feldstein (1983).
17. Cinematherapy was preceded by *bibliotherapy*, the use of books to promote therapeutic change (e.g., Pardeck, 1993). The term *cinematherapy* was first used by Berg-Cross, Jennings, and Baruch (1990) although the therapeutic use of film appeared earlier (Smith, 1974). Hesley and Hesley (2001), Rubin (2008), and Gregerson (2010) are all extensions of cinematherapy and other uses of popular culture in counseling.
18. Kuriansky *et al.* (2010).
19. Turley and Derdeyn (1990).
20. This is the approach of Hesley and Hesley in their *Rent Two Films and Let's Talk in the Morning*.
21. Shedler (2010).
22. Unfortunately Jones (2002) fails to consistently confront the studies on negative impacts of violence, an example of how the humanities and the social sciences remain segregated.
23. Madison and Schmidt (2001).

24. Grace (2006).
25. Niemiec and Wedding (2008).
26. Positive psychology encompasses many areas of psychology including clinical, personality, developmental, social, and neuropsychology. The movement was popularized by Seligman and Csikszentmihalyi (2000), building upon Csikszentmihalyi's (1997) work on "flow" (those moments when people are at their optimal level of functioning) and related concepts.
27. Peterson and Seligman (2004).
28. See Blumler and Katz (1974), Rosengren, Wenner and Palmgreen (1985), and Rubin (2009) for overviews of uses and gratifications research.
29. Katz, Blumler and Gurevitch (1974: pp. 21–22). Rubin (2009) points out that recent study has been more interested in practical implications.
30. See Chapter 7 for an overview of this issue.
31. See Zillmann (1988), and Knobloch-Westerick (2006).
32. Note that "media" is embedded in the term "*media*ted," a form of communication in which the text/screen/sound is a symbolic representation of its creator(s).
33. Perse and Rubin (1990).
34. Radway's (1991: p. 61) study is discussed in more detail in Chapter 7.
35. See Chapter 3 for discussion on portrayal of mental health professionals and mental illness.
36. Wright (1974).
37. Tesser, Millar, and Wu (1988).
38. Oliver and Woolley (2011).
39. Burke (1973: p. 304).
40. The importance of symbolism runs throughout Burke's (1966; 1973) writings.
41. See Dine Young (1996, 2000) for further discussion of this phenomenon.
42. See Chapters 6 and 7 for further exploration of these ideas.
43. Narrative approaches to knowledge are discussed in Chapter 2.
44. McAdams (1993).
45. Mar and Oatley (2008: p. 183).
46. Mar and Oatley (2008: p. 186).
47. Brummett (1985).
48. Qualitative audience response methods allow scholars to consider idiosyncratic experiences that may not be typical. For example, the notion of catharsis has been widely rejected in the effect tradition in regard to aggressive (Bandura, 2009) and sexual (Harris and Bartlett, 2009)

impulses. Given a broad sample of participants, it is difficult to systematically demonstrate that most people will experience a deflation of intense emotions (such as aggression) when exposed to emotional films (as opposed to assimilating the emotions of the film). This doesn't mean that catharsis never happens. Perhaps it is a more subtle, reflective process that occurs when people with sufficient ego strength are exposed to a well-done fictional narrative in a safe environment. Could such exposure help some people modulate aggressive tendencies in everyday life? Instances supporting this claim would me more accessible in open-ended interviews than they would be in social psych experiments.

49. See Rubin (1996) for an overview of autobiographical memory.
50. See Fivush and Haden (2003) for an edited volume exploring the relationship between narratives and autobiographical memory.
51. See section on psychiatric disturbances in Chapter 8.
52. Stein (1993).
53. McAdams (1993).
54. McMillan (1991).
55. Dine Young (2000).
56. All subjects from my interviews were assigned pseudonyms to insure confidentiality.
57. See Hills (2002) for overview of fan theory.
58. Austin (1981).
59. See Lieblich, McAdams, and Josselson (2004) and White and Epston (1990) as examples of narrative therapy and Payne (1989) for the therapeutic use of rhetoric.
60. Heinz Werner (1980) argues that development is more than just the aging process. What comes later cannot automatically be assumed to be more developed than what comes before. Instead, development is a conceptual framework that assumes that some modes of functioning have advantages over other modes and can therefore be said to have "progressed," become "higher developed" or even to be "better."
61. Dine Young (1996).

## Chapter 10

1. For the record, I am not a *Star Wars* purist. I don't mind Lucas tinkering with the special effects, and I enjoyed *Episodes I-III*. Nor I am particularly troubled by the imperious tone Lucas sometimes takes in interviews, and I am content with his decision to leave the series at six episodes. However, I was bothered when he started claiming in the 1990s

that he had never intended a third trilogy. This seemed like a violation of the accepted fact that my pre-adolescent friends and I pondered endlessly, like a rug being pulled out from under my thirty-something self.

2. This figure is essentially a combination of Figure 1.1 and Figure 8.1.

3. Two other important dimensions of the film experience (conscious versus non-conscious; social versus individual) that I have repeatedly emphasized cannot be captured in Figure 10.1 without going 3-D.

4. Actually, I do remember that *The Goodbye Girl* starred Richard Dreyfuss but that was only because he would soon end up in a kid-friendly Spielberg movie, *Close Encounters of the Third Kind*.

5. Filmmakers also engage in multiple levels of psychological processing as they employ perceptual technologies (cameras), write scripts, and draw upon themes that resonate in their own lives. More scholarly attention has been paid to viewers mostly because they are a larger and more accessible group than filmmakers.

6. See Ch. 8 for an overview of these dangers.

# Bibliography

Alexander, M., Lenahan, P., and Pavlov, A. (2005) *Cinemeducation: A Comprehensive Guide to using Film in Medical Education*. Radcliffe, Oxford.

Allport, G. (1965) *Letters from Jenny*. Harcourt Brace, New York, NY.

Althusser, L. (1977) *For Marx*. New Left Books, London.

American Film Institute. (2007) *AFI's 100 Years . . . 100 Movies-10th Anniversary Edition*. Available from http://www.afi.com/100years/movies10.aspx (accessed April 13, 2011).

American Psychiatric Association. (2000) *Diagnostic and Statistical Manual of the Mental Disorders*, 4th edn., text rev./DSM-IV. APA, Washington, DC.

Anderson, D.R., Fite, K.V., Petrovich, N., and Hirsch, J. (2006) Cortical activation while watching video montage: An fMRI study. *Media Psychology*, **8**, 7–24.

Anderson, J.A. (1998) Qualitative approaches to the study of the media: Theory and methods of hermeneutic empiricism, in *Research Paradigms, Television, and Social Behavior* (eds J.K. Asaman and G.L. Berry). Sage, Thousand Oaks, CA, pp. 205–268.

Anderson, J.D. (1996) *The Reality of Illusion: An Ecological Approach to Cognitive Film Theory*. Southern Illinois University Press, Carbondale, IL.

Andrew, J.D. (1976) *The Major Film Theories: An Introduction*. Oxford University Press, London.

Ang, I. (1985) *Watching* Dallas: *Soap Opera and the Melodramatic Imagination*. Methuen, New York, NY.

Aristotle (1967) *Poetics*. University of Michigan Press, Ann Arbor, MI.

Arnheim, R. (1957) *Film as Art*. University of California Press, Berkeley, CA.

Austin, B.A. (1981) Portrait of a cult film audience: *The Rocky Horror Picture Show.* *Journal of Communication,* **31** (2), 43–54.

Austin, B.A. (1989) *Immediate Seating: A Look at Movie Audiences.* Wadsworth, Belmont, CA.

Ballon, B. and Leszcz, M. (2007) Horror films: Tales to master terror or shapers of trauma? *American Journal of Psychotherapy,* **61** (2), 211–230.

Bandura, A. (2009) Social cognitive theory of mass communication, in *Media Effects: Advances in Theory and Research,* 3rd edn. (eds J. Bryant and M.B. Oliver), Routledge, Taylor and Francis, New York, NY, pp. 94–124.

Bandura, A., Ross, D., and Ross, S.A. (1963) Imitation of film-mediated aggressive models. *Journal of Abnormal and Social Psychology,* **66** (1), 3–11.

Banerjee, S.C., Greene, K., Krcmar, M., Bagdasarov, Z., and Ruginyte, D. (2008) The role of gender and sensation seeking in film choice: Exploring mood and arousal. *Journal of Media Psychology,* **20** (3), 97–105.

Barsam, R. and Monahan, D. (2010) *Looking at Movies: An Introduction to Film,* 3rd edn. W.W. Norton, New York, NY.

Baum, L.L. (F.) (2008) *The Wizard of Oz.* Puffin Books, London.

Baxter, J. (1999) *Woody Allen: A Biography.* Carroll & Graf, New York, NY.

Bazin, A. (1967) *What is Cinema?* University of California Press, Los Angeles, CA.

Berg-Cross, L., Jennings, P., and Baruch, R. (1990) Cinematherapy: Theory and application. *Psychotherapy in Private Practice,* **8** (1), 135–156.

Bertolucci, B., Shaw, F., and Mawson, C. (2003) The inner and outer worlds of the filmmaker's temporary social structure, in *The Couch and the Silver Screen: Psychoanalytic Reflections on European Cinema* (ed. A. Sabbadini), Brunner-Routledge, New York, NY, pp. 19–34.

Bettelheim, B. (1975) *The Uses of Enchantment: The Meaning and Importance of Fairy Tales.* Random House, New York.

Bischoff, R.J. and Reiter, A.D. (1999) The role of gender in the presentation of mental health clinicians in the movies: Implications for clinical practice. *Psychotherapy,* **36** (2), 180–189.

Bjorkman, S. (ed) (1994) *Woody Allen on Woody Allen.* Grove Press, New York, NY.

Bleich, D. (1978) *Subjective Criticism.* Johns Hopkins University Press, Baltimore, MD.

Bloch, R. (1989) *Psycho.* Tor Books, New York, NY.

Block, J.J. (2007) Lesson from Columbine: Virtual and real rage. *American Journal of Forensic Psychiatry,* **28** (2) 5–33.

Blumer, H. (1933) *Movies and Conduct.* Macmillan, New York, NY.

Blumer, H. and Hauser, P.M. (1933) *Movies, Delinquency, and Crime.* Macmillan, New York, NY.

Blumler, J.G. and Katz, E. (1974) *The Uses of Mass Communications: Current Perspectives on Gratifications Research.* Sage, Beverly Hills, CA.

Bordwell, D. (1985) *Narration in the Fiction Film.* University of Wisconsin Press, Madison, WI.

Bordwell, D. (1989a) *Making Meaning: Inference and Rhetoric in the Interpretation of Cinema*. Harvard University Press, Cambridge, MA.

Bordwell, D. (1989b) A case for cognitivism. *Iris*, **9**, 11–40.

Bordwell, D. and Carroll, N. (eds) (1996) *Post-Theory: Reconstructing Film Studies*. University of Wisconsin Press, Madison, WI.

Bordwell, D., Staiger, J., and Thompson, K. (1985) *The Classical Hollywood Cinema: Film Style and Mode of Production to 1960*. Columbia University Press, New York, NY.

Bozzuto, J.C. (1975) Cinematic neurosis following *The Exorcist*: Report of four cases. *Journal of Nervous and Mental Disease*, **161** (1), 43–48.

Brandell, J.R. (2004) *Celluloid Couches, Cinematic Clients: Psychoanalysis and Psychotherapy in the Movies*. State University of New York Press, Albany, NY.

Branigan, E. (1992) *Narrative Comprehension and Film*. Routledge, London.

Breuer, J. and Freud, S. (1957) *Studies on Hysteria*. Basic Books, New York, NY.

Brummett, B. (1985) Electronic literature as equipment for living: Haunted house films. *Critical Studies in Mass Communication*, **2**, 247–261.

Bruner, J. (1986) *Actual Minds, Possible Worlds*. Harvard University Press, Cambridge, MA.

Bruner, J. (1990) *Acts of Meaning*. Harvard University Press, Cambridge, MA.

Bryant, J. and Oliver, M.B. (eds) (2009) *Media Effects: Advances in Theory and Research*, 3rd edn. Routledge, Taylor & Francis, New York, NY.

Bryant, J. and Vorderer, P. (eds) (2006) *Psychology of Entertainment*. Lawrence Erlbaum, New York, NY.

Bryant, J. and Zillmann, D. (eds) (1991) *Responding to the Screen: Reception and Reaction Processes*. Lawrence Erlbaum, Hillsdale, NJ.

Bryant, J. and Zillmann, D. (2009) A retrospective and prospective look at media effects, in *The Sage Handbook of Media Processes and Effects* (eds R.L. Nabi and M.B. Oliver), Sage, Thousand Oaks, CA, pp. 9–18.

Burke, K. (1966) *Language as Symbolic Action*. University of California Press, Berkeley, CA.

Burke, K. (1973) *The Philosophy of Literary Form: Studies in Symbolic Action*. University of California Press, Berkeley, CA.

Burke, K. (1984) *Permanence and Change: An Anatomy of Purpose*, 3rd edn. University of California Press, Berkeley, CA.

Busselle, R. and Crandall, H. (2002) Television viewing and perception about race differences in socioeconomic success. *Journal of Broadcasting & Electronic Media*, **46** (2), 265–282.

Camp, M.E., Webster, C.R., Coverdale, T.R., Coverdale, J.H., and Nairn, R. (2010) The Joker: A dark night for depictions of mental illness. *Academic Psychiatry*, **34** (2), 145–149.

Campbell, J. (1968) *The Hero with a Thousand Faces*. Princeton University Press, Princeton, NJ.

Cantor, J. (1998) *'Mommy I'm Scared': How TV and Movies Frighten Children and What We Can Do To Protect Them.* Harcourt Brace, Orlando, FL.

Cantor, J. (2009) Fright reactions to mass media, in *Media Effects: Advances in Theory and Research*, 3rd edn (eds J. Bryant and M.B. Oliver), Routledge, Taylor & Francis, New York, NY, pp. 287–303.

Cantor, J. and Omdahl, B.L. (1999) Children's acceptance of safety guidelines after exposure to televised dramas depicting accidents. *Western Journal of Communication*, **63** (1), 57–71.

Cantor, J., Wilson, B.J., and Hoffner, C. (1986) Emotional responses to a televised nuclear holocaust film. *Communication Research*, **13** (2), 257–277.

Carroll, N. (1988) *Mystifying Movies: Fads and Fallacies in Contemporary Film Theory.* Columbia University Press, New York, NY.

Carroll, N. (1999) Film, emotion, and genre, in *Passionate Views: Film, Cognition, and Emotion* (eds C. Plantinga and G.M. Smith), John Hopkins University Press, Baltimore, MD, pp. 21–47.

Casetti, F. (1999) *Theories of Cinema: 1945-1995.* University of Texas Press, Austin, TX.

Cassirer, E. (1955–1957) *The Philosophy of Symbolic Forms*, Vol. 1-3. Yale University Press, New Haven, CT.

Centerwall, B.S. (1993) Television and violent crime. *Public Interest*, **111**, 56–70.

Chatman, S. (1978) *Story and Discourse: Narrative Structure in Fiction and Film.* Cornell University Press, Ithaca, NY.

Cocks, G. (1991) Bringing the Holocaust home: The Freudian dynamics of Kubrick's 'The Shining'. *Psychoanalytic Review*, **78** (1), 103–125.

Cohen, A.J. (2004) Woody Allen and Freud, in *Celluloid Couches, Cinematic Clients: Psychoanalysis and Psychotherapy in the Movies* (ed. J.R. Brandell), State University of New York Press, Albany, NY, pp. 127–146.

Cohen-Shalev, A. and Raz, A. (2008) Poetry of unadulterated imagination: The late style of Akira Kurosawa. *Psychology of Aesthetics, Creativity, and the Arts*, **2** (1), 34–41.

Cole, M. (1996) *Cultural Psychology: A Once and Future Discipline.* Harvard University Press, Cambridge, MA.

Collins, R.L., Elliott, M.N., Berry, S.H., Kanouse, D.E., Kunkel, D., Hunter, S.B., and Miu, A. (2004) Watching sex on television predicts adolescent initiation of sexual behavior. *Pediatrics*, **114** (3), 280–289.

Corliss, R. (1992, August 31) Scenes from a break up. *Time*, 54–58.

Cowan, G., Lee, C., Levy, D., and Snyder, D. (1988) Dominance and inequality in X-rated videocassettes. *Psychology of Women Quarterly*, **12**, 299–311.

Coyne, S. and Whitehead, E. (2008) Indirect aggression in animated Disney films. *Journal of Communication*, **58**, 382–395.

Crews, F. (1995) *The Memory Wars.* The New York Review of Books, New York, NY.

Csikszentmihalyi, M. (1997) *Finding Flow: The Psychology of Engagement with Everyday Life.* Basic Books, New York, NY.

D'Arminio, A. (2011, April 22/29) Harry Potter and the Deathly Hallows, Part II. *Entertainment Weekly*, 26–30.

Davis, G. (2008) *Praising it New: The Best of the New Criticism.* Swallow Press, Athens, OH.

Diamond, D., Wrye, H., and Sabbadini, A. (2007) Prologue. *Psychoanalytic Inquiry*, **27** (4), 367–380.

Dine Young, S. (1996) *Movies as Equipment for Living: Symbolic Action in the Viewing of Film* (unpublished doctoral dissertation). Clark University, Worcester, MA.

Dine Young, S. (2000) Movies as equipment for living: A developmental analysis of the importance of film in everyday life. *Critical Studies in Media Communication*, **17** (4), 447–468.

Dine Young, S., Boester, A., Whitt, M.T., and Stevens, M. (2008) Character motivation in the representations of mental health professionals in popular film. *Mass Communication and Society*, **11** (1), 82–99.

Domino, G. (1983) Impact of the film *One Flew Over the Cuckoo's Nest* on the attitudes towards mental illness. *Psychological Reports*, **53**, 179–182.

Dyer, R. (1998) *Stars.* British Film Institute, London.

Dylan, B. and Shepard, S. (1986) Brownsville Girl. On *Knocked Out Loaded* [CD]. Columbia, New York, NY.

Eber, M. and O'Brien, J. (1982) Psychotherapy in the movies. *Psychotherapy: Theory, Research, and Practice*, **19** (1), 116–120.

Ebert, R. (1986) *Roger Ebert's Movie Home Companion 1987 Edition.* Andrews, McMeel and Parker, Kansas City, MO.

Edelson, M. (1993) Telling and enacting stories in psychoanalysis and psychotherapy: Implications for teaching psychotherapy. *Psychoanalytic Study of the Child*, **48**, 293–325.

Ekman, P. (2007) *Emotions Revealed: Recognizing Faces and Feelings to Improve Communication and Emotional Life*, 2nd edn. Owl Books, New York, NY.

Elms, A.C. (1994) *Uncovering Lives: The Uneasy Alliance of Biography and Psychology.* Oxford University Press, New York, NY.

Elms, A.C. (2005) Freud as Leonardo: Why the first psychobiography went wrong, in *Handbook of Psychobiography* (ed. W.T. Schultz), Oxford University Press, New York, NY, pp. 210–222.

Erikson, E.H. (1962) *Young Man Luther: A Study in Psychoanalysis and History.* W.W. Norton, New York, NY.

Eron, L.D. (1963) Relationship of TV viewing habits and aggressive behavior in children. *The Journal of Abnormal and Social Psychology*, **67** (2), 193–196.

Farber, S. and Green, M. (1993) *Hollywood on the Couch: A Candid Look at the Overheated Love Affair between Psychiatrists and Moviemakers.* William Morrow, New York.

Fisch, S.M. (2009) Educational television and interactive media for children: Effects on academic knowledge, skills, and attitudes, in *Media Effects: Advances in Theory and Research*, 3rd edn. (eds J. Bryant and M.B. Oliver), Routledge, Taylor & Francis Group, New York, NY, pp. 402–435.

Fischoff, S., Dimopoulos, A., Nguyen, F., and Gordon, R. (2002–2003) Favorite movie monsters and their psychological appeal. *Imagination, Cognition, and Personality*, **22** (4), 401–426.

Fiske, J. (1989) *Understanding Popular Culture*. Unwin Hyman, Boston, MA.

Fivush, R. and Haden, C.A. (2003) *Autobiographical Memory and Construction of a Narrative Self: Developmental and Cultural Perspectives*. Lawrence Erlbaum, Mahwah, NJ.

Fleming, M. and Manvell, R. (1985) *Images of Madness: The Portrayals of Insanity in the Feature Film*. Associated University Presses, Cranbury, NJ.

Forrester, J. (1998) *Dispatches from the Freud Wars: Psychoanalysis and its Passions*. Harvard University Press, Cambridge, MA.

Fournier, G. (2007) Thelma & Louise *and Women in Hollywood*. McFarland, Jefferson, NC.

Freedberg, D. (1989) *The Power of Images: Studies in the History and Theory of Response*. University of Chicago Press, Chicago, IL.

Freedman, J.L. (2002) *Media Violence and its Effect on Aggression: Assessing the Scientific Evidence*. University of Toronto Press, Toronto.

Freud, S. (1955) The Uncanny, in *The Standard Edition of the Complete Psychological Works of Sigmund Freud*, Vol. 17 (ed. J. Strachey), Hogarth Press, London, pp. 217–256.

Freud, S. (1957) Leonardo da Vinci and a memory of his childhood, in *The Standard Edition of the Complete Psychological Works of Sigmund Freud*, Vol. 6 (ed. J. Strachey), Hogarth Press, London, pp. 63–137.

Freud, S. (1959) Creative writers and day-dreaming, in *The Standard Edition of the Complete Psychological Works of Sigmund Freud*, Vol. 9 (ed. J. Strachey), Hogarth Press, London, pp. 143–153.

Freud, S. (1960a) *Jokes and their Relation to the Unconscious*. W.W. Norton, New York, NY.

Freud, S. (1960b) *The Ego and the Id*.: W.W. Norton, New York, NY.

Fuller, K.H. (1996) *At the Picture Show: Small-Town Audiences and the Creation of Movie Fan Culture*. Smithsonian Institution Press, Washington, DC.

Gabbard, G.O. (2001) Psychotherapy in Hollywood cinema. *Australasian Psychiatry*, **9** (4), 365–369.

Gabbard, G.O. and Gabbard, K. (1999) *Psychiatry and the Cinema*, 2nd edn, American Psychiatric Press, Washington, DC.

Gentile, D.A. (2003) *Media Violence and Children: A Complete Guide for Parents and Professionals*. Praeger, Westport, CT.

Gerbner, G., Gross, L., Morgan, M., Signorielli, N., and Shanahan, J. (2002) Growing up with television: Cultivation processes, in *Media Effects: Advances in Theory and Research*, 2nd edn. (eds J. Bryant and D. Zillmann), Lawrence Erlbaum, Hillsdale, NJ, pp. 43–67.

Giles, D. (2003) *Media Psychology*. Routledge, Taylor and Francis, New York, NY.

Gladstein, G.A. and Feldstein, J.C. (1983) Using film to increase counselor empathetic experiences. *Counselor Education and Supervision*, **23** (2), 125–131.

Gladwell, M. (2005) *Blink: The Power of Thinking Without Thinking*. Little, Brown, New York, NY.

Gladwell, M. (2008) *Outliers: The Story of Success*. Little, Brown, New York, NY.

Glantz, S.A., Kacirk, K.W., and McCulloch, C. (2004) Back to the future: Smoking in movies in 2002 compared with 1950 levels. *American Journal of Public Health*, **94** (2), 261–262.

Grace, M. (2006) *Reel Fulfillment: A 12-Step Plan for Transforming your Life through Movies*. McGraw-Hill, New York, NY.

Granello, D.H., Pauley, P.S., and Carmichael, A. (1999) Relationship of the media to attitudes toward people with mental illness. *Journal of Humanistic Counseling, Education, and Development*, **38** (2), 98–110.

Gray, J. (1993) *Men are From Mars, Women are From Venus*. HarperCollins, New York, NY.

Greenberg, B.S. (1994) Content trends in media sex, in *Media, Children, and the Family: Social, Scientific, Psychodynamic, and Clinical Perspectives* (eds O. Zillmann and J. Bryant), Lawrence Erlbaum, Hillsdale, NJ, pp. 165–181.

Greenberg, H.R. (1975) The movies on your mind. *Saturday Review Press*, New York, NY and E.P. Dutton.

Greenberg, H.R. (1993) *Screen Memories: Hollywood Cinema on the Psychoanalytic Couch*. Columbia University Press, New York, NY.

Greenberg, H.R. (2003) La-La Land meets *DSM-IV*: The pleasures and pitfalls of celluloid diagnostics. *Psychiatric Services*, **54** (6), 807–808.

Gregerson, M.B. (2010) Story board: The 'Filmist' fall of the cinematic fourth wall, in *The Cinematic Mirror for Psychology and Life Coaching* (ed. M.B. Gregerson), Springer, New York, NY, pp. 1–16.

Grimes, T., Anderson, J.A., and Bergen, L. (2008) *Media Violence and Aggression: Science and Ideology*. Sage, Thousand Oaks, CA.

Grodal, T. (1997) *Moving Pictures: A New Theory of Film Genres, Feelings, and Cognition*. Oxford University Press, New York.

Gunter, B. (2002) *Media Sex: What are the Issues?* Lawrence Erlbaum, Mahwah, NJ.

Hall, C. (1999) *A Primer of Freudian psychology*. Meridian, New York, NY.

Hall, S. (1980) Encoding/decoding, in *Culture, Media, Language: Working Papers in Cultural Studies* (eds S. Hall, S. Hobson, A. Lowe, and P. Willis), Hutchinson Press, London, pp. 128–138.

Hamilton, J.W. (1978) Cinematic neurosis: A brief case report. *Journal of the American Academy of Psychoanalysis*, **6** (4), 569–572.

Harris, R.J. (1999) *A Cognitive Psychology of Mass Communication*, 3rd edn. Lawrence Erlbaum, Mahwah, NJ.

Harris, R.J. and Barlett, C.P. (2009) Effects of sex in the media, in *Media Effects: Advances in Theory and Research*, 3rd edn. (eds J. Bryant and M.B. Oliver), Routledge, Taylor & Francis, New York, pp. 362–401.

Harrison, K. and Cantor, J. (1999) Tales from the screen: Enduring fright reactions to scary media. *Media Psychology*, 1, 97–116.

Haskell, M. (1973) *From Reverence to Rape: The Treatment of Women in Movies*. Holt, Rinehart, and Winston, New York, NY.

Hazan, A.R., Lipton, H.L., and Glantz, S.A. (1994) Popular films do not reflect current tobacco use. *American Journal of Public Health*, 84 (6), 998–1000.

Hesley, J.W. and Hesley, J.G. (2001) *Rent Two Films and Let's Talk in the Morning: Using Popular Movies in Psychotherapy*, 2nd edn. John Wiley & Sons, Inc., New York, NY.

Hill, A. (1999) Risky business: Film violence as an interactive phenomenon, in *Identifying Hollywood's Audiences: Cultural Identity and the Movies* (eds M. Stokes and R. Maltby), British Film Institute, London, pp. 175–186.

Hill, G. (1992) *Illuminating Shadows: The Mythic Power of Film*. Shambhala, Boston, MA.

Hills, M. (2002) *Fan Cultures*. Routledge, Taylor & Francis, New York, NY.

Hinds, M. (1993, October 19) Not like the movie: A dare leads to death. *The New York Times*. Available from http://www.nytimes.com/ (accessed June 10, 2011

Hochberg, J. (1989) The perception of moving images. *Iris*, 9, 41–68.

Hoekstra, S.J., Harris, R.J., and Helmick, A.L. (1999) Autobiographical memories about the experience of seeing frightening movies in childhood. *Media Psychology*, 1, 117–140.

Hoffner, C. (1995) Adolescents' coping with frightening mass media. *Communication Research*, 22 (3), 325–346.

Hoffner, C. and Cantor, J. (1991) Factors affecting children's enjoyment of a frightening film sequence. *Communication Monographs*, 58, 41–62.

Hogan, P.C. (2003) *Cognitive Science, Literature, and the Arts: A Guide for Humanists*. Routledge, Taylor & Francis, New York, NY.

Holland, N. (1975) *Five Readers Reading*. Yale University Press, New Haven, CT.

Holland, N. (1986) I-ing Film. *Critical Inquiry*, 12, 654–671.

Holland, N. (1989) *The Dynamics of Literary Response*. Columbia University Press, New York, NY.

Holland, N. (2006) *Meeting Movies*. Associated University Presses, Cranbury, NJ.

Holling, H.C. (1980) *Paddle-to-the-Sea*. Sandpiper, Riverside, UT.

Hopcke, R.H. (1989) Dorothy and her friends: Symbols of gay male individuation in 'The Wizard of Oz'. *Quadrant: Journal of the C. G. Jung Foundation for Analytical Psychology*, 22 (2), 65–77.

Horowitz, J. (2008) *Woody Allen explains his love of Scarlett Johansson and why he doesn't do Broadway*. Available from http://www.mtvnews.com/articles/1579782/woody-allen-explains-his-love-scarlett-johansson.jhtml (accessed August 1, 2011).

Horrigan, P.E. (1999) *Widescreen Dreams: Growing Up Gay at the Movies*. The University of Wisconsin Press, Madison, WI.

Hubert, W. and de Jong-Meyer, R. (1991) Autonomic, neuroendocrine, and subjective responses to emotion-inducing film stimuli. *International Journal of Psychophysiology*, **11**, 131–140.

Huesmann, L.R. and Eron, L.D. (1986) *Television and the Aggressive Child: A Cross-National Comparison*. Lawrence Erlbaum, Hillsdale, NJ.

Huesmann, L.R. and Taylor, L.D. (2003) The case against the case against media violence, in *Media Violence and Children: A Guide for Parents and Professionals* (ed. D.A. Gentile), Praeger, Westport, CT, pp. 107–130.

Hyde, J. (2005) The gender similarities hypothesis. *American Psychologist*, **60** (6), 581–592.

Hyler, S.E., Gabbard, G.O., and Schneider, I. (1991) Homicidal maniacs and narcissistic parasites: Stigmatization of mentally ill persons in the movies. *Hospital and Community Psychiatry*, **42** (10), 1044–1048.

Iaccino, J.F. (1998) *Jungian Reflections within the Cinema: A Psychological Analysis of Sci-Fi and Fantasy Archetypes*. Praegers, Westport, CT.

Indick, W. (2004) *Movies and the Mind: Theories of Great Psychoanalysts Applied to Film*. McFarland, Jefferson, NC.

Internet Movie Database (2011) *IMDB Top 250 Movies as Voted by Our Users*. Available from http://www.imdb.com/chart/top (accessed April 13, 2011).

Iser, W. (1974) *The Implied Reader: Patterns of Communication in Prose Fiction from Bunyan to Beckett*. The John Hopkins University Press, Baltimore, MD.

Jamieson, P.E., Romer, D., and Jamieson, K.H. (2006) Do films about mentally disturbed characters promote ineffective coping in vulnerable youth? *Journal of Adolescence*, **29**, 749–760.

Johnson, B.R. (1980) General occurrence of stressful reactions to commercial motion pictures and elements in films subjectively identified as stressors. *Psychological Reports*, **47** (3, Pt 1), 775–786.

Jones, G. (2002) *Killing Monsters: Why Children Need Fantasy, Super Heroes, and Make-Believe Violence*. Basic Books, New York, NY.

Jorm, A.F. (2000) Mental health literacy: Public knowledge and beliefs about mental disorders. *British Journal of Psychiatry*, **177**, 396–401.

Jowett, G.S. and O'Donnell, V. (1992) *Propaganda and Persuasion*, 2nd edn. Sage, Newbury Park, CA.

Jung, C. (1964) *Man and his Symbols*. Dell, New York, NY.

Jung, C. (1969) *The Archetypes and the Collective Unconscious*. Princeton University Press, Princeton, NJ.

Kael, P. (1976) *Reeling*. Little, Brown, Boston, MA.

Kaplan, E.A. (1990) *Psychoanalysis and Cinema*. Routledge, New York, NY.

Katz, E., Blumler, J.G., and Gurevitch, M. (1974) Utilization of mass communication by the individual, in *The Uses of Mass Communications: Current Perspectives on*

*Gratifications Research* (eds J. G. Blumler and E. Katz), Sage, Beverly Hills, CA, pp. 19–34.

Kerby, J., Calton, T., Dimambro, B., Flood, C., and Glazebrook, C. (2008) Anti-stigma films and medical students' attitudes towards mental illness and psychiatry: Randomised controlled trial. *Psychiatric Bulletin*, **32**, 345–349.

Key, W.B. (1973) *Subliminal Seduction: Ad Media's Manipulation of a Not So Innocent America.* Signet, New York, NY.

Keyser, L. (1992) *Martin Scorsese.* Twayne, New York, NY.

Kirsh, S.J. (2006) *Children, Adolescents, and Media Violence: A Critical Look at the Research.* Sage, Thousand Oaks, CA.

Knobloch-Westerwick, S. (2006) Mood management: Theory, evidence, and advancements, in *Psychology of Entertainment* (eds J. Bryant and P. Vorderer), Lawrence Erlbaum, New York, NY, pp. 239–254.

Kondo, N. (2008) Mental illness in film. *Psychiatric Rehabilitation Journal*, **31** (3), 250–252.

Koukounas, E. and Over, R. (1997) Male sexual arousal elicited by film and fantasy matched in content. *Australian Journal of Psychology*, **49** (1), 1–5.

Kracauer, S. (1947) *From Caligari to Hitler: A Psychological History of the German Film.* Princeton University Press, Princeton, NJ.

Kracauer, S. (1960) *Theory of Film: The Redemption of Physical Reality.* Oxford University Press, New York, NY.

Kraft, R.N. (1991) Light and mind: Understanding the structure of film, in *Cognition and the Symbolic Processes: Applied and Ecological Perspectives* (eds R.R. Hoffman and D.S. Palermo), Lawrence Erlbaum, Hillsdale, NJ, pp. 351–370.

Krasner, D. (ed.) (2000) *Method Acting Reconsidered: Theory, Practice, Future.* St. Martin's Press, New York, NY.

Krippendorff, K.H. (2004) *Content Analysis: An Introduction to its Methodology*, 2nd edn. Sage, Thousand Oaks, CA.

Kristen, S. and Dine Young, S. (2009) A foreign sound to your ear: The influence of Bob Dylan's music on American and German-speaking fans. *Popular Music and Society*, **32** (2), 229–248.

Krugman, D.M. and Johnson, K.F. (1991) Differences in the consumption of traditional broadcast and VCR movie rentals. *Journal of Broadcasting and Electronic Media*, **35** (2), 213–232.

Kuriansky, J., Vallarelli, A., DelBuono, J., and Ortman, J. (2010) Cinematherapy: Using movie metaphors to explore real relationships in counseling and coaching, in *The Cinematic Mirror for Psychology and Life Coaching* (ed. M.B. Gregerson), Springer, New York, NY, pp. 89–122.

Laan, E., Everaerd, W., van Bellen, G., and Hanewald, G. (1994) Women's sexual and emotional responses to male- and female-produced erotica. *Archives of Sexual Behavior*, **23** (2), 153–169.

Lambert, M.J. and Bergin, A.E. (1994) The effectiveness of psychotherapy, in *Handbook of Psychotherapy and Behavior Change*, 4th edn (eds A.E. Bergin and S.C. Garfield), John Wiley & Sons, Inc., New York, NY. pp. 143–189.

Larsen, S. and Larsen, R. (2002) *Joseph Campbell: A Fire in the Mind*. Inner Traditions, Rochester, VT.

Lawson, A. and Fouts, G. (2004) Mental Illness in Disney Animated Films. *Canadian Journal of Psychiatry*, **49** (5), 310–314.

Lax, E. (2000) *Woody Allen: A Biography*. Da Capo Press, Cambridge, MA.

Levine, M.P. and Harrison, K. (2009) Effects of media on eating disorders and body image, in *Media Effects: Advances in Theory and Research*, 3rd edn. (eds J. Bryant and M. B. Oliver), Routledge, Taylor & Francis, New York, NY, pp. 490–516.

Lewis, M., Haviland-Jones, J.M., and Barrett, L.F. (2008) *Handbook of Emotion*. Guilford Press, New York, NY.

Liebes, T. and Katz, E. (1990) *The Export of Meaning: Cross-Cultural Readings of Dallas*. Oxford University Press, New York, NY.

Lieblich, A., McAdams, D.P., and Josselson, R. (eds) (2004) *Healing Plots: The Narrative Basis of Psychotherapy*. American Psychological Association, Washington, DC.

Lincoln, A.E. and Allen, M.P. (2004) Double jeopardy in Hollywood: Age and gender in the careers of film actors, 1926-1999. *Sociological Forum*, **19** (4), 611–631.

Linz, D. and Donnerstein, E. (1994) Sex and violence in slasher films: A reinterpretation. *Journal of Broadcasting & Electronic Media*, **38** (12), 243–246.

Linz, D., Donnerstein, E., and Penrod, S. (1988) Effects of long-term exposure to violent and sexually degrading depictions of women. *Journal of Personality and Social Psychology*, **55** (5), 758–768.

LoBrutto, V. (2008) *Martin Scorsese: A Biography*. Praeger, Westport, CT.

Madison, R.J. and Schmidt, C. (2001) *Talking Pictures: A Parents' Guide to Using Movies to Discuss Ethics, Values, and Everyday Problems with Children*. Running Press, Philadelphia, PA.

Mar, R.A. and Oatley, K. (2008) The function of fiction is the abstraction and simulation of social experience. *Perspectives on Psychological Science*, **3** (3), 173–192.

Marich, R. (2005) *Marketing to Moviegoers: A Handbook of Strategies Used by Major Studios and Independents*. Focal Press, Burlington, MA.

Martin, N.K. (2007) *Sexy Thrills: Undressing the Erotic Thriller*. University of Illinois Press, Chicago, IL.

Mastro, D. (2009) Effects of racial and ethnic stereotyping, in *Media Effects: Advances in Theory and Research*, 3rd edn (eds J. Bryant and M.B. Oliver), Routledge, Taylor & Francis, New York, NY, pp. 325–341.

Mathai, J. (1983) An acute anxiety state in an adolescent precipitated by viewing a horror movie. *Journal of Adolescence*, **6**, 197–200.

Mauss, I.B., Levenson, R.W., McCarter, L., Wilhem, F.H., and Gross, J.J. (2005) The tie that binds? Coherence among emotion experience, behavior, and physiology. *Emotion*, **5** (2), 175–190.

Mayne, J. (1993) *Cinema and Spectatorship*. Routledge, New York, NY.

McAdams, D.P. (1993) *The Stories We Live By: Personal Myths and the Making of the Self*. Guilford Press, New York, NY.

McDonald, A. and Walter, G. (2009) Hollywood and ECT. *International Review of Psychiatry*, **21** (3), 200–206.

McGilligan, P. (1994) *Jack's Life: A Biography of Jack Nicholson*. W.W. Norton, New York, NY.

McGinn, C. (2005) *The Power of Movies: How Screen and Mind Interact*. Pantheon Books, New York, NY.

McGowan, T. and Kunkle, S. (eds) (2004) *Lacan and Contemporary Film*. Other Press, New York, NY.

McIntosh, W.D., Murray, J.D., Murray, R.M., and Manian, S. (2003) What's so funny about a poke in the eye? The prevalence of violence in comedy films and its relation to social and economic threat in the United States, 1951-2000. *Mass Communication & Society*, **6** (4), 345–360.

McLuhan, M. (1964) *Understanding Media: The Extensions of Man*. McGraw-Hill Book, New York, NY.

McMillan, T. (1991) *The Wizard of Oz*, in *The Movie that Changed my Life* (ed. D. Rosenberg), Viking Penguin, New York, pp. 253–265.

Metz, C. (1974) *Film Language: A Semiotics of the Cinema*. Oxford University Press, New York, NY.

Metz, C. (1982) *The Imaginary Signifier: Psychoanalysis and the Cinema*. Indiana University Press, Bloomington, IN.

Modleski, T. (1988) *The Women who Knew Too Much: Hitchcock and Feminist Theory*. Routledge, New York, NY.

Molitor, F. and Sapolsky, B.S. (1993) Sex, violence, and victimization in slasher films. *Journal of Broadcasting & Electronic Media*, **37** (2), 233–242.

Molitor, F. and Sapolsky, B.S. (1994) Violence towards women in slasher films: A reply to Linz and Donnerstein. *Journal of Broadcasting & Electronic Media*, **38** (12), 247–249.

Morley, D. (1980) *The* Nationwide *Audience: Structure and Decoding*. British Film Institute, London.

Morton, A. (2010) *Angelina: An Unauthorized Biography*. St. Martin's Press, New York, NY.

Mulvey, L. (1986) Visual pleasure and narrative cinema, in *Narrative, Apparatus, Ideology* (ed. P. Rosen), Columbia University Press, New York, NY (pp. 198–209).

Munsterberg, H. (1970, 1916) *The Film: A Psychological Study*. Dover Publications, Inc., New York, NY. (1916, *The Photoplay*).

Murphy, M. (1996) 'The Wizard of Oz' as cultural narrative and conceptual model for psychotherapy. *Psychotherapy*, **33** (4), 531–538.

Murray, L. (1979) *The Celluloid Persuasion: Movies and the Liberal Arts*. William B. Eerdmans, Grand Rapids, MI.

Murray, R.L. and Heumann, J.K. (2009) *Ecology and Popular Film: Cinema on the Edge*. State University of New York Press, Albany, NY.

Nabi, R.L. and Oliver, M.B. (eds) (2009) *The Sage Handbook of Media Processes and Effects*. Sage, Thousand Oaks, CA.

Nasar, S. (2001) *A Beautiful Mind: The Life of Mathematical Genius and Nobel Laureate John Nash.* Touchstone, New York.

Nettle, D. (2001) *Strong Imagination: Madness, Creativity, and Human Nature.* Oxford University Press, New York, NY.

Niemiec, R.M. and Wedding, D. (2008) *Positive Psychology at the Movies: Using Film to Build Virtues and Character Strengths.* Hogrefe & Huber, Cambridge, MA.

Oliver, M.B. (1993) Adolescents' enjoyment of graphic horror: Effects of viewers' attitudes and portrayals of victim. *Communication Research,* **20** (1), 30–50.

Oliver, M.B. (2008) Tender affective states as predictors or entertainment preferences. *Journal of Communication,* **58**, 40–61.

Oliver, M.B. and Woolley, J.K. (2011) Tragic and poignant entertainment: The gratifications of meaningfulness as emotional response, in *The Routledge Handbook of Emotions and Mass Media* (eds K. Döveling, C. von Scheve, and E.A. Konijn), Routledge, Taylor & Francis, New York, NY, pp. 134–147.

Orchowski, L.M., Spickard, B.A., and McNamara, J.R. (2006) Cinema and the valuing of psychotherapy: Implications for clinical practice. *Professional Psychology: Research and Practice,* **37** (5), 506–514.

Packer, S. (2007) *Movies and the Modern Psyche.* Praeger, Westport, CT.

Paddock, J.R., Terranova, S., and Giles, L. (2001) SASB goes Hollywood: Teaching personality theories through movies. *Teaching of Psychology,* **28** (2), 117–121.

Page, J. and Plant, R. (1971) Stairway to Heaven. On *Led Zeppelin IV* [CD]. New York: Atlantic.

Pardeck, J.T. (1993) *Using Bibliotherapy in Clinical Practice: A Guide to Self-Help Books.* Greenwood Press, Westport, CT.

Payne, D. (1989a) *Coping with Failure: The Therapeutic Use of Rhetoric.* University of South Carolina Press, Columbia, SC.

Payne, D. (1989b) *The Wizard of Oz*: Therapeutic rhetoric in a contemporary media ritual. *Quarterly Journal of Speech,* **75**, 25–39.

Perlin, M.L. (1991) Power imbalances in therapeutic relationships, in *The Hatherleigh Guide to Psychotherapy.* Hatherleigh Press, New York, NY, pp. 215–229.

Perloff, R.M. (2009) Mass media, social perception, and the third-person effect, in *Media Effects: Advances in Theory and Research,* 3rd edn (eds J. Bryant and M.B. Oliver), Routledge, Taylor & Francis, New York, pp. 252–268.

Perse, E.M. (2001) *Media Effects and Society.* Lawrence Erlbaum, Mahwah, NJ.

Perse, E.M. and Rubin, A.M. (1990) Chronic loneliness and television use. *Journal of Broadcasting & Electronic Media,* **34** (1), 37–53.

Peterson, C. and Seligman, M. (2004) *Character Strengths and Virtues: A Handbook and Classification.* Oxford University Press, New York, NY.

Philaretou, A.G. (2006) Learning and laughing about gender and sexuality through humor: The Woody Allen case. *The Journal of Men's Studies,* **14** (2), 133–144.

Philo, G. (1996) *Media and Mental Distress.* Addison Wesley Longman, New York, NY.

Pirkis, J., Blood, R.W., Francis, C., and McCallum, K. (2006) On-screen portrayals of mental illness: Extent, nature, and impacts. *Journal of Health Communication*, **11** (5), 523–541.

Plantinga, C. (1999) The scene of empathy and the human face on film, in *Passionate Views: Film, Cognition, and Emotion* (eds C. Plantinga, and G.M. Smith), The John Hopkins University Press, Baltimore, MD, pp. 239–255.

Plantinga, C. (2009) *Moving Viewers: American Film and the Spectator's Experience.* University of California Press, Berkeley, CA.

Plantinga, C. and Smith, G.M. (eds) (1999) *Passionate Views: Film, Cognition, and Emotion.* The John Hopkins University Press, Baltimore, MD.

Pope, K.S. and Vasquez, M.J.T. (1998) *Ethics in Psychotherapy and Counseling: A Practical Guide*, 2nd edn. Jossey-Bass, San Francisco, CA.

Postman, N. (1984) *Amusing Ourselves to Death: Public Discourse in the Age of Show Business.* Viking Penguin, New York, NY.

Potter, W.J. and Riddle, K. (2007) A content analysis of the media effects literature. *Journalism & Mass Communication Quarterly*, **84** (1), 90–104.

Pouliot, L. and Cowen, P.S. (2007) Does perceived realism really matter in media effects? *Media Psychology*, **9**, 241–259.

Pritzker, S.R. (2009) Marketing movies: An introduction to the special issue. *Psychology & Marketing*, **26** (5), 397–399.

Rabkin, L.Y. (1998) *The Celluloid Couch: An Annotated International Filmography of the Mental Health Professional in the Movies and Television from the Beginning to 1990.* Scarecrow Press, Lanham, MD.

Radway, J. (1984) *Reading the Romance: Women, Patriarchy and Popular Literature*, 1st edn. University of North Carolina Press, Chapel Hill, NC.

Radway, J. (1991) *Reading the Romance: Women, Patriarchy and Popular Literature*, 2nd edn. University of North Carolina Press, Chapel Hill, NC.

Ray, R.B. (1985) *A Certain Tendency of the Hollywood Cinema, 1930-1980.* Princeton University Press, Princeton, NJ.

Rebello, S. (1990) *Alfred Hitchcock and the Making of* Psycho. Harper Perennial, New York, NY.

Rendleman, T. (2008) 'I know y'all think I'm pretty square, but I believe what I believe': Images of Evangelicals in American film. *Journal of Media and Religion*, **7**, 271–291.

Ricoeur, P. (1970) *Freud and Philosophy: An Essay on Interpretation.* Yale University Press, New Haven, CT.

Ricoeur, P. (1974) *The Conflict of Interpretations.* Northwestern University Press, Evanston, IL.

Ringel, S. (2004) Talk therapy: The representation of insight in the cinema, in *Celluloid Couches, Cinematic Clients: Psychoanalysis and Psychotherapy in the Movies* (ed. J. Brandell), State University of New York Press, Albany, NY, pp. 169–190.

Roberts, D.F. and Foehr, U.G. (2004) *Kids and Media in America.* Cambridge University Press, Cambridge.

Robinson, D.J. (2003) *Reel Psychiatry: Movie Portrayals of Psychiatric Conditions.* Rapid Psychler Press, Port Huron, MI.

Robinson, D.J. (2009) Reel psychiatry. *International Review of Psychiatry*, **21** (3), 245–260.

Rosengren, K.E., Wenner, L.A., and Palmgreen, P. (eds) (1985) *Media Gratifications Research: Current Perspectives.* Sage, Beverly Hills, CA.

Roskos-Ewoldsen, D.R. and Roskos-Ewoldsen, B. (2009) Current research in media priming, in *The Sage Handbook of Media Processes and Effects* (eds R.L. Nabi and M.B. Oliver), Sage, Thousand Oaks, CA, pp. 177–192.

Rothenberg, A. (1990) *Creativity and Madness: New Findings and Old Stereotypes.* The Johns Hopkins University Press, Baltimore, MD.

Rottenberg, J., Ray, R.D., and Gross, J.J. (2007) Emotion elicitation using films, in *Handbook of Emotion Elicitation and Assessment* (eds J.A. Coan and J.B. Allen), Oxford University Press, New York, NY, pp. 9–28.

Rubin, A.M. (2009) Uses-and-gratifications perspective on media effects, in *Media Effects: Advances in Theory and Research*, 3rd edn. (eds J. Bryant and M.B. Oliver), Routledge, Taylor & Francis, New York, NY, pp. 165–184.

Rubin, D.C. (1996) *Remembering our Past: Studies in Autobiographical Memory.* Cambridge University Press, Cambridge.

Rubin, L.C. (2008) *Popular Culture in Counseling, Psychotherapy, and Play-Based Interventions.* Springer, New York, NY.

Ryan, M. (2008) *Cultural Studies: An Anthology.* John Wiley & Sons, Inc., Malden, MA.

Sacks, O. (1987) *The Man Who Mistook his Wife for a Hat.* Harper Perennial, New York, NY.

Sacks, O. (2009) *The Mind's Eye.* Knopf, New York, NY.

Sarafino, E.P. (2008) *Health Psychology: Biopsychosocial Interactions.* John Wiley & Sons, Inc., Hoboken, NJ.

Schank, R.C. and Abelson, R. (1977) *Scripts, Plans, Goals, and Understanding: An Inquiry into Human Knowledge Structures.* Lawrence Erlbaum, Hillsdale, NJ.

Schill, T., Harsch, J., and Ritter, K. (1990) Countertranference in the movies: Effects on beliefs about psychiatric treatment. *Psychological Reports*, **67**, 399–402.

Schneider, I. (1987) The theory and practice of movie psychiatry. *American Journal of Psychiatry*, **144** (8), 996–1002.

Schore, A.N. (2003) *Affect Regulation and the Repair of the Self.* W.W. Norton, New York, NY.

Schultz, H.T. (2005) Hollywood's portrayal of psychologists and psychiatrists: Gender and professional training differences, in *Featuring Females: Feminist Analyses of Media* (eds E. Cole and J.H. Daniel), APA Books, Washington, DC, pp. 101-112.

Seligman, M. and Csikzentmihalyi, M. (2000) Positive psychology: An introduction. *American Psychologist*, **55** (1), 5–14.

Shaw, R.L. (2004) Making sense of violence: A study of narrative meaning. *Qualitative Research in Psychology*, **1**, 131–151.

Shedler, J. (2010) The efficacy of psychodynamic psychotherapy. *American Psychologist*, **65** (2), 98–109.

Siegel, J. (1999) Political correctness run amok? *APA Monitor*, **30** (1).

Silverman, K. (1986) Suture, in *Narrative, apparatus, ideology: A film theory reader* (ed. P. Rosen), Columbia University Press, New York, NY, pp. 219–235.

Simonton, D.K. (2011) *Great Flicks: Scientific Studies of Cinematic Creativity and Aesthetics*. Oxford University Press, New York, NY.

Singer, D.G. and Singer, J.L. (eds) (2001) *Handbook of Children and the Media*. Sage, Thousand Oaks, CA.

Singer, D.G. and Singer, J.L. (2005) *Imagination and Play in the Electronic Age*. Harvard University Press, Cambridge, MA.

Singh, G. (2009) *Film after Jung: Post-Jungian Approaches to Film Theory*. Routledge/Taylor & Francis, New York, NY.

Sleek, S. (1998) How are psychologists portrayed on screen? *APA Monitor*, **29** (11).

Smith, J.M. (1974) The movie as medium for the message (or movies, dreams, and schizophrenic thinking). *Perspectives in Psychiatric Care*, **12** (4), 157–164.

Smith, S.L. and Granados, A.D. (2009) Content patterns and effects surrounding sex-role stereotyping on television and film, in *Media Effects: Advances in Theory and Research*, 3rd edn (eds J. Bryant and M.B. Oliver), Routledge, Taylor & Francis, New York, NY, pp. 342–361.

Solomon, G. (2001) *Reel Therapy: How Movies Inspire You to Overcome Life's Problems*. Lebhar-Friedman Books, New York, NY.

Sparks, G.G. (2010) *Media Effects Research: A Basic Overview*, 3rd edn. Wadsworth, Cengage Learning, Boston, MA.

Sparks, G.G. and Cantor, J. (1986) Developmental differences in fright responses to a television program depicting a character transformation. *Journal of Broadcasting & Electronic Media*, **30** (3), 309–323.

Sparks, G.G., Sparks, C.W., and Sparks, E. A. (2009) Media violence, in *Media Effects: Advances in Theory and Research*, 3rd edn. (eds J. Bryant and M.B. Oliver), Routledge, Taylor & Francis Group, New York, NY, pp. 269–286.

Spoto, D. (1983) *The Dark Side of Genius: The Life of Alfred Hitchcock*. Little, Brown, Boston, MA.

Staiger, J. (1992) *Interpreting Films: Studies in the Historical Reception of American Cinema*. Princeton University Press, Princeton, NJ.

Staiger, J. (2000) *Perverse Spectators: The Practices of Film Reception*. New York University Press, New York, NY.

Stein, H.H. (1993) A screen memory: My recollections and distortions of the 1950 film, *Three Came Home*. *Psychoanalytic Quarterly*, **62**, 109–113.

Stein, H.H. (2003) Good psychoanalytic psychotherapy in film: Three unorthodox examples. *Psychoanalytic Psychology*, **20** (4), 701–709.

Sternberg, R.J. and Sternberg, K. (2011) *Cognitive Psychology*, 6th edn. Wadsworth Cengage Learning, Belmont, CA.

Sternberg, R.J. and Grigorenko, E.L. (2001) Unified psychology. *American Psychologist*, **56** (12), 1069–1079.

Stokes, M. and Maltby, R. (eds) (1999) *Identifying Hollywood's Audiences: Cultural Identity and the Movies*. British Film Institute, London.

Stoolmiller, M., Gerrard, M., Sargent, J.D., Worth, K.A., and Gibbons, F.X. (2010) R-rated movie viewing, growth in sensation-seeking and alcohol initiation: Reciprocal and moderation effects. *Prevention Science*, **11**, 1–13.

Storey, J. (2009) *Cultural Theory and Popular Culture: An Introduction*, 5th edn. Pearson Education, Upper Saddle River, NJ.

Strasburger, V.C. and Wilson, B.J. (2002) *Children, Adolescents, and the Media*. Sage, Thousand Oaks, CA.

Sullivan, H.S. (1953) *The Interpersonal Theory of Psychiatry*. W.W. Norton New York, NY.

Surette, R. (2002) Self-reported copycat crime among a population of serious and violent juvenile offenders. *Crime & Delinquency*, **48** (1), 46–69.

Sutherland, J. and Feltey, K. (2009) *Cinematic Sociology: Social Life in Film*. Pine Forge Press, Newbury Park, CA.

Tamborini, R. and Stiff, J. (1987) Predictors of horror film attendance and appeal: An analysis of the audience for frightening films. *Communication Research*, **14** (4), 415–436.

Tan, E.S. (1996) *Emotion and the Structure of the Narrative Film: Film as an Emotion Machine*. Lawrence Erlbaum, Mahwah, NJ.

Tavris, C. and Wade, C. (2001) *Psychology in Perspective*, 3rd edn. Prentice-Hall, Upper Saddle River, NJ.

Taylor, F.J. (2002) Big boom in outdoor movies, in *Moviegoing in America: A Sourcebook in the History of Film Exhibition* (ed. G.A. Waller), Blackwell Publishing Inc., Malden, MA, pp. 247–253.

Television Facts and Statistics, 1939 to 2000 (n.d.) *Television History*. Available from http://tvhistory.tv/facts-stats.htm (accessed July 27, 2011).

Tenyi, T. and Csizyne, C.N. (1993) The case of the crisis of adolescent identity induced by the movie *The Exorcist*. *Psychiatria Danubina*, **5** (3-4), 303–305.

Tesser, A., Millar, K., and Wu, C.H. (1988) On the perceived functions of movies. *Journal of Psychology*, **122** (5), 441–449.

Titus-Ernstoff, L., Dalton, M.A., Adachi-Mejia, A.M., Longacre, M.R., and Beach, M.L. (2008) Longitudinal study of viewing smoking in movies and initiation of smoking by children. *Pediatrics*, **121** (1), 15–21.

Tomarken, A.J., Davidson, R.J., and Henriques, J.B. (1990) Resting frontal brain asymmetry predicts affective responses to films. *Journal of Personality and Social Psychology*, **59** (4), 791–801.

Tompkins, J.P. (ed.) (1980) *Reader-Response Criticism from Formalism to Post-Structuralism*. Johns Hopkins University Press, Baltimore, MD.

Trend, D. (2007) *The Myth of Media Violence: A Critical Introduction*. Blackwell Publishing, Inc., Malden, MA.

Truffaut, F. (1985) *Hitchcock.* Touchstone, New York, NY.

Turley, J.M. and Derdeyn, A.P. (1990) Use of a horror film in psychotherapy. *Journal of the American Academy of Child and Adolescent Psychiatry,* **29** (6), 942–945.

Turner, M. (1996) *The Literary Mind: The Origins of Thought and Language.* Oxford University Press, New York, NY.

Twain, M. and Cooley, T. (ed.) (1998) *The Adventures of Huckleberry Finn,* 3rd edn. W.W. Norton, New York, NY.

Van Belle, D.A. and Mash, K.M. (2009) *A Novel Approach to Politics: Introducing Political Science through Books, Movies, and Popular Culture.* CQ Press, Washington, DC.

Wade, C. and Tavris, C. (2005) *Invitation to Psychology,* 3rd edn, Pearson Education, Upper Saddle River, NJ.

Wahl, O. (1995) *Media Madness: Public Images of Mental Illness.* Rutgers University Press, New Brunswick, NJ.

Wahl, O., Wood, A., Zaveri, P., Drapalski, A., and Mann, B. (2003) Mental illness depiction in children's films. *Journal of Community Psychology,* **31** (6), 553–560.

Walker, J. (1993) *Couching Resistance: Women, Film, and Psychoanalytic Psychiatry.* University of Minnesota Press, Minneapolis, MN.

Waters, R. (1973) Eclipse. On *The Dark Side of the Moon* [CD]. London: Abbey Road Studios.

Weaver, J.B. and Tamborini, R. (1996) *Horror Films: Current Research on Audience Preferences and Reactions.* Lawrence Erlbaum, Mahwah, NJ.

Wedding, D., Boyd, M.A., and Niemiec, R.M. (2010) *Movies and Mental Illness: Using Films to Understand Psychopathology,* 3rd edn. Hogrefe, Cambridge, MA.

Weissman, S. (2008) *Chaplin: A Life.* Arcade, New York, NY.

Welsh, A. (2010) On the perils of living dangerously in the slasher horror film: Gender differences in the association between sexual activity and survival. *Sex Roles,* **62** (11–12), 762–773.

Werner, H. (1980) *Comparative Psychology of Mental Development.* International Universities Press, New York, NY.

Werner, H. and Kaplan, B. (1984) *Symbol Formation.* Lawrence Erlbaum, Hillsdale, NJ.

Wertheimer, M. (1987) *A Brief History of Psychology,* 3rd edn Holt, Reinhart, and Winston, New York, NY.

White, D. and Robinson, J. (1991, June 14) The Great Debate over *Thelma and Louise. The Boston Globe,* 29 and 36.

White, M. and Epston, D. (1990) *Narrative Means to Therapeutic Ends.* W.W. Norton, New York, NY.

Wilson, B.J., Smith, S.L., Potter, W.J., Kunkel, D., Linz, D., Colvin, C. M., and Donnerstein, E. (2002) Violence in children's television programming: Assessing the risks. *Journal of Communication,* **52,** 5–35.

Wilson, W. and Hunter, R. (1983) Movie-inspired violence. *Psychological Reports,* **53,** 435–441.

Wilson, W. and Liedtke, V. (1984) Movie-inspired sexual practices. *Psychological Reports*, **54**, 328.

Winick, C. (1978) *Deviance and Mass Media*. Sage, Beverly Hills, CA.

Wiseman, R. (2002) *Queen Bees and Wannabes: Helping your Daughter Survive Cliques, Gossip, Boyfriends and other Realities of Adolescence*. Three Rivers Press, New York.

Wolfenstein, M. and Leites, N. (1970) *Movies: A Psychological Study*. Atheneum, New York, NY.

Wollen, P. (1976) The auteur theory, in *Movies and Methods*, Vol. 1 (ed. B. Nichols), Berkeley University Press, Berkeley, CA, pp. 529–542.

Wonderly, M. (2009) Children's film as an instrument of moral education. *Journal of Moral Education*, **38** (1), 1–15.

Worth, K.A., Chambers, J.G., Nassau, D.H., Rakhra, B.K., and Sargent, J.D. (2008) Exposure of US adolescents to extremely violent movies. *Pediatrics*, **122**, 306–312.

Wright, C.R. (1974) Functional analysis and mass communication revisited, in *The Uses of Mass Communications: Current Perspectives on Gratifications Research* (eds J.G. Blumler and E. Katz), Sage, Beverly Hills, CA, pp. 197–212.

Yearly Box Office (2011) *Box Office Mojo*. Available from http://boxofficemojo.com/yearly (accessed April 13, 2011).

Young, S. (1992) *Self-Reflection: A Proposal for a New Approach to Viewing Film* (unpublished master's thesis) Clark University, Worcester, MA.

Zillmann, D. (1988) Mood management through communication choices. *American Behavioral Scientist*, **31** (3), 327–340.

Zillmann, D. (2000) Humor and comedy, in *Media Entertainment: The Psychology of its Appeal* (eds D. Zillmann and P. Vorderer), Lawrence Erlbaum, Mahwah, NJ, pp. 37–58.

Zillmann, D. (2006) Empathy: Affective reactivity to others' emotional experiences, in *Psychology of Entertainment* (eds J. Bryant and P. Vorderer), Lawrence Erlbaum, New York, NY, pp. 151–181.

Zillmann, D. (2011) Mechanisms of emotional reactivity to media entertainments. In *The Routledge Handbook of Emotions and Mass Media* (eds K. Döveling, C. von Scheve, and E.A. Konijn), Routledge, Taylor & Francis, New York, NY, pp. 101–115.

Zillmann, D. and Bryant, J. (eds) (1985) *Selective Exposure to Communication*. Lawrence Erlbaum, Hillsdale, NJ.

Zillmann, D. and Vorderer, P. (eds) (2000) *Media Entertainment: The Psychology of its Appeal*. Lawrence Erlbaum, Mahwah, NJ.

Zimmerman, J. (2003) *People like Ourselves: Portrayals of Mental Illness in the Movies*. The Scarecrow Press, Oxford.

# Filmography

*10* (1979) Dir: B. Edwards. United States: Geoffrey Productions and Orion Pictures Corporation.

*1900* (1976) Dir: B. Bertolucci. Italy: Produzioni Europee Associati.

*Affair to Remember, An* (1957) Dir: L. McCarey. United States: Twentieth Century Fox Film Corporation and Jerry Wald Productions.

*Airport* (1970) Dir: G. Seaton. United States: Universal Pictures.

*Alien* (1979) Dir: R. Scott. United States: Brandywine Productions and Twentieth Century Fox Productions.

*Aliens* (1986) Dir: J. Cameron. United States: Twentieth Century Fox Film Corporation, Brandywine Productions, and SLM Production Group.

*Amelie* (2001) Dir: J. Jeunet. France: Claudie Ossard Productions.

*American Beauty* (1999) Dir: S. Mendes. United States: DreamWorks SKG and Jinks/Cohen Company.

*American History X* (1998) Dir: T. Kaye. United States: New Line Cinema, Savoy Pictures, and Turman-Morrissey Company.

*Amityville Horror* (1979) Dir: S. Rosenberg. United States: American International Pictures.

*Analyze This* (1999) Dir: H. Ramis. United States: Village Roadshow Pictures and Tribeca Productions.

*Animal House* (1978) Dir: J. Landis. United States: Universal Pictures, Oregon Film Factory, and Stage III Productions.

*Annie Hall* (1977) Dir: W. Allen. United States: United Artists.

*Another Woman* (1988) Dir: W. Allen. United States: Jack Rollins and Charles H. Joffe Productions.

*Anything Else* (2003) Dir: W. Allen. United States: Canal+, DreamWorks SKG, and Granada Film Productions.

*Apocalypse Now* (1979) Dir: F.F. Coppola. United States: Zoetrope Studios.

*As Good As It Gets* (1997) Dir: J.L. Brooks. United States: Gracie Films.

*Austin Powers: The Spy Who Shagged Me* (1999) Dir: J. Roach. United States: New Line Cinema.

*Avatar* (2009) Dir: J. Cameron. United States: Lightstorm Entertainment, Dune Entertainment, and Ingenious Film Partners.

*Bambi* (1942) Dir: D. Hand. United States: Walt Disney Productions.

*Basic Instinct* (1992) Dir: P. Verhoeven. United States: Carolco Pictures. France: Canal+.

*Basketball Diaries, The* (1995) Dir: S. Kalvert. United States: New Line Cinema and Island Pictures.

*Battleship Potemkin* (1925) Dir: S. M. Eisenstein. Soviet Union: Goskino.

*Beautiful Mind, A* (2001) Dir: R. Howard. United States: Imagine Entertainment.

*Beauty and the Beast* (1991) Dir: G. Trousdale and K. Wise. United States: Walt Disney Pictures.

*Big Sleep, The* (1946) Dir: H. Hawks. United States: Warner Bros. Pictures.

*Birth of a Nation, The* (1915) Dir: D.W. Griffith. United States: David W. Griffith Corp. and Epoch Producing Corporation.

*Black Swan* (2010) Dir: D. Aronofsky. United States: Fox Searchlight Pictures.

*Blade* (1998) Dir: S. Norrington. United States: Amen Ra Films, Imaginary Forces, Marvel Enterprises, and New Line Cinema.

*Blade Runner* (1982) Dir: R. Scott. United States: The Ladd Company and Warner Bros. Pictures.

*Blazing Saddles* (1974) Dir: M. Brooks. United States: Warner Bros. Pictures and Crossbow Productions.

*Blow-Up* (1966) Dir: M. Antonioni. United Kingdom: Bridge Films.

*Blue Lagoon, The* (1980) Dir: R. Kleiser. United States: Columbia Pictures Corporation.

*Blue Valentine* (2010) Dir: D. Cianfrance. United States: Hunting Lane Films and Silverwood Films.

*Blue Velvet* (1986) Dir: D. Lynch. United States: De Laurentiis Entertainment Group.

*Bride of Chucky* (1998) Dir: R. Yu. United States: Universal Pictures and Midwinter Productions, Inc.

*Bridge to Terabithia* (2007) Dir: G. Csupo. United States: Hal Lieberman Company, Lauren Levine Productions, Inc., and Walden Media.

*Bringing Up Baby* (1938) Dir: H. Hawks. United States: RKO Radio Pictures.

*Burning Bed, The* (1984) Dir: R. Greenwald. United States: Tisch/Avnet Productions, Inc.

*Butch Cassidy and the Sundance Kid* (1969) Dir: G.R. Hill. United States: Twentieth Century Fox Film Corporation.

*Cabinet of Dr. Caligari, The* (1920) Dir: R. Weine. Germany: Decla-Bioscop AG.

*Casablanca* (1942) Dir: M. Curtiz. United States: Warner Bros. Pictures.

*Casino* (1995) Dir: M. Scorsese. United States: Universal Pictures.

*Celebrity* (1998) Dir: W. Allen. United States: Sweetland Films and Magnolia Productions.

*Champ, The* (1979) Dir: F. Zeffirelli. United States: Metro-Goldwyn-Mayer (MGM).

*Children of Paradise* (1945) Dir: M. Carné. France: Pathé Consortium Cinéma.

*Chinatown* (1974) Dir. R. Polanski. United States: Paramount Pictures.

*Cinderella* (1950) Dir: C. Geronimi, W. Jackson, and H. Luske. United States: Walt Disney Productions.

*Citizen Kane* (1941) Dir: O. Welles. United States: RKO Radio Productions and Mercury Productions.

*Cleopatra* (1963) Dir: J. L. Mankiewicz. United States: Twentieth Century Fox Film Corporation.

*Close Encounters of the Third Kind* (1977) Dir: S. Spielberg. United States: Sony Pictures.

*Cool Hand Luke* (1967) Dir: S. Rosenberg. United States: Jalem Productions.

*Dark Knight, The* (2008) Dir: C. Nolan. United States: Legendary Pictures, Syncopy Film, and DC Comics.

*David and Lisa* (1962) Dir: F. Perry. United States: Lisa and David Company and Vision Associates Productions.

*Day After, The* (1983) Dir: N. Meyer. United States: ABC Circle Films.

*Deconstructing Harry* (1997) Dir: W. Allen. United States: Jean Doumanian Productions and Sweetland Films.

*Deer Hunter, The* (1978) Dir: M. Cimino. United States: EMI Films and Universal Pictures.

*Defending Your Life* (1991) Dir: A. Brooks. United States: Geffen Pictures.

*Dial 'M' for Murder* (1954) Dir: A. Hitchcock. United States: Warner Bros. Pictures.

*Dog Day Afternoon* (1975) Dir: S. Lumet. United States: Artists Entertainment Complex.

*Don't Look Back* (1967) Dir: D.A. Pennebaker. United States: Leacock-Pennebaker.

*Donnie Darko* (2001) Dir: R. Kelly. United States: Flower Films.

*Dr. Dippy's Sanitarium* (1906) United States: American Mutoscope and Biograph.

*Dr. Strangelove* (1964) Dir: S. Kubrick. United States: Columbia Pictures Corporation.

*Dreams* (1990) Dir: A. Kurosawa. Japan: Warner Bros. Pictures.

*Dressed to Kill* (1980) Dir: B. De Palma. United States: Filmways Pictures.

*E. T.: The Extra-Terrestrial* (1982) Dir: S. Spielberg. United States: Universal Pictures and Amblin Entertainment.

*Endless Love* (1981) Dir: F. Zeffirelli. United States: PolyGram Filmed Entertainment.

*Eternal Sunshine of the Spotless Mind* (2004) Dir: M. Gondry. United States: Focus Features.

*Exorcist, The* (1973) Dir: W. Friedkin. United States: Warner Bros. Pictures and Hoya Productions.

*Fahrenheit 9/11* (2004) Dir: M. Moore. United States: Miramax Films.

*The Fast and the Furious* (2001) Dir: R. Cohen. United States: Universal

*Fast Times at Ridgemont High* (1982) Dir: A. Heckerling. United States: Refugee Films and Universal Pictures.

*Fatal Attraction* (1987) Dir: A. Lyne. United States: Paramount Pictures.

*Fear Strikes Out* (1957) Dir: R. Mulligan. United States: Paramount Pictures.

*Field of Dreams* (1989) Dir: P. Robinson. United States: Gordon Company.

*Fight Club* (1999) Dir: D. Fincher. United States: Fox 2000 Pictures and Regency Enterprises.

*Final Destination* (2000) Dir: J. Wong. United States: New Line Cinema.

Final Frontier, The [Television series episode] (1992) Dir: T. Moore. In *Northern Exposure*. United States: Falahey/Austin Street Productions.

*Five Easy Pieces* (1970) Dir: B. Rafelson. United States: BBS Productions.

*Foxfire* (1996) Dir: A. Haywood-Carter. United States: Chestnut Hill Productions.

*Freud* (1962) Dir: J. Huston. United States: Universal Pictures.

*Friday the 13th* (1980) Dir: S. Cunningham. United States: Paramount Pictures.

*Girl, Interrupted* (1999) Dir: J. Mangold. United States: 3 Art Entertainment and Columbia Pictures Corporation.

*Godfather, The* (1972) Dir: F.F. Coppola. United States: Paramount Pictures.

*Golden Voyage of Sinbad, The* (1973) Dir: G. Hessler. United States: Columbia Pictures Corporation.

*Gone with the Wind* (1939) Dir: V. Fleming. United States: Metro-Goldwyn-Mayer (MGM) and Selznick International Pictures.

*Good Will Hunting* (1997) Dir: G. Van Sant. United States: Lawrence Bender Productions.

*Goodbye Girl, The* (1977) Dir: H. Ross. United States: Warner Bros. Pictures.

*Graduate, The* (1967) Dir: M. Nichols. United States: Embassy Pictures Corporation.

*Grand Illusion, The* (1937) Dir: J. Renoir. France: RAC.

*H.O.T.S.* (1979) Dir: G. Sindell. United States: The American Dream Machine Movie Company.

*Halloween* (1978) Dir: J. Carpenter. United States: Compass International Pictures and Falcon International Productions.

*Hancock* (2008) Dir: P. Berg. United States: Columbia Pictures Corporation.

*Hangover Part II, The* (2011) Dir: T. Phillips. United States: Warner Bros. Pictures.

*Harry Potter* [Film Series] (2001-2011) Dir: C. Columbus, A. Cuaron, M. Newell, and D. Yates. United States: Warner Bros. Pictures.

*Hello Dolly!* (1969) Dir: G. Kelly. United States: Chenault Productions.

*High Anxiety* (1977) Dir: M. Brooks. United States: Twentieth Century Fox Film Corporation.

*Home Alone* (1990) Dir: C. Columbus. United States: Twentieth Century Fox Film Corporation.

*Hostel* (2005) Dir: E. Roth. United States: Hostel LLC, International Production Company, Next Entertainment, and Raw Nerve.

*Hotel Rwanda* (2004) Dir: T. George. United States: United Artists.

*Husbands & Wives* (1992) Dir: W. Allen. United States: TriStar Pictures.

*Hustler, The* (1961) Dir: R. Rossen. United States: Twentieth Century Fox Film Corp.

*I Became a Criminal* (1947) Dir: A. Cavalcanti. United Kingdom: A. R. Shipman Productions and Alliance Film Corporation.

*I Still Know What You Did Last Summer* (1998) Dir: D. Cannon. United States: Mandalay Entertainment and Summer Knowledge LLC.

*Inception* (2010) Dir: C. Nolan. United States: Warner Bros. Pictures.

*Incredible Hulk, The* (2008) Dir: L. Leterrier. United States: Universal Pictures and Marvel Enterprises.

*Independence Day* (1996) Dir: E. Emmerich. United States: Twentieth Century Fox Film Corporation.

*Intolerance: Love's Struggle Throughout the Ages* (1916) Dir: D.W. Griffith. United States: Triangle Film Corporation and Wark Producing.

*Invasion of the Body Snatchers* (1978) Dir: P. Kaufman. United States: Solofilm.

*It Happened One Night* (1934) Dir: F. Capra. United States: Columbia Pictures Corporation.

*It's a Wonderful Life* (1946) Dir: F. Capra. United States: Liberty Films (II)

*Jackass: The Movie* (2002) Dir: J. Tremaine. United States: Paramount Pictures and MTV Films.

*Jaws* (1975) Dir: S. Spielberg. United States: Universal Pictures and Zanuck/Brown Productions.

*Killing Us Softly* (1979) Dir: M. Lazarus and R. Wunderlich. United States: Cambridge Documentary Films.

*King of Hearts* (1966) Dir: P. de Broca. France: Fildebroc.

*Kings Speech, The* (2010) Dir: T. Hooper. United States: See-Saw Films.

*Koyaanisqatsi* (1982) Dir: G. Reggio. United States: Institute for Regional Education.

*Lara Croft: Tomb Raider* (2001) Dir: S. West. United States: Paramount Pictures and Mutual Film Company.

*Last Temptation of Christ, The* (1988) Dir: M. Scorsese. United States: Universal Pictures.

*Life is Beautiful* (1997) Dir: R. Benigni. Italy: Cecchi Gori Group and Melampo Cinematografica.

*Lilith* (1964) Dir: R. Rossen. United States: Columbia Pictures Corporation.

*Lion King* (1994) Dir: R. Allers and R. Minkoff. United States: Walt Disney Pictures.

*Lord of the Rings, The* [Film Series] (2001-2003) Dir: P. Jackson. United States and New Zealand: WingNut Films, The Saul Zaentz Company, and New Line Cinema.

*Lorenzo's Oil* (1992) Dir: G. Miller. United States: Universal Pictures.

*Lovesick* (1983) Dir: M. Brickman. United States: The Ladd Company and Warner Bros. Pictures.

*Maltese Falcon, The* (1941) Dir: J. Huston. United States: Warner Bros. Pictures.

*Manhattan* (1979) Dir: W. Allen. United States: Jack Rollins and Charles H. Joffe Productions.

*March of the Penguins* (2005) Dir: L. Jacquet. United States: Warner Independent Pictures.

*Marnie* (1964) Dir: A. Hitchcock. United States: Universal Pictures.

*Matrix, The* (1999) Dir: A. Wachowski and L. Wachowski. United States: Warner Bros. Pictures and Silver Pictures.

*Me, Myself, and Irene* (2000) Dir: B. Farrelly and P. Farrelly. United States: Twentieth Century Fox Film Corporation.

*Mean Girls* (2004) Dir: M. Waters. United States: Paramount Pictures.

*Mean Streets* (1973) Dir: M. Scorsese. United States: Warner Brothers.

*Midnight Express* (1978) Dir: A. Parker. United States: Casablanca Filmworks.

*Midnight in Paris* (2011) Dir: W. Allen. United States: Gravier Productions and Mediapro.

*Mommie Dearest* (1981) Dir: F. Perry. United States: Paramount Pictures.

*Mr. Jones* (1993) Dir: M. Figgis. United States: TriStar Pictures.

*My Girl* (1991) Dir: H. Zieff. United States: Columbia Pictures Corporation and Imagine Entertainment.

*Naked Gun, The: From the Files of Police Squad!* (1988) Dir: D. Zucker. United States: Paramount Pictures.

*Natural Born Killers* (1994) Dir: O. Stone. United States: Warner Bros. Pictures.

*Nightmare on Elm Street 4: The Dream Master* (1988) Dir: R. Harlin. United States: New Line Cinema, Heron Communications, and Smart Egg Pictures.

*Nightmare on Elm Street, A* (1984) Dir: W. Craven. United States: New Line Cinema.

*North by Northwest* (1959) Dir: A. Hitchcock. United States: Metro-Goldwyn-Mayer (MGM)

*Notebook, The* (2004) Dir: N. Cassavetes. United States: New Line Cinema and Gran Via.

*Notorious* (1946) Dir: A. Hitchcock. United States: RKO Radio Pictures.

*Officer and a Gentleman, An* (1982) Dir: T. Hackford. United States: Lorimar Film Entertainment.

*Old Yeller* (1957) R. Stevenson. United States: Walt Disney Productions.

*One Flew Over the Cuckoo's Nest* (1975) Dir: M. Forman. United States: United Artists.

*Ordinary People* (1980) Dir: R. Redford. United States: Paramount Pictures.

*Paddle-to-the-Sea* (1969) Dir: B. Mason. United States: Favorite Films.

*Paranormal Activity* (2007) Dir: O. Peli. United States: Blumhouse Productions.

*Paris, Texas* (1984) Dir: W. Wenders. West Germany: Road Movies Filmproduktion. France: Argos Films.

*Passion of the Christ, The* (2004) Dir: M. Gibson. United States: Icon Productions.

*Pirate, The* (1948) Dir: V. Minnelli. United States: Metro-Goldwyn-Mayer (MGM)

*Poseidon Adventure, The* (1972) Dir: R. Neame. United States: Twentieth Century Fox Film Corporation.

*Pretty Woman* (1990) Dir: G. Marshall. United States: Touchstone Pictures.

*Prince of Tides, The* (1991) Dir: B. Streisand. United States: Columbia Pictures Corporation.

*Program, The* (1993) Dir: D.S. Ward. United States: The Samuel Goldwyn Company and Touchstone Pictures.

*Psycho* (1960) Dir: A. Hitchcock. United States: Paramount Pictures.

*Pulp Fiction* (1994) Dir: Q. Tarantino. United States: Miramax Films.

*Pursuit of Happyness, The* (2006) Dir: G. Muccino. United States: Columbia Pictures Corporation and Relativity Media.

*Raiders of the Lost Ark* (1981) Dir: S. Spielberg. United States: Paramount Pictures and Lucasfilm.

*Rashomon* (1950) Dir: A. Kurosawa. Japan: Daiei Motion Picture Company.

*Rebel Without a Cause* (1955) Dir: N. Ray. United States: Warner Bros. Pictures.

*Requiem for a Dream* (2000) Dir: D. Aronofsky. United States: Artisan Entertainment.

*Reservoir Dogs* (1992) Dir: Q. Tarantino. United States: Live America, Inc. and Dog Eat Dog Productions, Inc.

*Robe, The* (1953) Dir: H. Koster. United States: Twentieth Century Fox Film Corporation.

*Rocky Horror Picture Show, The* (1975) Dir: J. Sharman. United States: Twentieth Century Fox Film Corporation.

*Rome, Open City* (1945) Dir: R. Rossellini. Italy: Excelsa Film.

*Romeo + Juliet* (1996) Dir: B. Luhrman. United States: Bazmark Films and Twentieth Century Fox Film Corporation.

Rosebud [Television series episode] (1993) Dir: M. Fresco. In *Northern Exposure*. United States: Falahey/Austin Street Productions.

*Saturday Night Fever* (1977) Dir: J. Badham. United States: Robert Stigwood Productions.

*Saving Private Ryan* (1998) Dir: S. Spielberg. United States: Amblin Entertainment.

*Saw* (2004) Dir: J. Wan. United States: Evolution Entertainment, Saw Productions, Inc., and Twisted Productions.

*Scary Movie* (2000) Dir: K. Wayans. United States: Dimension Pictures, Wayans Bros. Entertainment, and Gold/Miller Productions.

*Schindler's List* (1993) Dir: S. Spielberg. United States: Universal Pictures and Amblin Entertainment.

*Scream* (1996) Dir: W. Craven. United States: Dimension Films.

*Searching for Bobby Fischer* (1993) Dir: S. Zaillian. United States: Mirage Entertainment.

*Seven Samurai* (1954) Dir: A. Kurosawa. Japan: Toho Company.

*Sex and the City* (2008) Dir: M.P. King. United States: New Line.

*Shakespeare in Love* (1998) Dir: J. Madden. United States: Universal Pictures, Miramax Films, and Bedford Falls Productions.

*Shining, The* (1980) Dir: S. Kubrick. United States: Warner Bros. Pictures.

*Shutter Island* (2010) Dir: M. Scorsese. United States: Paramount Pictures.

*Silence of the Lambs, The* (1991) Dir: J. Demme. United States: Orion Pictures.

*Sixth Sense, The* (1999) Dir: M. Night Shyamalan. United States: Kennedy/Marshall/ Barry Mendel Production, Hollywood Pictures, and Spyglass Entertainment.

*Social Network, The* (2010) Dir: D. Fincher. United States: Columbia Pictures Corporation.

*Sound of Music, The* (1965) Dir: R. Wise. United States: Twentieth Century Fox Film Corporation and Robert Wise Productions.

*Speed* (1994) Dir: J. de Bont. United States: Twentieth Century Fox Film Corporation.

*Spellbound* (1945) Dir: A. Hitchcock. United States: Vanguard Films, Selznick International Pictures, and United Artists.

*Spider-Man* (2002) Dir: S. Raimi. United States: Columbia Pictures.

*Stagecoach* (1939) Dir: J. Ford. United States: Walter Wanger Productions.

*Stand By Me* (1986) Dir: R. Reiner. United States: Columbia Pictures Corporation.

*Star Wars: Episodes I-III* (1999-2005) Dir: G. Lucas. United States: Lucasfilm.

*Star Wars: Episode IV—A New Hope* (1977) Dir: G. Lucas. United States: Lucasfilm.

*Star Wars: Episode V—The Empire Strikes Back* (1980) Dir: I. Kershner. United States: Lucasfilm.

*Star Wars: Episode VI—Return of the Jedi* (1983) Dir: R. Marquand. United States: Lucasfilm.

*Steel Magnolias* (1989) Dir: H. Ross. United States: Rastar Films.

*Story of O, The* (1975) Dir: J. Jaeckin. France: AD Productions and S.N. Prodis.

*Straw Dogs* (1971) Dir: S. Peckinpah. United States: ABC Pictures.

*Sucker Punch* (2011) Dir: Z. Snyder. United States: Warner Bros. Pictures.

*Taxi Driver* (1976) Dir: M. Scorsese. United States: Columbia Pictures Corporation.

*Ten Commandments, The* (1956) Dir: C.B. DeMille. United States: Paramount Pictures and Motion Picture Associates.

*Terms of Endearment* (1983) Dir: J.L. Brooks. United States: Paramount Pictures.

*Texas Chainsaw Massacre, The* (2003) Dir: M. Nispel. United States: Radar Pictures, Platinum Dunes, and Next Entertainment.

*Thelma & Louise* (1991) Dir: R. Scott. United States: Pathé Entertainment.

*Three Came Home* (1950) Dir: J. Negulesco. United States: Twentieth Century Fox Film Corporation.

*Three Faces of Eve, The* (1957) Dir: N. Johnson. United States: Twentieth Century Fox Film Corporation.

*Tin Cup* (1996) Dir: R. Shelton. United States: Regency Enterprises and Warner Bros. Pictures.

*Titanic* (1997) Dir: J. Cameron. United States: Paramount Pictures, Twentieth Century Fox Film Corporation, and Light Storm Entertainment.

*To Kill a Mockingbird* (1962) Dir: R. Mulligan. United States: Universal International Pictures.

*Town Without Pity* (1961) Dir: G. Reinhardt. United States: The Mirisch Corporation.

*Toy Story 3* (2010) Dir: L. Unkrich. United States: Pixar Animation Studios and Walt Disney Pictures.

*Transformers* (2007) Dir: M. Bay. United States: DreamWorks SKG and Paramount Pictures.

*Tree of Life* (2011) Dir: T. Malick. United States: Cottonwood Pictures, Plan B Entertainment, and River Road Entertainment.

*Triumph of the Will* (1935) Dir: L. Riefenstahl. Germany: Leni Riefenstahl-Produktion & Reichspropagandaleitung der NSDAP.

*Tromeo & Juliet* (1996) Dir: L. Kaufman. United States: Troma Entertainment.

*Twilight* (2008) Dir: C. Hardwicke. United States: Summit Entertainment.

*Un Chien Andalau* (1929) Dir: L. Buñuel. France.

*Usual Suspects, The* (1995) Dir: B. Singer. United States: PolyGram Filmed Entertainment and Spelling Films International.

*Vertigo* (1958) Dir: A. Hitchcock. United States: Paramount Pictures.

*Virgin Suicides, The* (1999) Dir: S. Coppola. United States: American Zoetrope, Eternity Pictures, Muse Productions, and Virgin Suicides, LLC.

*Waiting for Superman* (2010) Dir: D. Guggenheim. United States: Electric Kinney Films, Participant Media, and Walden Media.

*What About Bob?* (1991) Dir: F. Oz. United States: Touchstone Pictures.

*When Harry Met Sally* (1989) Dir: R. Reiner. United States: Castle Rock Entertainment and Nelson Entertainment.

*White Christmas* (1954) Dir: M. Curtiz. United States: Paramount Pictures.

*Why We Fight* (1942-1945) Dir: F. Capra. United States.

*Wizard of Oz, The* (1939) Dir: V. Fleming. United States: Metro-Goldwyn-Mayer (MGM)

*Workers Leaving the Lumière Factory* (1895) Dir: A. Lumière and L. Lumière. France.

*Wrong Man, The* (1956) Dir: A. Hitchcock. United States: Warner Bros. Pictures.

# Index

*Psychology at the Movies*, First Edition. Skip Dine Young
© 2012 John Wiley & Sons, Ltd. Published 2012 by John Wiley & Sons, Ltd.